DESIGNING
SECOND
LANGUAGE
PERFORMANCE
ASSESSMENTS

TECHNICAL REPORT #18

DESIGNING SECOND LANGUAGE PERFORMANCE ASSESSMENTS

JOHN M. NORRIS
JAMES DEAN BROWN
THOM HUDSON
JIM YOSHIOKA

SECOND LANGUAGE TEACHING & CURRICULUM CENTER
University of Hawai'i at Mānoa

01 02 03 04 05 06 6 5 4 3 2

The contents of this Technical Report were developed under a grant from the Department of Education (CFDA 84.229, P229A60007). However, the contents do not necessarily represent the policy of the Department of Education, and one should not assume endorsement by the Federal Government.

ISBN 0–8248–2109–2

∞™ The paper used in this publication meets the minimum requirements of the American National Standard for Information Sciences–Permanence of Paper for Printed Library Materials.

ANSI Z39.48–1984

Book design by Deborah Masterson

Distributed by
University of Hawai'i Press
Order Department
2840 Kolowalu Street
Honolulu, HI 96822

ABOUT THE NATIONAL FOREIGN LANGUAGE
RESOURCE CENTER

THE SECOND LANGUAGE TEACHING AND CURRICULUM CENTER of the University of Hawai'i is a unit of the College of Languages, Linguistics, and Literature. Under a grant from the US Department of Education, the Center has since 1990 served as a National Foreign Language Resource Center (NFLRC). The general direction of the Resource Center is set by a national advisory board. The Center conducts research, develops materials, and trains language professionals with the goal of improving foreign language instruction in the United States. The Center publishes research reports and teaching materials; it also sponsors a summer intensive teacher training institute. For additional information about Center programs, write:

Dr. Richard Schmidt, Director
National Foreign Language Resource Center
1859 East-West Road #106
University of Hawai'i
Honolulu, HI 96822

or visit our Web site: http://www.lll.hawaii.edu/nflrc

NFLRC ADVISORY BOARD

CONTENTS

CHAPTER ONE: ALTERNATIVES IN SECOND LANGUAGE ASSESSMENT 1

"Alternative Assessments" 2

Alternatives in Assessment 3

CHAPTER TWO: PERFORMANCE ASSESSMENTS 7

What Are Performance Assessments? 7

What Should a Performance Assessment Look Like? 9

How Are Performance Assessments Developed? 10

Why Bother With Performance Assessment? 14

What Problems Occur in Performance Assessment? 16

What Steps Can Be Taken to Avoid Performance Assessment Problems? 21

Where Do Performance Assessments Fit Into a Language Curriculum? 27

What Examples Exist of Actual Performance Assessment Projects? 30

Summary 30

CHAPTER THREE: TASK-BASED LANGUAGE TEACHING 31

What Are Tasks? 32

What Is the Role of Needs Analysis in Task Selection? 35

What Are the Factors that Affect Task Difficulty and Sequencing? 39

CHAPTER FOUR: TASK-BASED ASSESSMENT 53

How Do We Assess Task-based Performance? 53

What Are the Factors that Affect Task-based Assessment Reliability? 60

What Are the Factors that Affect Task-based Assessment Validity? 61

What Are the Factors that Affect Task-based Assessment Practicality? 64

What Are the Steps Involved in Developing Task-based Assessment? 65

CHAPTER FIVE: TEST AND ITEM SPECIFICATIONS 69

Test Specifications 70

Item Specifications 82

CHAPTER SIX: ITEM PROMPTS _____ 99

CHAPTER SEVEN: CONCLUSIONS _____ 137
       Immediate Plans for Research 137
       Suggestions for Future Research 141

REFERENCES _____ 143

APPENDIX: EXAMPLE ITEMS AND ITEM GENERATION _____ 151

ABOUT THE AUTHORS AND HOW TO CONTACT THEM _____ 227

chapter one

ALTERNATIVES IN
SECOND LANGUAGE ASSESSMENT

The primary goal of this project is to provide guidelines for designing performance assessments for second or foreign language classes at all levels of university instruction. Through our efforts towards this goal, we hope to achieve three fundamental objectives: (a) to provide means whereby student performance on real-world language tasks can be validly assessed in terms of real-world criteria, (b) to elucidate the potential for using task-based performance assessment to generalize about students' L2 abilities, and (c) to facilitate a direct link between classroom L2 instruction and real-world language use. Given these objectives and the consequent scope of this project (described in chapter 7), we have decided to report on our progress and findings in a series of publications. The following chapters have been included in this first volume:

Chapter 1 —Alternatives in Second Language Assessment

Chapter 2 — Performance Assessments

Chapter 3 — Task-Based Language Teaching

Chapter 4 — Task-Based Language Assessment

Chapter 5 — Test and Item Specifications

Chapter 6 — Item Prompts

Chapter 7 — Conclusions

Appendix — Example Items and Item Generation

In this first chapter, we will begin by exploring the general topic of so-called "alternative assessments" and how they contrast with our notion of *alternatives in assessment*. In chapter 2, we will turn to the issues involved in performance assessment as it is covered in general education circles as well as in the language testing literature. In chapter 3, we will explore the literature on task-based teaching and demonstrate its relevance for the current project. In chapter 4, we discuss the issues in the literature that are directly related to task-based language assessment. In chapter 5, we will provide test specifications that describe a number of variables which contribute to task difficulty and apply that knowledge to the process of grading the difficulty of prototypical performance assessment items in item specifications. In chapter 6, we will provide detailed descriptions of prototype item

Norris, J. M., Brown, J. D., Hudson, T., & Yoshioka, J. (1998). *Designing second language performance assessments*. (Technical Report #18). Honolulu: University of Hawai'i, Second Language Teaching & Curriculum Center.

prompts generated in this project. In chapter 7, we will summarize our project, discuss our immediate plans for research, and provide suggestions for other future research. In the appendix, we will demonstrate the generative process involved in creating test and item specifications.

"ALTERNATIVE ASSESSMENTS"

A variety of so-called "alternative assessment" procedures have become popular in recent years: performance assessments, portfolios, student-teacher conferences, diaries, self-assessments, peer-assessments, and so forth. But what are "alternative assessments," and how are they different from more traditional assessment procedures?

Within the mainstream educational assessment literature, the characteristics of "alternative assessments" seem to differ depending on who is describing them. Aschbacher (1991) lists several common characteristics that all alternative assessment procedures seem to share: (a) problem solving and higher level thinking are required, (b) the required tasks are worthwhile as instructional activities, (c) real-world contexts or simulations are used, (d) focus is given to processes as well as products, and (e) public disclosure of standards and criteria is encouraged.

Herman, Aschbacher, and Winters (1992, p. 6) list six characteristics of alternative assessments, which:

1. Ask students to perform, create, produce, or do something.

2. Tap higher-level thinking and problem-solving skills.

3. Use tasks that represent meaningful instructional activities.

4. Invoke real-world applications.

5. Use human judgments, not machine scoring.

6. Require new instructional and assessment roles for teachers.

Huerta-Macías (1995) points out that one benefit of alternative assessments is that they are non-intrusive in that they merely extend and reflect the day-to-day classroom curriculum. She goes on to suggest that, more importantly, students are therefore evaluated on what they ordinarily do in class every day. Alternative assessment provides information not only on learners' weaknesses, but also on their strengths, as they are manifested in class over time. In addition, appropriately administered alternative assessment should be multiculturally sensitive (thus particularly suited for second or foreign language populations). The alternative assessment procedures listed by Huerta-Macías include checklists, journals, logs, videotapes and audiotapes, self-evaluation, teacher observations, and so forth. In addition, Huerta-Macías (1995) argues that:

ld borrow terminology from qualitative research.
consists of its credibility and auditability. Alternative
hemselves valid, due to the direct nature of the
sured by the auditability of the procedure (leaving
processes), by using multiple tasks, by training judges
iangulating any decision-making process with varied
le, students, families, and teachers). Alternative
and reliable procedures that avoid many of the
al testing including norming, linguistic, and cultural

ALTERNATIVES IN ASSESSMENT

possibilities of developing new assessment
es for students to demonstrate their abilities to
inication (in ways that are consonant with the
y are studying), we must take issue with the
s" are somehow completely new and different
e before. We also reject the notion that *any*
assessment procedure can be held to be inherently valid.

Alternative assessments, especially in the form of performance assessments, are nothing new. We feel that the use of the phrase "alternative assessments" may be somewhat counterproductive, as it is often taken to mean that these assessment procedures are somehow a completely new way of doing assessment, that they are somehow completely different, and that they are somehow exempt from the requirements of responsible decision making. We would like to view procedures like performance assessments, portfolios, conferences, diaries, self-assessments, peer-assessments, and so forth, not as alternative assessments, but rather as *alternatives in assessment*. Language testers have always done assessment in one form or another in conjunction with language teaching (including procedures like multiple-choice, composition, dictation, cloze, etc.), and the recent "alternative assessment" procedures are just new alternatives in that long tradition.

At the moment, others would seem to hold a different view. For instance, from the language testing literature, Huerta-Macías (1995) talks rather dismissively about "problems inherent in traditional testing including norming, linguistic, and cultural biases" (p. 10). Two problems jump to mind with such a statement: first, *norming* is not in-and-of-itself a bad thing, and second, the idea of *traditional testing* seems to be too narrowly defined.

Norming

If the purpose of a test is to make norm-referenced decisions (for say proficiency or placement decision making), that test must be normed in one way or another because each student's performance will ultimately be compared with the

---

performances of other students. How the test is normed is another issue. Norming is only a statistical procedure. How it is done and who is used as the norm population are separate issues. There are many options from among which educators can and should choose, but there is nothing inherently bad about norming itself. Norming is a necessary part of developing norm-referenced tests, and such tests are often necessary for distinguishing among peoples' abilities for purposes of admissions or placement. There may be valid political reasons for arguing against making such norm-referenced admissions and placement decisions, but these are separate political issues rather than inherent characteristics of entire types of tests. In a perfect world, with unlimited resources, such decisions would indeed be unnecessary. In the world we live in, such decisions are, and will continue to be, made on a daily basis. We advocate that they be made in a responsible manner.

Traditional testing

In 1962, another branch of *traditional* testing called criterion-referenced testing was born with the publication of an article by Glaser and Klaus (1962). This approach to educational testing has nothing to do with norming. Instead, in this line of work, strategies and statistical procedures have been developed for improving the relationship of tests to the curriculum actually being taught, to the objectives involved, and to the learning that students are doing. Criterion-referenced testing is not some peripheral movement that will soon disappear. As mentioned earlier, it began with Glaser and Klaus (1962), but it continued with Glaser's (1963) paper, and year by year, criterion-referenced testing has been gaining acceptance (for instance, see Popham, 1978 & 1981 and Berk, 1980 & 1984 for much more on the history of criterion-referenced testing; or see almost any recent issue of *Journal of Educational Measurement* or *Applied Psychological Measurement*).

Criterion-referenced testing has also become increasingly important in language testing circles. The concept of criterion-referenced testing first appeared in the language testing literature as far back as 1968 with an article by Cartier in the *TESOL Quarterly*. While criterion-referenced testing did not reappear until the 1980s, a considerable number of articles have appeared since then (e.g., Cziko, 1982, 1983; J. D. Brown, 1984; Hudson & Lynch, 1984; Henning, 1987; J. D. Brown, 1988; Bachman, 1989; J. D. Brown, 1989 a & b; Hudson, 1989 a & b; Bachman, 1990; J. D. Brown, 1990 a & b; Cook, 1990; Hudson 1991, J. D. Brown, 1992, 1993; Griffee, 1995; and J. D. Brown, 1995 a & b, 1996).

Given its decades-long history and general acceptance, criterion-referenced testing can now be considered rather *traditional*, and this branch of testing answers many of the problems that traditional norm-referenced multiple-choice tests did indeed create in language testing. In addition, criterion-referenced testing procedures, statistics, and theory in general are consonant with the various alternative types of assessment advocated by Aschbacher (1991), Herman, Aschbacher, and Winters (1992), Huerta-Macías (1995), and many others.

Indeed, the authors of this report are comfortable with the ideas and procedures of criterion-referenced testing and find nothing particularly new in the types of assessments advocated by those on the "alternative assessments" bandwagon. *Traditional* testing methods in language testing diverged from multiple-choice years ago with explorations of integrative tests (cloze, dictation, etc.) and performance tests (compositions, interviews, etc.). Research on integrative and performance tests dates back to the 1970s, so they too can be considered quite traditional. How is it that such *traditional* measures are therefore inherently problematic?

We also feel compelled to take issue with the notion that "alternative assessments" are somehow "in and of themselves valid, due to the direct nature of the assessment" (Huerta-Macías, 1995, p. 10). Such an attitude ignores the fact that, like all other forms of assessment, the so-called alternative assessments are used to make decisions (sometimes very high-stakes in nature) about students. Hence, as with all other forms of assessment, the designers and users of alternative assessment procedures must make every effort to structure such decisions so that they are shown to be reliable and valid. Indeed, we feel that designers of alternatives in assessment would do well to attend to and meet the guidelines for reliability and validity set forth in the *Standards for Educational and Psychological Testing* (APA, 1985, 1986).

Precedents exist for demonstrating the reliability and validity of such procedures in the performance assessment branch of the educational testing literature, and we want to adapt those reliability and validity procedures to the purposes of developing sound alternatives in language assessment. The existing techniques for showing reliability and validity of performance assessments, including certain statistical procedures, a variety of observational procedures, and techniques for triangulation of decision making, are not particularly new, nor are they particularly difficult from a technical point of view. Hence, we feel that it is no longer acceptable to take the view that alternatives in assessment are "in and of themselves valid." Such a stance can only lead to smug self-satisfaction and irresponsible decisions being made about the very language students that we claim to care so much about. The issues of reliability and validity must be dealt with for "alternative assessments" just as they are for any alternative in assessment — in an open, honest, clear, demonstrable, and convincing way.

The point of view represented here, then, is that using demonstrably reliable and valid alternatives in assessment can only expand our capacity to make responsible decisions in language programs (for admitting students to the program through aptitude or proficiency testing or for placing them into levels of language study once they are in the program) and classrooms (for diagnosing strengths and weaknesses, checking progress, or assessing achievement). In order to meet this wide variety of decision-making needs, we maintain that a variety of assessment approaches must be used. While our focus in this report will be on a particular decision-making role for L2 performance assessments, we hope that the guidelines set down here and in subsequent reports for test development and validation will also be more generally applicable to other alternatives in language assessment.

chapter two

PERFORMANCE ASSESSMENTS

The purpose of this chapter is to define and explore the issues involved in performance assessment. To that end, we examined performance assessment as it exists in both the educational measurement literature and in the language testing literature. As a result of this process, we have identified a number of questions that are central to the design and administration of performance assessments:

1. What are performance assessments?

2. What should a performance assessment look like?

3. How are performance assessments developed?

4. Why bother with performance assessment?

5. What problems occur in performance assessment?

6. What steps can be taken to avoid performance assessment problems?

7. Where do performance assessments fit into a language curriculum?

8. What examples exist of actual performance assessment projects?

These eight questions will serve as the organizational basis for this chapter. We will answer them directly from the literature and summarize our findings, primarily in concise outlines, based both on what we found in the literature and on our professional experience as testers. Now, we will turn to the first question.

WHAT ARE PERFORMANCE ASSESSMENTS?

Certain types of performance assessments have been used in language testing for years. In fact, virtually all language tests have some degree of performance included. It might be more appropriate to think of tests as more performance oriented or less performance oriented along a continuum from least direct and least real-world or authentic to most direct and most real-world or authentic.

Given this view, we argue that language teachers have used forms of performance assessment for years, that is, forms of performance assessment that would fall fairly close to the most direct and authentic end of the continuum. For instance, teachers are using performance assessments fairly close to the authentic end of the continuum when they test writing ability more-or-less directly by having students write essays similar to the ones they would write in their university classrooms, or when they test speaking and listening abilities by conducting interviews with their students — interviews like the ones they might encounter in a job search, and so forth. For years, testers have not known exactly how to label these types of tests. We sometimes labeled them integrative tests because: (a) they were not discrete-point in nature (that is, they did not test easily identifiable and distinctly separate parts of the grammar, vocabulary, or pronunciation of the language); (b) they did indeed integrate two or more of the language skills of listening, speaking, reading, and writing; and (c) they also integrated the various aspects of language like grammar, pronunciation, and vocabulary, as well as other less-well-understood aspects of language like cohesion and coherence, suprasegmentals, paralinguistics, kinesics, proxemics, pragmatics, and culture in ways that we did not particularly understand.

However, many language testers recognized that performance tests like compositions and interviews were different from other tests like dictations and cloze procedures, which were also labeled integrative tests. For instance, J. D. Brown (1996) discussed a category of test items called "tasks," that was quite distinct from items like the fill-in items of a cloze test. These task-based tests were different from other types of tests in that the students taking them were asked to perform tasks much like what would be expected of them in the real-life situations in which they would eventually be expected to use the language.

Such a description of a task-based test (also see chapter 3) is quite similar to occupational assessments in which the candidates are expected to perform a sampling of job-related tasks in a testing situation. For example, candidates for police work might be asked to: (a) interview a hysterical citizen trying to report a crime in an apartment building, (b) work their way through a maze of hostile and innocent pop up targets, (c) fill out a police report, and so forth. A similar EOP (English for occupational purposes) test could be developed to assess the English as a second language ability of police candidates who happened to be non-native speakers of English. An existing example of this type of occupation related task-based assessment is the test described in McNamara (1990), which examines an occupational English test for health professionals in Australia (also see expanded discussion of this topic in McNamara, 1996).

Such occupational tests have long been labeled performance assessments. What distinguishes performance assessments from other types of tests, then, appears to be that (a) examinees must perform tasks, (b) the tasks should be as authentic as possible, and (c) success or failure in the outcome of the tasks, because they are performances, must usually be rated by qualified judges. These three characteristics might just as well serve as a working definition for performance assessments — a working definition that will help us to distinguish already existing performance assessments, such as essays, interviews, extensive reading tasks, and so forth from integrative tests like dictations and cloze tests which do not fully meet any of the three criteria. Readers will see in subsequent sections of this chapter (as well as in the next chapter) how this three-part definition also fits other types of performance assessments and how it is related to other definitions found in the literature.

WHAT SHOULD A PERFORMANCE ASSESSMENT LOOK LIKE?

The three characteristics listed above help to distinguish performance assessments from other types of tests, but what are some of the other characteristics of performance assessments? In short, what should a performance assessment look like?

Wiggins (1989) advocates widespread use of authentic tests for educational measurement. According to him, such tests should (a) have collaborative elements, (b) be contextualized and complex, (c) measure real-world tasks, and (d) have standards that are authentic and clear to students. These seem to us to be key characteristics for consideration in designing second language performance assessments.

More recently and with specific reference to second language applications, Shohamy (1995) pointed out that performance assessments should be viewed more broadly by addressing the following considerations:

1. Needs analysis (What criteria should be used? What content and contexts? Should a task or item pool be used? How should experts be used?)

2. Nature of instrument (Which and how many tasks should be used? How long should they last? How often should they be used? And, so forth)

3. Raters (Who and how many?)

4. Integration of skills with content

5. Student input in selection of content

6. Methods for accountability (Should self-assessment, portfolio, multiple judgments, etc. be used?)

Based on review of the literature and our experience, we feel that a performance assessment should include the characteristics summarized in the following section.

CHARACTERISTICS OF PERFORMANCE ASSESSMENTS

Performance assessments will typically be based on tasks, which will be judged by raters on the basis of some form of rating scale.

1. The tasks should:
   a. Be based on needs analysis (including student input) in terms of rating criteria, content, and contexts
   b. Be as authentic as possible with the goal of measuring real-world activities
   c. Sometimes have collaborative elements that stimulate communicative interactions
   d. Be contextualized and complex

e. Integrate skills with content

f. Be appropriate in terms of number, timing, and frequency of assessment

g. Be generally non-intrusive, that is, be aligned with the daily actions in the language classroom

2. Raters should be appropriate in terms of:

   a. Number of raters

   b. Overall expertise

   c. Familiarity and training in use of the scale

3. The rating scale should be based on appropriate:

   a. Categories of language learning and development

   b. Appropriate breadth of information regarding learner performance abilities

   c. Standards that are both authentic and clear to students

4. To enhance the reliability and validity of decisions as well as accountability, performance assessments should be combined with other methods for gathering information (for instance, self-assessments, portfolios, conferences, classroom behaviors, and so forth)

HOW ARE PERFORMANCE ASSESSMENTS DEVELOPED?

In order to ensure the presence of the broad range of characteristics identified in the previous section, and given the more direct and subjective nature of performance assessments, we reasonably expected a number of special issues to arise in developing them. The literature offered some guidance. For instance, Stiggins (1987) suggests using the following steps to create a blueprint for a performance assessment:

1. Clarify the reasons for assessment by: specifying the decisions to be made (individual or group needs diagnosis, grading, grouping, selection, certification); identifying the decision makers; specifying how the results will be used (for instance, ranking examinees as opposed to determining mastery); and describing the examinees to be assessed.

2. Clarify performance characteristics by: specifying the content or skill focus; selecting the type of performance (for instance, a behavioral process, or a performance product); and listing performance criteria (including at least a definition and performance continuum for each performance dimension).

3. Design exercises by: selecting the form (consider the availability of dependable evidence and the importance of the decision that will result); determining the obtrusiveness of the assessment (Should it be announced or not announced? Public or not? A surreptitious observation?); and determining the amount of evidence needed (consider the importance of

the decision, the need for representative information, and the amount of available time).

4. Design the performance rating plan by: determining the type of score needed (holistic, rank order, or analytic?); determining who will rate the performance (teacher, professional, expert, self, or peer rating?); and clarifying the score recording method to be used (checklist, scale, anecdotes, portfolio, etc.).

More specifically focused on language education, Wesche (1987) describes the development of the Ontario Test of ESL (OTESL), a university-level ESL diagnostic/placement exam, which follows these steps:

1. Identify homogeneous need groups and corresponding procedures and details (including what to do with outliers).

2. Determine the discourse types, subject matter, and authentic tasks to sample, and the degree to which they should be emphasized.

3. Create scoring criteria that reflect authentic, academic scoring criteria, consequences, and judgments.

4. Implement individualized administration and scoring procedures (especially for productive skills testing), including the training of scorers for all phases of testing and efforts to maintain reliability.

5. Determine the reliability and validity.

Allaei and Connor (1991) suggest, with respect to writing performance assessment, that the following steps are necessary:

1. Identify the knowledge and skills that students are expected to command with regard to specific types of writing tasks.

2. Create test tasks that supply content and elicit desired skills and knowledge.

3. Develop scoring rubrics in terms of the desired sub-skills and levels of proficiency within those sub-skills.

Shohamy (1992) suggests that the implementation of second language performance assessments should be done in the following steps:

1. Describe the curriculum in terms of language learning objectives (for skills, content, etc.).

2. Develop tests that cover the four language skills from both school-based and real-world perspectives.

3. Administer the test.

4. Analyze the test data from multiple perspectives (keeping in mind the various types of decisions that will be made with the scores).

5. Summarize and interpret the results.

6. Initiate reform based on deliberation about the results.

Shohamy concludes by pointing out that tests should not be used alone to implement change, but should instead be used as part of a dynamic system in which they can provide valuable information for affecting changes in instruction and learning.

These four sources, which do well at exemplifying the literature, reveal a pattern of recommendations for performance assessment development. Although we concur with their general components of a development framework, we suggest the need for a greater degree of specificity in the various developmental phases, in order to facilitate hands-on test development. Having developed our own performance assessments at various stages of our careers, we would suggest a more comprehensive list of steps including at least those summarized in the following section.

DEVELOPING PERFORMANCE ASSESSMENTS

1. Use needs analysis to define the purposes of the assessment in terms of the
   a. Types of examinees who will be assessed
   b. Types of decisions that will be made and their consequences (admissions, individual or group diagnosis, grading, grouping, certification)
   c. People who will make the decisions (not necessarily restricted to program administrators)
   d. Uses to which the resulting scores/information will be put
   e. The criteria by which a given performance will be judged (based on input from a variety of stakeholders)

2. Design the performances that will be required in terms of the
   a. Type of performance (e.g., a set of behaviors, or a performance product)
   b. Knowledge, skill, and/or content focus, and how they will be elicited
   c. Types of discourse, subject matter, and authenticity of tasks
   d. Degree of warning (Will students be told in advance about assessments? Will assessment be in front of other students or done individually? Will covert observations be made without telling students until afterwards? Etc.)
   e. Amount of evidence needed (based on the importance of the decisions, the need for representative performances, and the amount of time available) (How much language will be elicited?)

3. Describe how the performance will be rated in terms of the
   a. Type of score needed (holistic or analytic)
   b. People who will rate the performances (i.e., the students' teacher, other teachers, experts, peer raters, a combination of the above, etc.)
   c. Training that raters will receive in the rating process (i.e., any rubrics they will be given, other information they will receive, practice ratings they will give, recalibration they will experience during the rating processes, etc.)
   d. Performance criteria that will be applied (in a scoring rubric if appropriate) including description of the categories of language or behavior that will be rated and description of what successful performance at each score level means (based on needs analysis)
   e. Score recording method to be used (checklist, numerical scale, portfolio, etc.)

4. Administer the performance assessments, while insuring that
   a. Directions are clearly given for each performance to each student
   b. Physical conditions (in terms of space, light, noise, temperature, etc.) are the same for each student's performance
   c. Administration conditions (in terms of timing, equipment, realia, language stimulus, etc.) are the same for each student's performance

5. Rate the performances by
   a. Following the guidelines described in number 3 above
   b. Training the raters
   c. Using multiple raters
   d. Checking the ratings as they are made for aberrant raters
   e. Recalibrating the raters on a regular basis if necessary
   f. Recording the results
   g. Reporting the results to students and other interested parties in a manner that is thorough, easily understood, and conducive to productive change (e.g., in terms of emphasis on an individual's future studies)

6. Analyze the resulting data making sure to
   a. Estimate rater (and other types) of consistency/reliability
   b. Consider (from multiple perspectives) the validity of the performance assessment procedures as well as the resulting decisions
   c. Summarize and interpret the results in view of the types of decision involved

7. Initiate change based on the results, in terms of
   a. Making any appropriate curriculum revisions or policy reforms based on the results

b. Keeping in mind that performance assessments are only one source of information and that many other sources of information should be used in making such decisions (see J. D. Brown, 1995a, p. 46 for a list of other such sources)

WHY BOTHER WITH PERFORMANCE ASSESSMENT?

In promoting any alternative in testing, especially testing that is relatively difficult to administer and score like performance assessment, advocates are likely to spend a good deal of energy explaining why we should bother with it. A number of articles have addressed this issue. This section includes a sampling of different perspectives on the reasons why performance assessment is useful.

According to Miller and Legg (1993), performance assessment can compensate for the negative washback effect of standardized testing (that is, the negative impact on teaching practices and curriculum content produced by teaching to standardized tests). They also point out that performance assessment can be used effectively in diagnostic situations and as a part of multi-faceted approaches to information gathering. Moss (1992) further points out that performance assessments can be used to "document and encourage critical, creative, and self-reflective thought" (pp. 229–230).

In language education, Jones (1985) argues that the value of language performance assessment is that it measures students' abilities to respond to real-life language tasks. In other words, unlike other types of tests, performance assessments can be used to approximate the conditions of a real task in a real-life situation. As a result, performance assessments have value in that their scores can be used to predict students' abilities in future, real-world situations, unlike other tests where scores are only very indirect predictors of ability to perform a real-life language task. We suggest that this potential for predicting or generalizing to future, real-world language use is one of the key contributions that performance assessment might make as an alternative form of language assessment.

Along these lines, Shohamy (1995) agrees that the value of language performance assessments is that they are more valid (predictively) with respect to students' abilities to use language in real situations in the future. In addition, she suggests that, having realized that testing effects are unavoidable, we can use that knowledge to justify inclusion of non-standard testing procedures and indicators (records reviews, observations, portfolios, etc.) in order to construct more valid decision-making processes. Positive washback effects are another instructional benefit that she mentions.

Short (1993) adds that non-standardized, alternative assessment (incorporating open-ended questions, portfolios, authentic assessments, and performance-based measurements) offers a more accurate picture of student knowledge and ability than traditional (short answer, multiple-choice, and so forth) assessment.

However, not everyone agrees that performance assessments are worth the effort involved. For instance, Mehrens (1992) rather skeptically considers the following factors that are purported to support the use of performance assessment:

1. Traditional criticisms of multiple-choice tests: bias in testing; irrelevant content; lack of inclusiveness of test content and correlation with curricular goals; multiple-choice tests measure ability to recognize only and cannot measure higher order thinking skills.

2. Delimited domain coverage in multiple choice tests.

3. Lake Wobegon effects, or teaching too closely to the test.

4. Deleterious instruction due to multiple-choice formats; that is, excessive focus on mastering abilities needed to score well on achievement tests.

Having listed the factors often cited in support of performance assessment (and against multiple-choice tests), Mehrens then counters: that charges of bias against well-constructed multiple-choice tests are misguided; that standardized multiple-choice achievement tests are effective and representative; that evidence exists that multiple-choice tests can indeed test higher-order thinking skills; that performance assessments may be capable of measuring in more depth, but most likely with narrower domain coverage than multiple-choice tests; that performance assessments will not overcome problems caused by excessive focus on mastering only those abilities needed to obtain high scores on any kind of achievement tests. We will consider these and similar problems in more detail below. In general, however, we hold that while many of Mehren's points are indeed valid arguments that demand consideration in the design of any performance assessment, such arguments also further support the need for incorporating a variety of alternative assessment techniques into effective classroom decision making.

Based on review of the literature and our own experiences, we would characterize the benefits of using performance assessments as summarized in the following section.

BENEFITS OF USING PERFORMANCE ASSESSMENTS

1. Performance assessments can compensate for the following negative aspects of standardized testing (note that Mehrens, 1992 argued against these):

    a. Negative washback (i.e, any negative effects of testing on teaching, curriculum development, or educational policies)

    b. Lake Wobegon effects (i.e., teaching too closely to the test, or excessive focus on the teaching of abilities needed to score well on standardized tests)

    c. Bias in testing

    d. Irrelevant content
       i. Delimited domain coverage in multiple-choice tests (lack of inclusiveness of test content)
       ii. Lack of relationship with curriculum goals and objectives
    e. Multiple-choice tests measure ability to recognize only and cannot measure higher order thinking skills
    f. Multiple-choice tests lack obvious and real-world criteria for selection and scoring

2. Performance assessments can have positive washback effects by:
    a. Providing diagnostic information in functional, or task-based curriculums
    b. Supplying achievement information in functional, or task based curriculums
    c. Documenting critical thought, creativity, and self-reflection
    d. Encouraging critical thought, creativity, and self-reflection
    e. Aligning classroom assessment and instructional activities with authentic, real-life activities
    f. Showing students' strengths and weaknesses in detailed and real-world terms

3. Performance assessments approximate the conditions of real-life tasks so they can:
    a. Measure abilities to respond to real-life language tasks
    b. Create more accurate assessments of student's knowledge and ability than traditional multiple-choice tests
    c. Predict students' abilities in future, real-world situations
    d. Be more valid than traditional tests in terms of predicting students's abilities to use language in the future real-life situations

WHAT PROBLEMS OCCUR IN PERFORMANCE ASSESSMENT?

In contrast to the discussion above of the benefits of performance assessment, much of the literature addresses instead the problems that performance assessments create. For instance, Aschbacher (1991) points out, with respect to large-scale performance assessments, that state governments in the United States are worried primarily about:

1. Costs — including test development, training of teachers and raters, extensive rating sessions, transportation, public education about the new assessments, and score reporting, among others.

2. Logistics — large amounts of collected material, special equipment, storage and transportation of tests, and increased time commitment.

3. Technical reliability and validity — especially given that decisions must be defended to multiple interested parties.

4. Support for implementation — which is lacking in most states because of the difficulty of comparing traditional, inexpensive, easy-to-administer, norm-referenced tests with new alternatives.

In addition to Mehrens' criticisms listed in the previous section, Mehrens (1992) discusses the following accountability problems that performance assessments raise:

1. The small number of questions leads to a lack of examination content security, which further leads to a need to develop new questions each year (and related costs).

2. Development, administration, and scoring of performance assessments are all much more costly that traditional multiple-choice testing.

3. Increased costs will negatively affect public acceptance.

4. Legal defensibility of performance assessments could become an issue, especially if documentation of the scoring and decision-making processes are limited.

5. Professional credibility of performance assessments will be determined through interactions between teachers, teacher trainers, and psychometricians, all of whom have different views of what constitutes a credible test.

6. The validity of the performance assessments (in view of the necessarily limited domain sampling and the lack of generalizability of the performance sample) could be limited by lack of precision in inferences based on lower-level scores on a performance test.

7. The reliability of judgments in performance assessment could be jeopardized by the limited number of observations, subjectivity of the scoring processes, as well as lack of internal consistency and generalizability.

Miller and Legg (1993) also address a number of potential problems:

1. The validity of performance assessments for measuring higher-order thinking skills (for instance, hypothesizing, searching for alternatives, self-monitoring, etc.) may be affected by test method, task type, and scoring criteria.

2. Reliability may be problematic because it hinges on rater consistency and task-specific variance.

3. The various testing formats and tasks may not be equivalent.

4. Fairness may be an issue because of lack of task relevancy or because of bias or offensiveness for certain populations.

5. True costs of the testing may not be immediately evident.

6. Test security may also be more difficult for this type of testing particularly due to the difficulty of reproducing limited items.

7. The safety, ethics, and legality of alternative techniques are also potential problems.

According to Messick (1994, 1996), two major threats to validity exist for performance assessments, as well as for any evaluation procedure: construct underrepresentation and construct-irrelevant variance. He also points out that performance assessments risk problems of adequate content coverage and construct generalizability. More specifically, do scores represent processes of approaching tasks? What knowledge and skills are required to address the task? How broad is the domain definition? Does the test adequately cover all skills, processes, and knowledge related to the task? Or is the performance taken to be representative of the extended range of possible tasks, including all of their inherent skills, processes, and knowledge as well?

In the language testing literature, Henning (1996) focuses on issues of rater reliability in making scoring judgments on a six-point performance assessment scale. He finds that rater agreement (in the form of interrater reliability estimates) may not be a dependable estimate of performance assessment reliability and that the practice of seeking additional raters to raise score reliability may not always be the most appropriate strategy. More interestingly, he finds that, though error is most abundant in the mid-range of scores, most of that error is canceled out by averaging ratings. As a result, the most serious need for adjudication of scores may fall at the extremes of the scale range.

McNamara (1995) identifies the following four problems that language testers must face in developing performance assessments:

1. Difficulty in generalizing from one observed instance of language behavior to other instances.

2. Difficulty in spelling out the actual criteria for assessment.

3. Difficulty in accounting for the role of non-linguistic factors and the fact that native speaker performance cannot be assumed to be representative of the top level of performance.

4. Difficulty in establishing a theoretical background to inform research and implementation.

Shohamy (1995) points to the following problems that language testers should grapple with:

1. Discrepancies between level descriptors and rater decisions.

2. Excessive influence of linguistic accuracy in the assignment of ratings.

3. Deciding who is an expert.

4. Determining what constitutes authentic measurement, and for whom? (contextual bias).

5. Deciding whether to use live testing or other methods.

6. Understanding the test situation effect and interviewer effect.

7. Using native speakers as models or as experts.

In short, the difficulties and problems in developing, implementing, scoring, and interpreting performance assessments are many. However, a similar array of problem areas exist for virtually all alternatives in assessment; indeed, without first identifying such a set of difficulties in assessment design, we would argue that the validity of any test-based inferencing must be seriously challenged. Based on our review of the literature and our experiences with performance assessment, we would therefore characterize the problems as summarized in the following section.

PROBLEMS WITH PERFORMANCE ASSESSMENT

1. Considerable increased costs in:
   a. Developing the tests
   b. Administering the tests
   c. Training teachers and raters
   d. Transporting tests (for large-scale assessments)
   e. Conducting extensive rating sessions
   f. Reporting scores
   g. Educating the public education about the procedures
   h. Many other factors not be immediately evident

2. Increased logistical problems of:
   a. Dealing with large amounts of collected material
   b. Providing special equipment
   c. Storing and transporting the tests
   d. Increasing time commitments
   e. Providing test security

3. Reliability may be problematic because it depends on:
   a. Rater consistency
   b. Task-specific variance
   c. A limited number of observations
   d. Subjectivity in the scoring process

4. Validity of performance tests is subject to the following threats:

   a. Construct underrepresentation — In language testing terms, this means the problem of generalizing from one or a few observations of language behavior to other real-life instances

   b. Construct-irrelevant variance (i.e., performance attributes that have little to do with language ability per se)

   c. Inadequate content coverage

   d. Lack of construct generalizability

   e. Sensitivity of performance tests to test method, task type, and scoring criteria considerations especially in terms of their validity for measuring higher-order thinking skills

   f. Differing views on what constitutes evidence for validity (including the perspectives of and interactions between teachers, teacher trainers, psychometricians, students, the general public, and any other stakeholders in the assessment process)

5. Test security may be problematic because of:

   a. The small number of test items which endangers test security and leads to the need for ongoing item development

   b. The difficulty of creating new items year after year

   c. Potential effects of "teaching to the test"

6. Political considerations that must be taken into account include the facts that:

   a. It may prove difficult to marshal support for implementation of new alternative procedures when they are compared to traditional, inexpensive, easy-to-administer, norm-referenced tests

   b. Increased costs will negatively affect public acceptance

   c. Decisions may have to be defended to multiple stake holders

   d. Safety, ethics, and legal defensibility of performance tests could become problematic

   e. The equivalence of the various testing formats and tasks may be difficult to create and defend

   f. Fairness may be an issue because tasks lack relevancy or because of offensiveness or bias for certain populations

7. Language performance testing, in particular, may prove problematic because:

   a. In trying to create reliable procedures, it may be difficult to:

      i. Create the descriptors of language behaviors which must serve as the criteria for assessment

      ii. Judge real-time language performance because it moves quickly

      iii. Deal with differences between level descriptors and actual rater decisions

    iv. Deal with discrepancies between level descriptors and actual second language performance

    v. Deal with excessive influence of accuracy on ratings

    vi. Decide who is an expert and who should rate

b. In trying to create valid procedures, it may be difficult to:

    i. Account for the role of non-linguistic factors

    ii. Deal with the fact that native-speaker norms cannot be taken to be representative of the highest levels of language performance

    iii. Implement language performance tests in light of the general lack of necessary theoretical background

    iv. Determine what constitutes authentic measurement, and for whom? (contextual bias)

    v. Assess receptive skills because they can only be observed indirectly

    vi. Decide whether to use live testing or other methods

    vii. Understand the test situation effect and interviewer effect

    viii. Use native speakers as models or as experts

WHAT STEPS CAN BE TAKEN TO AVOID PERFORMANCE ASSESSMENT PROBLEMS?

Refreshingly, several authors also suggest steps that can be taken to help test developers/users avoid many of the problems discussed in the previous section. We will begin by examining solutions to the reliability and validity problems associated with performance assessments.

Stiggins (1988) suggests that the "two keys to the success of this kind of judgment-based assessment are developing clear, explicit performance criteria and using systematic procedures for rating performances" (p. 365). Following these two recommendations should lead directly to enhanced reliability of the subjective rating process that is necessitated in performance assessments.

More specifically, Dunbar, Koretz, and Hoover (1991) point out that interrater reliability can be improved by using:

1. detailed scoring protocols

2. explicit criteria for different score levels

3. samples of work rated at different levels to guide raters

4. intensive rater training

They also warn that validity must be carefully studied in large-scale performance assessments, especially with regard to domain representativeness (i.e., the degree to which a task or a few tasks in a testing situation represent the many tasks that will be required in the real world). However, they do see some hope in the fact that, within the classroom, teachers are able to take variables like group differences and task types into account; hence, classroom-based performance assessment validity is not so seriously threatened by such factors. Indeed, individual variation in ability to handle different tasks may provide valuable diagnostic information for classroom teachers. We would also add that, given a principled method for comparisons of task types and task difficulty, generalizability of learner performances based on assessment tasks can be greatly enhanced.

Miller and Legg (1993) suggest a number of solutions to the problems they raise. For instance, they suggest: (a) that the reliability of performance assessments can be improved by using standard scoring procedures and by using multiple tasks; (b) that various testing formats and tasks should be carefully equated; (c) that fairness should be established by comparing task relevancy for different populations and by conducting reviews for bias and offensiveness; (d) that comparisons of the costs of various forms of testing should include all implementation costs (time, effort, reusability of items, and so forth); (e) that tasks and scoring criteria should be clearly described, but test users should also be made aware that such descriptions delimit what the scores can mean; (f) that multiple sources of information can be used to compensate for that delimitation; (g) that the teaching-to-the-test issue can be addressed by making sure that everybody involved understands the scoring criteria, while at the same time making sure that it is *not* possible to compromise the scoring criteria by using rote memorization strategies; (h) that test security will be essential, especially due to the more unwieldy nature of much performance assessment; and (i) that the safety, ethics, and legality of performance assessment techniques should be established prior to implementation.

Messick (1994) suggests a number of ways that performance assessments can be improved, especially during the test development process:

1. The breadth and depth of coverage by individual performance assessments should be increased by using multiple and varied tests, although he admits that this must be tempered by the availability of time.

2. Open-ended and structured-response item prompts and task descriptions, as well as various types of response formats (for instance, checklists, multiple-choice questions, and essays) can be combined in varying ways to achieve acceptable levels of content coverage and generalizability.

3. Transparency and meaningfulness should be maintained (that is, tests should be meaningful educational experiences that motivate and guide learning).

4. The focus in developing performance assessments should be either on constructs or on tasks:

   a. Construct-based test development should begin with the construct of interest and then tasks should be based on the performance attributes of the construct, scoring exigencies, and so forth.

b. Task-centered test development should begin by determining which performances are the desired ones. Then, scoring criteria and performance rubrics become part of the performance itself.

5. Complex, integrated skills should be assessed in addition to component skills.

6. Individual processes as well as complex performances are both components of authentic situations, hence both should be assessed.

7. Classifying all performance assessments as inherently direct is inappropriate because scores are always mediated by some kind of outside judgment. Any kind of measurement is indirect: "...a claim that a particular performance assessment is authentic and direct is tantamount to a claim of construct validity and needs to be supported by empirical evidence of construct validity" (p. 21).

8. Finally, the consequences, costs, and efficiency must also be considered in thinking about construct validity.

Quellmalz (1991) suggests a detailed set of characteristics to help insure the validity of performance assessment criteria:

1. Significance — criteria should represent a sample of knowledge and strategies from the real-world target domain, including cognitive, metacognitive, and dispositional components of the performance task.

2. Fidelity — criteria should be maintained by creating real-world tasks, conditions, expectations, and quality levels.

3. Generalizability — rubrics should be representative within domains, but also across domains when appropriate, and should represent instructional practices. A common understanding of the criteria should be shared by raters, students, and teachers.

4. Developmental appropriateness — criteria should be consistent with theory-based stages in learner development. In addition, criteria should be described in bands of developmental abilities, while emphasizing accomplishments at each level rather than weaknesses.

5. Accessibility — criteria should be written in a style that will be clear to all audiences involved (including at least students, teachers, parents, administrators, etc.).

6. Utility — criteria should concentrate on performance features that instruction can address within reasonable time constraints.

Quellmalz further argues that construction of assessment criteria should begin early in the process of creating performance assessments, utilizing professional advice, information from previous performance assessments, and comparisons of real student work with the performance levels found on the test.

Finally, Scott, Stansfield, and Kenyon (1996) demonstrate how situational and interactional authenticity (originally suggested by Bachman, 1991) as well as convergent/divergent validity can be used to validate a performance assessment. We will return to the components of performance assessment validation when discussing the current research project.

Based on the foregoing literature review and our experiences with developing performance assessments, we would conclude that a number of steps can be taken to avoid the problems of performance assessment (listed under "Problems with performance assessment" above) as summarized in the following section.

STEPS THAT CAN BE TAKEN TO AVOID THE PROBLEMS OF PERFORMANCE ASSESSMENT

1. Considerable increased costs of performance tests
   a. Make sure that any comparisons of the costs of performance testing and the standardized tests to which they will inevitably be compared include *all* of the implementation costs of the standardized tests, including time, staff costs, reusability of items, and so forth.
   b. Use existing resources to the greatest degree possible; for example, do the testing during school time using school facilities, supplies, and teachers

2. Increased logistical problems
   a. Designate a single person responsible for collecting and organizing materials and reward that person in some way for doing the task
   b. Write grant proposals for grants to pay for any necessary special equipment
   c. Store and transport the tests using school space and school transportation
   d. Decrease teachers' time commitments to other less essential work related items and tasks (e.g., needless, repetitive paperwork)
   e. Use the same test security precautions that would be used in a standardized test
   f. Use an item bank of performance tasks from which various forms of the test (in various years) can be drawn

3. Reliability can be improved by doing the following:
   a. Create clear, explicitly explained performance criteria
      i. Produce them early in the test development process
      ii. Obtain professional advice on criteria
      iii. Examine already exising performance test criteria from the literature
      iv. Pilot criteria with a special focus on comparing real student work with performance levels found on pilot test

b. Be systematic in using procedures for rating students' performances
   i. Use clear and detailed scoring criteria in written form
   ii. Provide explicit criteria for different categories of language if an analytic approach is to be used
   iii. Provide explicit criteria for different score levels (within categories of language if appropriate)
   iv. Give raters example work samples at various levels to help them get a feel for the relationship between the criteria and real work
   v. Train the raters intensively
   vi. Retrain the raters as necessary
   vii. Periodically monitor rater agreement
c. Use the following general guidelines to improve the reliability of performance assessments:
   i. Provide clear task descriptions and directions
   ii. Use standard scoring procedures
   iii. Use multiple tasks (generally, the more, the better)
   iv. Marshal and utilize multiple sources of information in decision making

4. Threats to the validity of performance assessments can be minimized as follows:
   a. In developing a performance assessment, focus either on constructs or on tasks:
      i. Begin construct-based test development by focusing on the construct of interest and then develop tasks based on the performance attributes of the construct, score uses, scoring constraints, and so forth.
      ii. Begin task-centered test development by deciding which performances are the desired ones. Then, score uses, scoring criteria, and so forth become part of the performance test itself.
   b. Carefully study the validity of the performance test, especially with regard to domain representativeness (i.e., the degree to which a task or a few tasks in a testing situation represent the many real-world tasks that will be required later)
   c. Increase the breadth and depth of coverage in performance tests by using numerous tasks and subtests of varied content
   d. Receptive-response and productive-response item prompts and task descriptions, as well as various types of formats (for instance, multiple-choice items, checklists, self-ratings, essays, etc.), can effectively be combined to maximize acceptable content coverage and score generalizability
   e. Complex, interrelated, and integrated skills should be assessed in addition to the discrete component skills (component processes as well

as complex, integrated performances are all part of authentic situations, hence they should all be tested)

    f. Several of the authors suggest novel ways that validity should be viewed if it is to be adequate for assessing performance tests and comparing them to other forms of testing

        i. Significance, that is, scoring criteria should represent a sample of knowledge and strategies from the real-world target domain

        ii. Fidelity, that is, tasks should involve real-world activities, conditions, purposes, and expectations

      iii. Generalizability

           (a) Scoring criteria should be representative of specific domains

           (b) Scoring criteria should also include several domains when that is appropriate

           (c) Scoring criteria should represent instructional practices

           (d) Raters, teachers, and students should share a common understanding of what the scoring criteria mean

           (e) Scoring criteria should be based on input from multiple perspectives drawn from all stakeholders in the decision-making process

      iv. Developmental appropriateness, that is, scoring criteria should be consistent with theoretical stages of development and should be described in terms of those bands of development (while emphasizing accomplishments at each level rather than weaknesses)

        v. Accessibility, that is, scoring criteria should be written in a clear and accessible writing style so that, at minimum, students, teachers, parents, and even administrators will be able to understand them

      vi. Utility, that is, scoring criteria should concentrate on aspects of performance that instruction can realistically address within the instructional time available

     vii. Finally, the consequences, costs, and efficiency of the performance testing must also be considered in thinking about validity

5. Test security can be maximized by:

    a. Using numerous and varied tasks and task prompts

    b. Minimizing teaching-to-the-test by making sure that all parties involved understand the scoring criteria

    c. Considering that it is *not* possible to compromise the scoring criteria by using rote memorization strategies

    d. Maintaining test clarity and meaningfulness (i.e., insuring that the performance tests are meaningful educational experiences that motivate and guide learning)

6. Political problems can be avoided in part by making sure that:

    a. Various testing formats and tasks are equated

b. Fairness is established and maintained by comparing task relevancy for different populations and by performing periodic reviews for bias and offensiveness

c. The safety, ethics, and legality of the performance tests are considered prior to implementation

d. Extensive documentation is maintained throughout the process

e. Test results are thoroughly studied and documented on a periodic basis

f. Rating criteria are made explicit from the outset and are in line with classroom activities and real-world objectives

WHERE DO PERFORMANCE ASSESSMENTS FIT INTO A LANGUAGE CURRICULUM?

The fundamental role of assessment within a language curriculum has been discussed in detail by a number of authors over the past decade (see, e.g., Bachman, 1990; J. D. Brown, 1996). However, the express potential that is offered by performance assessment and other alternatives in assessment for informing curricular decision making has received less attention. Recently, the National Standards in Foreign Language Education Project (1996) proposed that new kinds of performance assessment should be developed in order to effectively assess students' abilities to communicate in the L2s that they are learning. Such performance assessments should facilitate decision making with respect to individual learners' progress and performance levels in terms of the *Standards for foreign language learning* (National Standards in Foreign Language Education Project, 1996). Performance assessment assumes a central role, therefore, in this nationwide (US) approach to foreign language curriculum design.

In the ESL literature, Short (1993) proposes an assessment framework within an integrated content/L2 curriculum that utilizes a variety of alternative measures which, "should be incorporated into lesson planning frequently and informally as a significant part of instruction" (p. 634). For Short, alternative forms of assessment (see Table 1) are particularly well-suited for enabling effective curricular decision making regarding language minority classrooms (e.g., ESL classes in the US), where students may not respond well to more traditional forms of testing and where a variety of types of information are needed by teachers and administrators. She advises selection of assessment types after careful consideration of curricular objectives, and she offers the set of alternatives shown in Table 1 as possibilities for integrating assessment with content/language objectives based within a given curriculum. Table 1 illustrates how performance assessments fit into the range of possible alternatives for assessing language and content learning in L2 classrooms.

Table 1: Integrated language and content assessment: WHAT and HOW (from Short, 1993, p. 636)

	checklist, inventory	anecdotal record, teacher observation	student self-evaluation	portfolios	peformance, manipulatives	written essays, reports	oral reports	student interviews
problem solving								
content-area skills								
concept comprehension								
language use								
communication skills								
individual behavior								
group behavior								
attitudes								

H O W

W H A T

Shohamy (1992) views specifically performance assessment as essential for sound L2 curricular decision making, and she proposes a model for L2 performance testing that is based on:

1. Stressing both achievement and proficiency testing

2. Providing multidimensional diagnostic information

3. Connecting teaching and learning by paying attention to the effect of tests on teaching

4. Involving teachers

5. Supplying both norm-referenced and criterion-referenced information

6. Basing test development on theories of language learning

7. Testing repeatedly in order to affect change

According to this model, performance assessment can be seen to function within the curriculum not only as a source of diagnostic feedback regarding students' L2 abilities, but also as an impetus for instructional change.

Within the task-based language teaching literature (see following chapter), performance assessment is generally held to provide essential feedback regarding student L2 acquisition, the effectiveness of instruction, and the outcomes of learner efforts at accomplishing real-world tasks, and as such it forms an essential curricular component. For example, Long and Crookes (1992) propose such a role for performance assessment in their discussion of task-based syllabus design:

> Such task-based syllabuses would usually, although not exclusively, imply assessment of student learning by way of task-based criterion-referenced tests, whose focus is whether or not students can perform some task to criterion, as established by experts in the field, not their ability to complete discrete-point grammar items. (p. 45)

We generally concur with the roles for performance assessments within L2 curricula as proposed by these various authors, and we feel that the potential for criterion-referenced task-based assessments is particularly important. In the following two chapters, we will outline a rationale for task-based performance assessment based on recent empirical findings as well as theoretical justification from the task-based language teaching literature.

Performance assessments have also found use within certain L2 curricula in very specific roles. The following section discusses several examples of the implementation of L2 performance assessments.

WHAT EXAMPLES EXIST OF ACTUAL PERFORMANCE ASSESSMENT PROJECTS?

While most of the articles reviewed here discuss performance assessments in terms of characteristics, developmental steps, benefits, problems, solutions, and place in curriculum, a small number discuss examples of actual performance assessments that have been put into practice. For example, Bailey (1985) describes a foreign teaching assistant performance assessment, while Clark and Grognet (1985) discuss a survival skills performance assessment. Other examples include McNamara (1990), which examines an occupational English test for health professionals, and Paltridge (1992), which describes an EAP placement test development project. Fulcher (1996) describes the development of task-based oral assessments using groups of EFL students in Cyprus. We direct the reader to any of these references for further insight into performance assessment development issues peculiar to these specific language programs. However, unlike these five examples, the project described in this volume focuses more generally on performance assessment for second and foreign language students at the university level in the United States.

SUMMARY

Zessoules and Gardner (1991) pretty much sum up the issues raised by advocates of alternative assessments when they argue that the dominance of standardized testing in American schools tends to lead to a standardized approach to learning and evaluation, and that curriculum and instruction also may tend to be driven by such standardization. Unfortunately, such standardization may not match the actual effective processes and performances that occur in typical teacher assessment practices and student learning. In reaction to standardization, new forms of assessment have evolved: "Currently taking the form chiefly of portfolios and performance-based tasks, these measures are often referred to as authentic assessment; and they are designed to present a broader, more genuine picture of student learning" (p. 49). After arguing strongly for the use of alternative assessments, Zessoules and Gardner conclude with the reminder that "Authentic assessment does not eradicate, but in fact inherits, many of the problems of standardized testing. Educators still need to confront issues of cultural bias, teacher fairness, validity, and reliability" (p. 70). We will return to these issues in subsequent chapters addressing a proposed framework for the development of second language performance assessments.

chapter three

TASK-BASED LANGUAGE TEACHING

Given their recurrence in the previous discussion, it should be obvious by now that *real-world* tasks play a central role in the design of various types of performance assessments. Ultimately, it seems that task accomplishment is the ultimate focus for evaluating human performance. It follows that L2 performance assessment and task-based approaches to language teaching and assessment will likely share a great deal of theoretical and practical common ground. In order to further explore this relationship, we review here the task-based language teaching (TBLT) literature with specific focus on the implications that task-based theory, research findings, and teaching practice might have for performance assessment design. This chapter considers general issues that have arisen from the task-based language teaching literature, and chapter 4 addresses issues specific to task-based assessment. Each set of issues is discussed in terms of consequences for L2 performance assessment.

Task-based language teaching has received increasing recognition in the second language acquisition and second language pedagogy literature over the past two decades. By employing the communicative task as the basic unit of analysis for motivating syllabus design and L2 classroom activities, advocates claim that contemporary theories of language learning and acquisition which are supported by empirical findings (e.g., regarding the need for a focus on form while maintaining an overall focus on the conveyance of meaning in the L2) can be effectively implemented. For example, Pica, Kanagy, and Falodun (1993) draw on studies of interaction-based pedagogy as well as input and interactionist theories in SLA; they suggest that the best way to learn and teach a language is through social interactions. According to these authors, social interactions allow students to work toward a clear goal, share information and opinions, negotiate meaning, get the interlocutor's help in comprehending input, and receive feedback on their language production. In the process, learners not only use their interlanguage but also modify it, which in turn promotes acquisition. The authors hold that communicative *tasks* are particularly well-suited for this job because of their two main features: communication goals and interactional activities (however, they caution that these two task features alone do not necessarily insure that all of the above processes will result). Pica, Kanagy, and Falodun (1993) offer a rationale that is rather representative of recent task-based approaches to language teaching.

Within such TBLT approaches, several authors have directly addressed some of the issues involved in assessment of task-based language performance, and we will discuss their specific recommendations in due course (in the following chapter on task-based assessment). However, on the whole, the TBLT literature only implicitly addresses issues in assessment. This growing body of pedagogic and theoretical

TBLT literature does, nonetheless, provide a basis for important considerations in informing assessment design parameters. Within this body of work, we found ourselves looking for answers to three general questions:

1. What are tasks?
2. What is the role of needs analysis in task selection?
3. What are the factors that affect task difficulty and sequencing?

It is beyond the scope of the current report to examine in detail the range of theoretical and empirical responses to such questions that have emerged over the past few years, and we direct the reader to recent work by Peter Skehan (1998) and a fothcomng book by Michael Long for thorough discussions of the range of issues related to task-based language teaching. However, brief answers to each of the above questions do seem necessary in order to better explain the role of tasks in designing second language performance assessments. The three questions will each be answered in turn in this chapter, so they will quite appropriately serve as subsection headings. We will address each question based on what we found in the literature and based on our experiences in language testing. We will also summarize the implications that these findings have for task-based assessment of L2 performance. We turn now to the first question.

WHAT ARE TASKS?

Within a task-based approach to language teaching (e.g., the previous rationale from Pica, Kanagy, and Falodun, 1993), what is it that constitutes a task? A convenient and oft-cited point of departure is provided by Long (1985), who defines task generically as:

> a piece of work undertaken for oneself or for others, freely or for some reward. Thus examples of tasks include painting a fence, dressing a child, filling out a form, buying a pair of shoes, making an airline reservation, borrowing a library book, taking a driving test, typing a letter, weighing a patient, sorting letters, taking a hotel reservation, writing a check, finding a street destination and helping someone across a road. In other words, by 'task' is meant the hundred and one things people *do* in everyday life, at work, at play, and in between. (p. 89)

For Long (1985), then, a task is fundamentally something that is accomplished or done, and language is involved insofar as it is inherently necessary for accomplishment of the task. We also consider this a suitable definition of task for L2 performance assessment; that is, we are interested in assessing the performances of L2 speakers in using language to accomplish the things that people do in everyday life. This emphasis on the everyday nature of performance assessment tasks will become more apparent in subsequent chapters dealing with item-specifications and item prototypes that reflect real-world language use.

Crookes (1986) also offers a broad definition of tasks in the real world, but he specifically includes the possibility of classroom and laboratory applications:

> A piece of work or an activity, usually with a specified objective, undertaken as part of an educational course, at work, or used to elicit data for research. (p. 1)

With respect to communicative tasks, then, this definition includes not only so-called *real-world* language tasks that involve the fundamental necessity of conveying meaning, but also the express application of task as an activity, the sole purpose of which is in some sense didactic. Hence, in a communicative task, the conveyance of meaning may take a back seat to pedagogic or research-related concerns. For example, one kind of task might be conceived of as a means for eliciting learner use of a particular syntactic structure (such as subject-verb inversion in German) or a particular morpheme (such as third-person *s* in English) in order to identify stages in learner L2 development. The objective of such a task might not be to engage the learner in everyday communication for the purpose of conveying meaning, rather it might be to provide diagnostic feedback for pedagogic decisions or to gather data for investigating theories of L2 development. Although such a notion of the potential role of tasks as primarily pedagogic or research-oriented tools is appropriate in some situations, the significance of such tasks in motivating performance assessment design is limited.

The approach to assessment discussed in this report does not focus on how or why learners produce specific syntactic structures or morphemes (for example), nor on the relationship between task performance and particular L2 syllabuses or particular theories of language acquisition (although these may be quite valid foci for other types of evaluation). The notion of task is defined in the current project as those activities that people do in everyday life and which require language for their accomplishment. Although task performances from the current assessment instrument will be used for research purposes, they are primarily intended to be possible real-world language tasks, and the research that will be accomplished by using them is concerned only with the performance of L2 speakers when doing these tasks.

Crookes further discusses the notion of *real-world* tasks as related to task-based pedagogy by borrowing the interpretation of curriculum as a set of tasks from Doyle (1983), whose definition of academic tasks bears repeating here:

> [t]he term "task" focuses attention on three aspects of students' work: (a) the products students are to formulate...; (b) the operations that are to be used to generate the product...; and (c) the "givens" or resources available to students while they are generating a product. (p. 161)

We find this three-part definition of academic tasks to be particularly useful with respect to the elements involved in item specifications within a task-based performance assessment, and we will return to operationalization of these elements in chapters 5, 6, and in the appendix. We also concur with Crookes, who cites parallels in Mohan (1986), in finding that such a conception of task essentially "reflects the structure of human activities" (p. 5). As with Long (1985), a task is still basically a real-world activity.

More recently, discussion of tasks has come to reflect more specific applications of the idea of task as a pedagogic tool. Nunan (1989) draws on a number of different definitions to define a communicative task as "a piece of classroom work which involves learners in comprehending, manipulating, producing or interacting in the target language while their attention is principally focused on meaning rather than form" (p. 10). Later he discusses two categories of tasks:

1. Real-world tasks, which are designed to practice or rehearse those tasks which are found to be important in a needs analysis and turn out to be important and useful in the real world, and

2. Pedagogic tasks, which have a psycholinguistic basis in SLA theory and research but do not necessarily reflect real-world tasks. (pp. 40–41)

Nunan's definition, then, can be seen to de-emphasize the real-world nature of tasks and focus instead on their pedagogic manipulation in line with purported relationships to theories of second language acquisition or a particular teaching methodology. Even in point 1 above, the notion of task is not allowed to transcend the classroom context (e.g., tasks are seen as "practice" or rehearsal). Although we are in basic agreement with the usefulness of this and similar definitions for the purposes of classroom language learning and research into processes of second language acquisition, we contend that such a definition is not particularly useful for operationalizing the notion of task within L2 performance assessments. In other words, following this definition, task-based assessment could be taken to measure in some way the results of the task in terms of the psycholinguistic processes that a learner engages in when attempting a task, the developmental stage revealed by certain structures produced during the task, and so forth. Although we certainly acknowledge the importance of these measurement objectives as they might affect immediate teaching practice or contribute to theories of L2 development (for example), we cannot be concerned with these and similar objectives when measuring the performance of an individual in accomplishing a given real-world task. What we are (and, we maintain, must be) concerned with is only the ability of an individual to successfully (or unsuccessfully) accomplish real-world tasks that require language use. If we conceive of performance assessment as a bridge between classroom learning and real-world language use, then our performance assessment tasks must convey with the greatest possible fidelity the real-world conditions of everyday task accomplishment. This fundamental assumption underlies a number of assessment design issues throughout the remainder of this book.

For the purpose of comparing a more recent definition, we would like to note that Skehan (1998) condenses previous definitions of tasks in task-based language teaching from the work of Candlin (1987), Long (1989), and Nunan (1989) by presenting the following parameters for a task activity: (a) meaning is primary, (b) learners are not given other people's meanings to regurgitate, (c) there is some sort of relationship to comparable real-world activities, (d) task completion has some priority, and (e) the assessment of the task is done in terms of outcome (p. 147). Skehan's very recent definition, then, is distinctly different from Nunan's definition. Whereas in Nunan's definition the primary interpretation of task is as a pedagogic tool, in Skehan's definition only implicit mention is made of the pedagogic role of the task, and the result is a picture of task as a daily activity in which language is used for the accomplishment of some kind of work that requires an outcome (much more in line with the earlier definition from Long). For considerations in L2 performance assessment design, we will adhere to these two definitions from Skehan (1998) and Long (1985).

It should be noted that the definition and description of tasks for the purposes of task-based pedagogy further involves a number of issues that will not be considered here. For example, in order to inform task-selection in language syllabus construction and classroom activity design, a variety of components that contribute to the nature of a task are important. Some of the many components that have been addressed in the literature include: task finiteness, goal orientation, outcome options, interaction requirements, interactant relationships, input form, activity types, teacher and learner roles, task and learning settings, integration possibilities, linguistic support, modification and feedback opportunities, accuracy/complexity/fluency requirements, and attentional demand (see Honeyfield, 1993; Lee, 1995; Long & Crookes, 1993; Nunan, 1989; Pica, Kanagy, & Falodun, 1993; Robinson, 1995; Skehan, 1996; and Van Patten, 1994 among others). Based on various combinations of these and similar task components, several pedagogic task types have emerged from the literature, each task type reflecting particular pedagogic concerns and desired learning outcomes. However, these task components and task types do not seem to us to be particularly salient in the design of task-based assessment, where concern is focused, not on the *process of learning* how to accomplish real-world tasks, but rather on the manner in which tasks are accomplished using language. Therefore, we will now turn to the very pertinent role of needs analysis in task selection and the related implications for L2 performance assessment.

WHAT IS THE ROLE OF NEEDS ANALYSIS IN TASK SELECTION?

Given our definition of tasks and our emphasis on maintaining their real-world essence, how are relevant tasks to be identified and sampled for the purposes of assessing learner L2 performance? Looking again to the TBLT literature, we find that a thorough analysis of the real-world needs that learners have in terms of tasks, task elements, and task types plays a central role in selecting pedagogic tasks. Long and Crookes (1992) suggest that:

> It is impossible for anyone to verify the appropriacy of particular pedagogic tasks for a given group of learners without objective evaluation criteria, one of which must surely be relevance to learner needs. (p. 37)

Fundamentally, the same requirement can be made for assessment tasks, that is, in order for a performance assessment to be designed so that it taps learner language abilities for accomplishing particular real-world tasks, relevant language needs must first be identified and described. Such needs analysis would investigate the domains of language use associated with a particular population of learners, and it would result in a set of real-world target tasks that would be used in developing various aspects of the syllabus for those students. Indeed, an effective needs analysis should indicate both pedagogic-oriented and assessment-oriented tasks.

Long and Crookes (1993) cite a number of sources from the ESP literature which detail how a needs analysis might be carried out, and we will leave it to the reader's discretion to investigate the needs analysis process in more detail (see also J. D. Brown, 1995a, for discussion of needs analysis at the program level). Long and Crookes (1993) suggest that, once identified, target tasks serve more as pedagogic goals than as the actual tasks students will undertake in the classroom, mainly because target tasks "would often be too difficult, inefficient in terms of class time, logistically impossible, and irrelevant for some learners in heterogeneous classes when students' future needs vary" (p. 40). Instead, in task-based syllabus construction, target tasks are often collapsed and classified into more general task types. "To take a simple example, serving breakfast, serving lunch, serving dinner and serving snacks and refreshments, might be classified into 'serving food and beverages' in a course for trainee flight attendants" (p. 40). Once organized, such task types can then provide the basis for developing pedagogic tasks, which are later sequenced to create a task-based syllabus — all of which Long and Crookes suggest to be quite a complex task in itself.

However, in terms of task-based performance assessments, which are designed to test the real-world outcomes of such task-based pedagogy, use of the actual tasks in authentic situations (to the extent that it is feasible) is called for. Here, then, assessment tasks must diverge from pedagogic tasks. We contend that it is imperative for assessment tasks to be preserved with as much authenticity as possible, in order to legitimately reflect learner abilities to perform under real-world conditions. Therefore, needs analysis is crucial not only for determining pedagogic sequencing and emphasis but also for establishing desired outcomes in terms of task performance (expert judgments of what constitutes success or failure, minimal criteria to be met in accomplishing the task, etc.). Several examples of large-scale needs analysis for university-level L2 learners offer interesting points of departure for the current project.

Horowitz (1986), for example, argues that too much emphasis has been placed on the psycholinguistic, "process" approaches to ESL writing and that not enough research has been done to determine the actual EAP (English for Academic Purposes) writing tasks and genres students must deal with in college. Thus, he implies that such a "missing half" approach does a disservice to the students. According to Horowitz, a number of surveys on writing tasks have been conducted, but the data collection instruments (usually a questionnaire or interview) were often too narrow or focused to give an accurate indication of the full range of writing tasks at US universities. For this new study, Horowitz contacted 750 faculty members at Western Illinois University, asking for the writing assignments they used in class. Only 38 people (a mere five percent) responded, representing 29 courses taught across 17 departments, and only 36 of those responses were usable. Such a weak return rate notwithstanding, Horowitz analyzed patterns in the data and found seven different writing task classifications: (a) summary of/reaction to a reading, (b) annotated bibliography, (c) report on a specified participatory experience, (d) connection of theory and data, (e) case study, (f) synthesis of multiple sources, and (g) research project. After considering the characteristics common across these task types, Horowitz developed a synthesized and generalized American academic writing task:

> Given a topic, topicless thesis statement, or full thesis statement, an indication of the audience's expectations (in terms of what questions are to be covered and in what order they should be answered), specified sources of data, and a lexis constrained (to some extent) by all of the above, find data which are relevant to each question and then reorganize and encode those data in such a way that the reader's expectations of relevance, coherence, and etiquette are fulfilled. (p. 455)

In the process of identifying the seven academic writing tasks above, Horowitz also identified three important sets of skills that are subsumed in each of the writing tasks and which would serve as important preparatory activities:

1. Selecting relevant data from sources;

2. Reorganizing data in response to a question; and

3. Encoding data into Academic English.

Although Horowitz's study provides a set of general EAP writing tasks, it probably leaves out a number of other important writing tasks, judging from the very small sample of respondents. If a large number of faculty members had responded, the number of categories might have increased and been more informative. Also, since his study focuses on one university, his results may only be applicable to that context. Similar samplings at a number of universities nationwide would perhaps provide more reliable categorizations of different types of writing tasks, as the author mentions. Nonetheless, his approach offers one interesting example of a large-scale needs analysis that was attempted for the purposes of determining relevant task types as well as expectations of the products, operations, and "givens" in a range of university-level academic writing tasks (cf. Doyle, 1983, above).

Although much research has focused on surveys of the academic reading/writing tasks that university professors require and ESL students must deal with in their courses, Ferris and Tagg (1996) point out that little similar information exists on academic listening/speaking tasks. To fill that gap, Ferris and Tagg reviewed the research on academic listening/speaking skills, as well as the survey literature on EAP, and pursued the following three research questions:

1. What types of listening and speaking tasks do professors expect or require of college/university students?

2. In what way(s) do the academic listening/speaking abilities of ESL students fall short in enabling them to complete these classroom tasks successfully?

3. What could university and university-preparatory ESL classes do to better fit their students for the oral/aural tasks they will face in their college and university classes? (p. 302)

Their survey was conducted across a broad range of schools: Sacramento City College; California State University, Sacramento; the University of California, Davis; and the University of Southern California. Of the 921 professors who received the survey, 234 responded (for a 25.6% rate of response).

The two important findings that emerged from their data were that students should have adequate general listening and speaking skills to comprehend what is being discussed or covered in class, and they should be able to participate and collaborate with their native English speaking peers. More generally, students should have the skills to be able to carry out vital classroom activities, particularly ones tied to the demands of their particular course or field. In their own words:

> Content-area professors wish that ESL teachers would better prepare their students for the expectations of the US university classroom by impressing upon them the importance of communication skills in general, by teaching them to ask and respond to questions effectively, by giving them practice speaking, and by encouraging class participation. In addition, many commented that ESL students should have opportunities and encouragement to interact with native speakers (or at least classmates who do not speak the same language). (p. 311)

Both of the previous examples show the potential for large-scale needs analysis in determining aspects of target tasks that are related to the goals of given language curricula and given learner populations (in this case university ESL classes). Based on the results of these efforts, performance assessment tasks could be sampled for use in determining learner ability to accomplish such academic tasks to an expected criterion level. However, one general criticism that could be leveled at each of these approaches to needs analysis would concern the fact that data were gathered from only one point of view, that of the university professor, and using only one method for collecting data, the survey questionnaire. It could be argued, therefore, that potential alternative methods of analysis based on input from various concerned parties might produce a divergent set of task types and criteria (cf. Lynch, 1996, for multiple theories and methods for needs analysis in the context of program evaluation). Such concerns also weaken the generalizability of the findings to other situations. We would suggest, therefore, that careful attention be given to the steps taken in a needs analysis in order to insure appropriate and valid findings in terms of pedagogic or assessment tasks. A wide variety of relevant examples for L2 needs analyses exist, and we direct the reader to any of these sources for further information (e.g., Benson, 1989; Berwick, 1989; Brindley, 1984; Cathcart, 1989; Hale, Taylor, Bridgeman, Carson, Kroll, & Kantor, 1996; Jacobson, 1986; Jasso-Aguilar, forthcoming; Kimzin & Proctor, 1986; Long, forthcoming; Prince, 1984; and West, 1994)

Long and Crookes (1992, 1993) explain how needs analysis of real-world tasks is related to classroom task-based syllabus design, and Horowitz (1986) as well as Ferris and Tagg (1996) provide examples of such needs analyses in academic settings for writing and listening/speaking, respectively. Subsequent sections in this book will outline the specific role that needs analysis plays for our prototypical performance assessment tasks. It should be noted, given the fact that the current performance assessment and related real-world tasks are intended to indeed be prototypes (and are not, therefore, tied to any one language curriculum), the impact of needs analysis is predictably limited. We reiterate, nonetheless, that rigorous investigation of learner language needs be included as an integral component of performance assessment design for specific language programs.

Once the students' needs have been determined and task selection and organization have taken place, it is still necessary to sequence the tasks following some principled understanding of the components of task difficulty and the effects of task difficulty and tasks types on language performance. Accordingly, factors affecting task sequencing and task difficulty will be addressed in the following section.

WHAT ARE THE FACTORS THAT AFFECT TASK DIFFICULTY AND SEQUENCING?

Thus far we have shown that setting task parameters (through task definition) and selecting appropriate tasks (through needs analysis) are integral, feasible, and well-motivated components of performance assessment design. The final task-related factor to be considered from the TBLT perspective involves the notion of differentiating among tasks based on their difficulty. The following chapters will show that this endeavor plays a central role in the performance assessment design presented in this report, especially if the potential for sequencing of tasks based on components of difficulty provides a basis for the predictive utility of L2 performance assessments.

Within the TBLT literature, a principled and empirically supported conceptualization of task difficulty has been long considered a primary goal and has, for just as long, proved to be elusive. Early TBLT proponents noted the necessity of describing difficulty components, in order to sequence task presentation within the classroom, and they proposed various sets of determinants. Crookes (1986), citing Long (1985), suggests that within task-based syllabus design, "difficulty is a prime consideration," and he lists the following possible contributors:

1. number of steps needed
2. number of parties involved

3. presupposed knowledge
4. intellectual challenge
5. spatio-temporal displacement (p. 24)

Crookes also notes that these possible contributors to task difficulty are hypothesized rather than founded on empirical evidence. Nevertheless, such possibilities, which are grounded in classroom observation of learner performances with various tasks, do offer valuable points of reference for motivating investigations into actual performance effects of different aspects of task difficulty. Difficulty components like these have inspired an expanding (if still limited) line of research into factors that affect a learner's ability to accomplish a given L2 task.

According to Nunan (1989), once a number of related tasks have been designed, they need to be graded (ranked in order of difficulty) so they can later be sequenced and appropriately integrated into the syllabus. Such grading, he maintains, is not an easy endeavor because it is affected by a great number of factors. The level of difficulty of the input, for example, may vary depending on the grammatical complexity involved, as well as the following:

> ...the length of the text, the propositional density (how much information it contains and the extent to which this information is recycled), the amount of low frequency vocabulary, the speed of spoken texts and the number of speakers involved, the explicitness of the information, the discourse structure and the clarity with which this is signaled (for example paragraphs in which the main point is buried away will probably be more difficult to process than those in which the main idea is clearly presented in the opening sentence). (p. 98)

Furthermore, Nunan asserts that the way a text may be modified and the genre it is written in can also affect the difficulty of the input.

Nunan (1989) points to factors other than input that can influence the level of task difficulty:

1. *Learner factors*, including their confidence, motivation, prior learning experience, learning pace, observed ability in language skills, cultural knowledge or awareness, linguistic knowledge (pp. 102–103); as well as
2. *Activity factors*, including relevance, complexity, amount of context provided prior to task, processability of the language of the task, amount of help available to the learner, degree of grammatical accuracy/contextual appropriacy, time available to learner, cognitive load, communicative stress, particularity and generalizability, code complexity and interpretive density, and process continuity. (pp. 109–111)

Nunan offers no empirical evidence for the potential combined effects of his list of factors on overall task difficulty. In other words, he gives no principled rationale for understanding or estimating the effects on difficulty of the variable contributions of such manifold factors within a given L2 task.

Nevertheless, by using his proposed task sequences (and his numerous examples of graded tasks), teachers could probably develop their own systematic task-based instruction framework. However, two vital aspects would be missing from such a framework: assessment of learner performance on the tasks and empirical evidence supporting the asserted difficulty and sequencing of tasks described in the book. For the purposes of informing classroom methodology, then, such work provides teachers with specific pedagogic options and a plan for implementing one version of task-based language teaching. Indeed, Thompson (1992) reports on the "successful" implementation of Nunan's framework for designing a task-based language syllabus in Singapore. However, success in Thompson's terms is not measured in terms of student performances on real-world tasks as compared with some set of real-world criteria, rather success in this case is indicative of learner enjoyment, investment in the pedagogical process, apparent motivation, and so forth.

Although this type of TBLT framework can inform L2 pedagogical methods, it does not have much to offer in terms of *evidence* for the presentation of tasks within the classroom (sequencing), nor does it contribute to our understanding of the effect of difficulty components on task performances. Nunan (1993) acknowledges this *difficulty* with task difficulty:

> Grading and sequencing are carried out with reference to priority of learner needs and also with reference to notions of difficulty. Determining difficulty is a major problem because of the number of factors involved... In addition, these factors interact. (p. 60)

Although he again provides no suggestions for how we might determine such interaction, he does cite a variety of studies that have investigated the implications for syllabus design and pedagogic practice of various aspects of task difficulty. These studies offer some evidence regarding what aspects of a task have certain kinds of effects on the learning and acquisition processes. However, assessment of differential effects on performance of the different aspects of task difficulty has largely been ignored (we will return shortly to the empirical issue of task difficulty and performance assessment).

Other authors have suggested particular types of task difficulty that can be motivated by language acquisition and linguistic theories. For example, drawing on research from first language acquisition, second language development, and functional linguistic theory, Robinson (1995) also determined a number of specific areas and measures for task complexity, with specific reference to two task types:

1. *Referential complexity* — a task can be referentially more or less complex. As Robinson puts it, "The ability to make displaced reference — that is, to events not in the Here-and-Now — involves a number of cognitive operations, conversational abilities, and linguistic resources not necessary when talking about objects and events that are visible while the

---

conversation is taking place (e.g., the varied discussions on this topic in R. W. Brown, 1973; Eisenberg, 1985; Givón, 1985; Gruber, 1967)" (p. 102).

2. *Structural complexity*, is basically a shift from a pragmatic mode to a syntactic mode. In Robinson's words:

> Givón (1979, 1985, 1989) has described the shift from the earliest, context-supported use of an 'undercoded' language system to acquisition of a later, more coded version as a process of 'syntactization' motivated by functional and processing demands of language users. Givón referred to the early language of the child as being in the 'pragmatic' mode; being contextually rooted, it tends to preserve a one-to-one, or iconic, correspondence between code structure and message meaning. Although it is structurally simple, its processing is slow. Later language development moves toward the more structurally complex 'syntactic' mode, which is more economic in terms of processing effort, but correspondingly less clear. (p. 104)

3. *Processing complexity*, which is evidenced during production, can be measured in a number of ways. In Robinson's words:

> Two measures of the complexity of the two narrative tasks, then, that relate to processing complexity, are the number of pauses in each narrative and the number of words per pausally defined unit. Narratives performed in the There-and-Then condition should exhibit greater dysfluency and therefore more pausing, as well as relatively fewer words per pause, than narratives performed in the Here-and-Now conditions. These measures of relative fluency of periods of phonation and nonphonation cannot be captured in measures of the time spent on narration, or of the rate of narration that is, Givón's (1985) third characteristic of the pragmatic/syntactic distinction. Time spent on narration is a function not simply of the amount of pausing but also of the speed of delivery or articulation. If an accurate measure of rate of delivery is to be made, the possible differential effects of pausing on the narratives need to be taken into account. (p. 106)

4. *Lexical load and memory*. Robinson notes that there are two kinds of memory that are drawn on differently depending on the contextual needs and task at hand as follows:

> Tulving (1985) has distinguished procedural memory from declarative memory, which itself consists of semantic and episodic subsystems. Procedural memory 'enables organisms to retain learned connections between stimuli and responses. . . and to respond adaptively to the environment' (p. 387). Episodic memory 'affords the . . . capability of acquisition and retention of knowledge about personally experienced events and their temporal relations in subjective time and the ability to mentally 'travel back' in time' (p. 387). Consequently, retrieval from declarative memory (episodic and semantic) probably requires more effort in the case of There-and-Then narratives than in the case of Here-and-Now narratives. During Here-and-Now narratives, on the other hand, participants can allocate more effort to retrieval from procedural memory that they can during There-and-Then narratives. In other words, the There-and-Then condition requires participants to expend

more effort remembering the details of the narrative, whereas the Here-and-Now condition allows them the freedom to concentrate on fluent production. (p. 107)

This detailed breakdown of types of task complexity is obviously tied directly to theories regarding the development of language. As such, this analysis of task complexity is not necessarily applicable to the assessment of language performance, although it may provide certain dimensions along which task difficulty can be seen to affect performance.

Honeyfield (1993) takes a different approach to pedagogic task difficulty. He discusses general "instructional strategies" that can be used to design tasks that make new demands on learners while doing so in a feasible way. One such instructional strategy deals mainly with task difficulty and how learner factors and task factors can be combined and modified to make a given task easier or more difficult depending on the need. As a simple illustration, Honeyfield provides a list which includes the following considerations:

1. Procedure, or what the learners have to do to derive output from input
2. Input text
3. Output required [note that points a.–d. below may need to be considered for both input and output]
   a. Language items: vocabulary, structures, discourse structures, processability, and so forth
   b. Skills, both macro-skills and sub-skills
   c. World knowledge or "topic content"
   d. Text handling or conversation strategies
4. Amount and types of help given
5. Roles of teacher and learners
6. Time allowed
7. Motivation
8. Confidence
9. Learning styles (p. 129)

These factors can then be accounted for and manipulated to make a given task easier or more difficult for a particular group of learners to handle. Points 7 through 9, although perhaps crucial from a pedagogic point of view, would likely have little to do with the grading of task difficulties in terms of desired performance outcomes in an assessment situation. Here again, evidence for differentiation of tasks according to such a difficulty framework does not exist.

In designing TBLT syllabuses, then, sequencing of tasks for presentation to learners can be influenced not only by the difficulty of individual tasks selected through a needs analysis, but also by theories of the language learning process and approaches to language pedagogy. Long and Crookes (1992) point out that, "[t]he grading and sequencing of pedagogic tasks is also partly a function of which various pedagogic options are selected to accompany their use" (p. 45), and they cite possible sources for these options from the body of work on classroom research. However, we would like to reiterate here a point made earlier, that is, in order to assess the performance of an L2 user on a given task, assertions regarding the process involved in learning to accomplish a task should not affect judgments of success with a task. Instead, real-world criteria that are directly related to the task itself must be used for judgments regarding task performance, success, or accomplishment. Sequencing decisions for performance assessment purposes should therefore be based on aspects of difficulty that issue from the tasks themselves, not from theories of learning processes. Along these lines, Long and Crookes (1992) add the important qualification that, "[s]implicity and complexity will not result from application of traditional linguistic grading criteria, however, but reside in some aspects of the tasks themselves" (p. 44). Thus, in order to validly sequence tasks in L2 performance assessment, those components of difficulty that issue from a task itself must first be investigated in terms of how they affect learners' L2 performance as judged according to real-world criteria. An understanding of the effects of various difficulty components will further enable the generalization of learner L2 performances to related real-world task conditions.

Before moving to possible sources of evidence for task-inherent difficulty, one further distinction in approaches to understanding task difficulty merits discussion. Crookes (1986), primarily citing work in human performance research by Fleishman (1978), indicates that task-based performances can be analyzed from two perspectives: (a) investigating individual difference characteristics that humans bring to task performance and (b) investigating task-inherent characteristics that affect performance. Crookes suggests that the first of these areas would likely be of interest to L2 researchers who are investigating outcomes of task performances, whereas the second area holds the most promise for sequencing tasks (e.g., in syllabus design). We would add to this effective analysis by suggesting that the first of these perspectives would be most beneficially applied in pedagogic situations wherein human individual differences must be addressed in order to support *learning* of abilities to accomplish real-world tasks. In contrast, the second perspective would prove particularly applicable for determining the components of difficulty that a task presents to any L2 user.

Within this second approach to task performance analysis, Crookes further identifies two strands for task classification: (a) based on descriptions of task characteristics and (b) based on human ability requirements of tasks. The first of these, "assumes tasks can be described and differentiated in terms of the intrinsic objective properties they possess (such as 'goals, input stimuli, procedures, responses and stimulus-response relationships')" (p. 27). The second strand addresses the "ability requirements (characteristics of the operator) necessary for tasks varying in complexity on a number of factors" (p. 27). He concludes that each of these strands are beneficial in producing descriptors of tasks, "which should be operationally defined, and at least capable of objective identification" (p. 28). Given such descriptors, which are based on those difficulty components that are inherent in a task, tasks can be classified and sequenced in a principled manner and used to predict consequent human performance. We would add, in terms of the assessment of L2 task performances, that these strands play an interactive role and should be considered as a set when classifying tasks according to difficulty. Thus, abilities that are required for successful task completion (e.g., command of certain L2 politeness structures) are often inherently tied to non-ability characteristics of the task (e.g., interlocutor status). Descriptors based on the *task characteristics* strand and the *ability requirements* strand, taken together, should effectively approximate an item specification, each strand contributing crucial information to the performance parameters inherent in a given assessment task. We will return to the use of such descriptors in subsequent chapters.

Robinson (1996a) discusses a similar approach to the classification and grading of tasks for syllabus design purposes, but he advises important conceptual differences in using the terms *task difficulty* and *task complexity*. He summarizes these differences as follows:

> task *difficulty* is determined by learner variables (affect, e.g., confidence, and physical abilities, e.g., eyesight); task *complexity* is determined by task factors (its point along a dimension of complexity, e.g., that of planning time, and task conditions, e.g., the one way or two way direction of information flow). (p. 4)

Essentially, Robinson seems to be making the same initial distinction as Fleishman (1978, above) between individual differences that affect individual performances and task-inherent characteristics that affect performance in general. However, Robinson's reasons for drawing this distinction are directly tied to the application of task complexity differences to investigations of their impact on task-based learning, that is, the distinction is not motivated by concerns with the assessment of L2 learner performances on real-world tasks. This interpretation is supported by Robinson's fundamental assumption, that:

> greater complexity of tasks in terms of their cognitive demands will facilitate greater attention to form and planning of production and lead, therefore, to greater accuracy in the use of morphosyntax and greater complexity of production. (p. 5)

This assumption ties the definition of task complexity directly to theories of task-based learning, which effectively serves Robinson's explicit ends of investigating these theories.

We would argue, then, that this conception of task *complexity* cannot be adopted for assessment that is designed to tap performances on tasks according to real-world criteria (and Robinson, 1996b, draws a similar conclusion; see following chapter on task-based assessment). The previous quote suggests that greater task complexity always facilitates or requires greater accuracy and complexity in performance of the task. However, we would argue that tasks can be conceived of wherein complexity of production is not correlated with the difficulty or complexity of the task or with successful versus unsuccessful performance. Indeed, real-world criteria for task success might specify that, regardless of the relative difficulty or complexity of the task, successful performance on the task would necessitate *less* complexity in production and, for example, greater emphasis on fluency, amount of information delivered, pragmatic requirements, and so forth. Such performance variables, including complexity of production, can all be included within the broader *ability requirements* strand of task classification (noted above). However, direct association of overall task difficulty or complexity with the resulting complexity of production (a single performance variable) eliminates the possibility of a framework that integrates ability requirements with task characteristics for the purposes of classifying tasks according to their inherent difficulty. For L2 performance assessment design, and in order to avoid potential terminological confusion, we recommend the use of the term task *difficulty* to represent the classification of tasks according to an integration of ability requirements and task characteristics (as taken from Crookes, 1986, above). Given this definition of task difficulty, we turn now to several sources of evidence for the classification of L2 task difficulty, with specific emphasis on the sequencing of tasks for assessment purposes.

Several authors have pointed to the need for development of sound assessment practices, in addition to pedagogical practices, motivated by findings from TBLT research into task difficulty and sequencing. For instance, Long and Crookes (1993) hold that, after task selection and sequencing, the final concern in a task-based syllabus is assessment. As we have seen (above), they suggest moving away from the more norm-referenced, discrete-point tests of the past and instead toward the use of task-based, criterion-reference tests, which will offer a better match to a task-based curriculum. However, matching such criterion-referenced tests to a particular syllabus also requires a valid means of determining task difficulty in order to sequence assessment tasks (as is the case with pedagogic tasks) in a manner relevant to learner progress in performing with the L2. Long and Crookes point out along these lines that, although a number of studies have expressed avenues that might be pursued, determining task difficulty and the factors involved in it still remains a challenge: "Little empirical support is yet available for the various proposed parameters of task difficulty, either, and little effort has been made even to define some of them operationally (but see J. D. Brown, 1989c). Indeed, identification of valid, user-friendly sequencing criteria is one of the oldest unsolved problems in language teaching of all kinds..." (p. 42). More recently, several studies have attempted to provide empirical evidence regarding a variety of proposed components of L2 task difficulty.

For example, Robinson (1995) designed an empirical study of the language produced on tasks that varied according to certain complexity parameters. Following "speculation by Long (1985) that tasks requiring present tense, context-supported reference are simpler than those requiring the management of reference to objects and events dislocated in time and space" (p. 102), Robinson set out to investigate this notion by devising two types of narrative tasks, one using a *Here-and-Now* perspective and the other using a *There-and-Then* perspective to describe a series of three comic strip (no words, just pictures) stories, creating a total of six possible tasks (see Table 1, p. 109). Robinson's specific hypotheses were that the There-and-Then narratives would elicit greater propositional complexity of production (i.e., higher numbers of multipropositional utterances), greater syntactic complexity of production (i.e., higher numbers of S-nodes per T-unit), more dysfluent performance (greater numbers of pauses per narrative and fewer words per pausally defined unit), more lexical content (i.e., higher rations of lexical to grammatical words), and more accurate production (i.e., greater target-like use of articles) than Here-and-Now narratives (p. 108).

Considering the amount of theoretical rationale and support Robinson gives to support his measures for task difficulty, it is surprising that almost all of his hypotheses turned out to be not significant. Only the hypothesis that There-and-Then narratives will elicit greater lexical content than Here-and-Now narratives is supported and significant across all the tasks involved. The last hypothesis, that there will be more accurate production in the former than the latter, is "nearly supported" [sic] and "almost significant" [sic] according to Robinson (p. 119).

His results (particularly all of the null hypotheses) may ultimately have occurred because of problems with the design of the study. Robinson points out that any of the following could have adversely affected his study:

1. The study was small in scale (12 intermediate-level international students)
2. The participant assignments were not random although measures that require random selection, ANOVA and MANOVA, were used
3. The students had relatively low levels of language proficiency
4. The contextual referents were not clearly established
5. The tasks were one-directional and open.

In terms of this last problematic area, Robinson notes that:

> ...There-and-Then tasks differ from Here-and-Now tasks to the extent that the speaker is forced to code presuppositions that cannot be assumed to be available from a shared context...Specifying the hearer's needs more precisely and setting closed narrative tasks, in which the speaker has to deliver information necessary for the hearer, with predetermined correct solutions — as in the information gap activities described by Pica et al. (1993) — may have overcome this deficiency." (p. 127)

Robinson's approach to the analysis of task performance in this study can be taken as characteristic of studies of task-based learning which seek to investigate theories of task complexity and its effect on the language learning process. As is demonstrated above, L2 performance on Robinson's tasks is measured using linguistic analysis of specific variables of language production (e.g., operationalizations of syntactic complexity, accuracy, and fluency). Findings from this and similar studies can be effectively used to further motivate decisions regarding task-based learning and pedagogy. However, findings in terms of such specific linguistic analysis do not necessarily contribute to the design of performance assessments that are to be referenced to real-world criteria. Here again, for example, an L2 learner might show high values on several measures of complexity in production while demonstrating little ability to apply pragmatic knowledge that is called for in a particular task. Analyses similar to those in Robinson (1995) would show that the learner was able to produce complex language, but assessment of the learner's attempt might show that the learner was nonetheless unsuccessful. Regardless of these critical differences in analysis or assessment of L2 performance for very different purposes, studies of task-based learning can be effectively used to motivate task difficulty considerations for performance assessments. In this sense, Robinson's study does provide some evidence for the greater difficulty of *There-and-then* language tasks.

Other studies have taken different approaches to analysis of task difficulty, utilizing, for example, observational techniques and post-task interviews. Such studies provide promising data regarding potential task factors that contribute to performance difficulty.

For example, Fulcher's (1996) study investigated the viability of group oral discussion as an alternative task type to be used in oral test batteries. To that end, he conducted a study of 47 EFL students in Cyprus (average age 15 years and 7 months) in which the students performed three different oral tasks, which were recorded on videotape and rated by five raters using a six-band fluency rating scale. Task 1, a one-on-one interview, required each student to describe a picture prompt and discuss a topic related to it with the interviewer. Task 2, another one-on-one interview, involved giving the students a certain text (the topic was "Poverty in the third world") prior to the test, allowing them thirty minutes to read it for gist, having them answer a few multiple-choice questions on it afterwards, and then two days later, discussing the reading with their interviewer. Task 3 was the group oral discussion task where the students had ten minutes to prepare for a discussion on education in their country and then spent fifteen minutes discussing the topic with each other. The tasks were administered in a different sequence, one-third of the students beginning with Task 1, 2, and 3, respectively, to control for any ordering effect.

On completing each task, the students were invited to fill out a questionnaire about their experience with the task, and after the entire test was finished, were also asked to compare the three tasks and indicate which they favored. Almost all the students (45) participated in the questionnaire, and eight of them later attended debriefing interviews where they were asked to watch video recordings of one of the tasks and then "retrospect" on them.

Fulcher's (1996) results indicate that group oral discussion as a task type offers a potentially more enjoyable, anxiety-reducing, perceptively valid alternative for students, regardless of ability level, than one-on-one interviews in oral testing. This study represents an important first step toward investigating the variety of task types that can be used in performance assessment, but more empirical research, of course, needs to be conducted. Fulcher suggests the following areas for future research:

1. Comparative analysis of the discourse produced by different task types, keeping participant variables steady

2. The assessment of the comparative difficulty of a variety of oral task types

3. Studies of the relative factors contributing to task design which account for the 'success' or 'failure' of the task in a test

4. An examination of student perceptions of task validity and difficulty in relation to student ability, and enjoyment of taking tasks

5. An investigation of the hypothesis that the more trait and method are confounded in rating scale descriptors, the lower the equivalent forms generalizability coefficient and the higher the outfit statistics will be in a G-study and a Rasch partial analysis, respectively." (pp. 38–39)

We will be considering all of these factors at various points in the present project. One of the primary contributions of the Fulcher (1996) study was the introduction and use of retrospective data from the students to aid in task development and modification. Such feedback is often left untapped when it could be used to inform better task design.

A number of studies that cover issues similar to those addressed by Robinson and Fulcher have recently appeared in the TBLT literature, and we leave it to the reader's discretion to examine their specific findings regarding aspects of task difficulty (e.g., Crookes, 1989; Foster & Skehan, 1996; Robinson, Ting, & Urwin, 1995; Skehan & Foster, 1996; Yule & Powers, 1994). We must first point out that we feel that many of these studies have serious methodological problems (for an exception, see Ortega, 1995), primarily of the following types: (a) lack of interrater reliability in coding various measures of L2 production, (b) lack of adequate N-sizes for application of the characteristic multivariate analyses that are used to test hypotheses, (c) disregard for other critical assumptions in drawing inferences based on such statistical analysis (e.g., basing conclusions on ANOVA calculations even after MANOVA calculations have shown no significant differences), and (d) inconsistency between studies in operationalizations of task difficulty or complexity components. As such, we believe that drawing any concrete conclusions regarding difficulty for L2 task performance is at best a risky endeavor; empirical evidence of various aspects of task difficulty must be taken as still incipient. Nevertheless, findings from these studies do offer at least the beginnings of evidence for task difficulty components, and they therefore provide valid points for further investigation. We will now turn to one framework for the description of task difficulty which is based on such early findings.

Thus far, the current chapter has demonstrated that the issue of determining task difficulty for theoretical, pedagogic, or assessment purposes is a long way from being resolved. Research into the variable effects of a wide number of potential factors is necessary before any claims can be made regarding the principled sequencing of tasks according to their difficulty. Since this is the case, the current performance assessment design project also takes as one of its objectives the investigation of several proposed components of task difficulty. We decided to motivate our selection of task difficulty components by seeking out a very recent approach to task difficulty that: (a) seemed based on appropriate theories, (b) was grounded in research findings, to the extent possible, (c) incorporated previous work in the TBLT field, and (d) was directly applicable to performance assessment. Recent work by Skehan seemed to best fit these criteria, and in concluding this chapter, we outline Skehan's (1996) approach to delineating task difficulty components.

Based on a variety of both empirical and theoretical sources, including much of the literature that has been presented here, Skehan (1996) develops a general scheme of task sequencing features (for details on the basis for his approach, we direct the reader to the examples of his work referenced at the end of this book). This scheme involves the description of factors that can affect the difficulty of a given task (ostensibly for all learners, regardless of individual differences) and which can be manipulated to increase or decrease task difficulty:

1. Code complexity, which is "concerned with traditional areas of syntactic and lexical difficulty and range" (p. 52). Differentiating a task according to this difficulty continuum involves identifying the relative complexity or simplicity of the language code that is required (in both receptive and productive ways) for task success.
2. Cognitive complexity, which is affected by both cognitive processing and cognitive familiarity. "Processing is concerned with the amount of on-line computation that is required while doing a task, and highlights the extent to which the learner has to actively think through task content. Familiarity, in contrast, involves the extent to which the task draws on ready-made or pre-packaged solutions. It is implicated when all that is required is the accessing of relevant aspects of schematic knowledge if such knowledge contains relevant, already-organized material, and even solutions to comparable tasks, e.g., sensitivity to macrostructures in narratives." (p. 52)
3. Communicative stress, which includes time pressure, modality (reading, writing, speaking, or listening), scale (number of participants or relationships involved), stakes (either low or high, depending on how important it is to do the task and to do it correctly), and control (how much learners can "control" or influence the task). (pp. 52–53)

Clearly, these task difficulty features comprise the *ability requirements* and *task characteristics* inherent in a given L2 task. As such, they offer a convenient and well-motivated starting point for gradation of task difficulty in order to predict performance outcomes, that is, by analyzing tasks (pre-selected based on needs analysis) according to these factors, the difficulty imposed by a given task might prove predictable, and the performance on that task might therefore prove generalizable to future real-world task performances. This framework forms the basis in the current project for differentiating among tasks according to task difficulty components. In subsequent chapters on test and item specifications (chapter 5) and performance task generation (appendix), these task difficulty components will be described in slightly altered and more curriculum-specific versions, and they will be applied to the generation, selection, and gradation of L2 performance assessment tasks.

chapter four

TASK-BASED ASSESSMENT

The previous chapter discussed a number of issues from the task-based language teaching literature that are relevant for designing L2 performance assessments: (a) a definition of task and several parameters for delimiting assessment tasks; (b) the importance of a needs analysis for identification of tasks, task types, and criteria for judging task success; and (c) a potential set of task difficulty components that may contribute to the predictive utility of L2 performance assessments. In addition to these central issues, several authors writing from a TBLT perspective have also directly addressed issues specific to task-based language assessment, which in turn have direct bearing on L2 performance assessment. In this chapter, we will focus on the contributions of these authors by addressing the following five questions:

1. How do we assess task-based performance?

2. What are the factors that affect task-based assessment reliability?

3. What are the factors that affect task-based assessment validity?

4. What are the factors that affect task-based assessment practicality?

5. What are the steps involved in developing task-based assessment?

Each of these questions will be answered in turn based on what the literature has to offer, and again, the questions themselves will function as section headings. Within each section we will also relate the findings to L2 performance assessment design.

HOW DO WE ASSESS TASK-BASED PERFORMANCE?

Several approaches to task-based testing can be found within the TBLT literature, and, as with any kind of language assessment, these various approaches are tied to a range of decision-making purposes. Each of these approaches also incorporates specific procedures for the analysis and/or evaluation of task performance.

One approach to task-based testing involves the assessment of task outcomes in terms of learner/examinee success or failure to accomplish the task. Such an outcomes-referenced approach would be utilized for the purposes of certifying that learners can accomplish particular tasks that have been identified (through a needs analysis) as seminal within a particular curriculum. This approach draws from occupational performance testing for certification purposes, and it has parallels in language testing within the English for Specific Purposes literature (see Clark &

Grognet, 1985 for an example of task-based outcomes testing within an English for survival purposes program). Robinson (1996b) also notes that such tests have been utilized for some time in order to make exit decisions in vocational training programs, and he cites similar efforts at task-based exit testing in language programs (e.g., Hauptman, LeBlanc, & Wesche, 1985).

Performances on such outcomes-referenced tests are evaluated in terms of simple yes/no decisions; that is, the pivotal question is *Did the examinee accomplish the goal of the task or not?* Further analysis of the performance is not undertaken, the yes/no distinction considered sufficient for supporting decisions regarding the examinee's ability to accomplish the given task. Finally, the tasks that are utilized in outcomes-referenced tests are necessarily drawn directly from an analysis of the real-world needs that learners have in terms of language tasks that they will be faced with upon exit or certification. Criteria for the yes/no decision also issue from the needs analysis, and they are based on those aspects specific to a given task that prove to be essential in its accomplishment.

Robinson (1996b) has noted the limitations of outcomes-referenced testing for second language pedagogical purposes:

1. They are often difficult to design and administer.
2. They lack generalizability across programs.
3. They are considered to be uneconomical. (p. 96)

We would add to these pedagogic limitations by suggesting that outcomes-referenced testing does not provide the learner/teacher with useful feedback in terms of the particular aspects of a task that prove more or less difficult for an examinee, nor does it necessarily reflect the efficiency with which a learner utilizes the L2 for task accomplishment. Another problem inherent in outcomes-referenced testing is that it obviates the possibility for differential success with some real-world tasks, that is, for certain real-world language tasks it is possible that multiple outcomes or various stages within the outcome could be considered in reaching success/failure decisions (as opposed to a single yes/no decision regarding the entire task). Thus, for L2 *pedagogic* purposes, the outcomes-referenced approach offers a means for certifying learner ability to accomplish a given task, but not much else. We agree, however, that there are certainly valid applications of outcomes-referenced testing (as in the examples mentioned above).

With respect to L2 performance assessment, we concur with Robinson that task-based testing in general is difficult and uneconomical to design and administer, although we feel that (a) these problems can be solved (see discussion in chapter 2 of solutions to problems with performance assessment), and (b) task-based testing is nonetheless requisite for claims regarding learners' abilities to use a given L2 under real-world conditions. However, Robinson's point number 2 above, which poses the greatest limitation for outcomes-referenced testing, is also one of the central issues for any approach to task-based testing that seeks to do more than certify learner abilities with respect to isolated real-world tasks. We turn therefore to other suggestions from the literature in search of solutions to the problem of generalizability in task-based assessment.

Robinson (1996b) distinguishes between performance-referenced and system-referenced testing as two possible approaches to task-based assessment related to a task-based language curriculum (see also Robinson & Ross, 1996). Drawing on Baker (1990), Robinson indicates that system-referenced tests attempt to tap a particular psychological construct (e.g., developmental level) which underlies a language task, without analyzing the accomplishment of the task itself. Although these tests do not provide feedback regarding real-world task performances, it is held that they can provide generalizable information regarding some component of a learner's language ability that might underlie the accomplishment of any number of different tasks. Performance-referenced tests, on the other hand, approximate as closely as possible the conditions of a future language task, and they therefore retain high face validity. However, generalizing to other task performances or L2 abilities from such performance-referenced tests is problematic (as we have mentioned above).

Robinson then suggests that each of these approaches to assessment is tied to a particular language syllabus type. Performance-referenced testing is most obviously related to ends-focused, analytic syllabuses, of the type discussed by Long and Crookes (1992), whereas system-referenced testing is closely related to aspects of means-focused, synthetic syllabuses, of the type proposed by Nunan (1989). Robinson maintains, however, that both of these assessment types should be integrated for effective task-based assessment of L2 ability and performance. For example, he suggests that interlanguage-sensitive, system-referenced testing (e.g., the assessment of stages in L2 development) could be effectively imbedded in the direct assessment of performance on L2 tasks. Each aspect of such a test could then be evaluated according to its own criteria, using criterion-referenced evaluation methods. For performance-referenced decisions, the criterion would be much the same as that suggested above for outcomes-referenced testing, whereas for system-referenced decisions, the criterion might be based on cut scores for minimal levels of production of particular aspects of the L2 (e.g., at a given developmental level). Finally, Robinson implies that such an integrative approach to task-based assessment could reconcile different decision-making needs, incorporating the generalizability and pedagogic relevance from system-referenced testing and the face validity and directness from performance-referenced testing.

We are in fundamental agreement with this integrative framework proposed by Robinson, although we would add several qualifications for the purposes of exercising L2 performance assessment to its fullest potential (and we will address these qualifications shortly). Essentially, this type of framework can be taken as one example of the emphasis made earlier in this book on the importance of considering *alternatives* in assessment. The system-referenced and performance-referenced testing approaches described by Robinson offer two alternatives for decision making in task-based language teaching classrooms and programs. As Robinson (1996b) suggests (and provides preliminary evidence in support of), these two alternatives can be effectively integrated to facilitate various pedagogic decisions.

Although Robinson's integrative approach to assessment may offer much promise for pedagogic decision making as well as for research into task complexity issues (as previously described according to Robinson), we find that several qualifications need to be made for effectively assessing learner performance on L2 tasks. If the goal of L2 performance assessment is to evaluate learner accomplishment on a variety of real-world tasks and according to real-world criteria, then the *a priori* expectation of a relationship between aspects of the language system and aspects of language performance unnecessarily delimits the possible range of tasks and evaluative criteria that can be implemented in L2 performance assessment. We suggest, therefore, that aspects of the language system only be considered as they occur in terms of task-inherent *ability requirements*. Furthermore, L2 performance assessment should encompass evaluation of learner performance within the range of such *ability requirements* as well as *task characteristics* that are found in a given task. For the purposes of evaluating learner L2 performance on real-world tasks, assessments should be designed and referenced with respect to needs analyses and resulting real-world criteria for success, but they should also remain independent of direct ties to non-real-world and non-task-inherent criteria. However, this approach still leaves us with the issue of generalizing from finite task-based performances to other potential real-world tasks. We turn now to one final example for dealing with the generalizability issue.

It was noted at the end of the previous chapter that Skehan's (1996) task sequencing features offer one approach to grading tasks according to processing difficulty. The proposed components of code complexity, cognitive complexity, and communicative stress offer viable rubrics under which both L2 *ability requirements* and *task characteristics* can be located and assessed for contribution to overall difficulty in task accomplishment. Skehan (1998) advises the sequencing of task difficulty according to these rubrics for the purposes of syllabus design. He also provides a rationale for performance assessment that incorporates these elements of difficulty into a system for generalizing from task-based assessment to future L2 performances.

Skehan (1998) reasons that predominant approaches to language testing (e.g., Bachman's, 1990, and Bachman and Palmer's, 1996, models of strategic competence) have over-emphasized the search for an underlying "structure-of-abilities" that L2 learners acquire — structures that determine their performances on L2 tasks (p. 263). In response, Skehan suggests:

> As an alternative it is central to investigate performance and processing in their own right, because these factors are fundamental for generalisations that need to be made about how language will actually be used. Such an approach would also broaden methods of establishing construct validity considerably… (p. 264)

As we noted at the beginning of this book, one of the fundamental objectives of the current research project is to explore specifically these issues in L2 performance assessment. Accordingly, Skehan's rationale provides further important motivation to the central issue of task-based assessment and generalizability.

Skehan goes on to note that, as tasks themselves enact an influence on an individual's L2 performance and therefore on judgments or ratings of their L2 proficiency, tasks must be analyzed for a better understanding of exactly how they affect a given performance. He indicates that, based on evidence from studies of the influence of task factors on resulting L2 performances, the processing dimensions noted above can serve as a useful system for task difficulty analysis. According to Skehan, as "[c]onditions of task implementation are likely to be the central influence upon how performance can be predicted" (p. 280) a focus on task difficulty features will thus make it "possible to base generalisations on task characteristics that are shared, or not, across the different contexts" (p. 281). As such, Skehan concludes:

> Tasks and processing need to be understood if results are to be interpreted. Tasks and processing provide guidance for the sampling that is necessary for generalisation to be possible: we need to know what sorts of performances people are capable of. (p. 281)

Sampling of L2 performance assessment tasks, then, would necessarily come out of an understanding of the processing attributes that are inherent in real-world tasks selected from a needs analysis. Such sampling would facilitate prediction of the effects of components of task difficulty on L2 performance, and generalizations regarding probable accomplishment of future tasks could then be based on learner performance with respect to these carefully sampled tasks.

Essentially, we concur with Skehan's notions regarding the contribution of processing demands to task difficulty, and we see in his processing components the potential for a principled analysis of task difficulty components. What remains to be completed, then, is an investigation of the actual, observable contribution of these proposed elements of task difficulty as they actually affect L2 performance of learners at various levels of L2 acquisition. Moreover (and this point is generally ignored in current literature), investigation is also necessary into the interface between predictions of task difficulty and judgments of task success according to real-world criteria (which issue from a needs analysis). Nonetheless, Skehan does address the evaluation of task-based performance, and his approach warrants mention here.

Skehan (1998) comments that task difficulty factors will interact with rating scales. He suggests, therefore, that an approach to the evaluation of task performances should stress those "areas which have some linkage to the nature of processing" (p. 274). Such areas, for Skehan, issue directly from his theories regarding the effects of competing attentional and processing demands. Thus, Skehan (1996) indicates the implications for evaluation of task performance based on what he sees as the three primary goals of a task-based language syllabus: accuracy, complexity, and fluency in communication. In his words,

> If we consider the processing implications of having these three goals, it is clear that there is not sufficient capacity for learners to devote resources to each of them so that they can be met simultaneously. As a result, decisions about the prioritization of attentional resources have to be made during communication and learning, leading us to need to explore the consequences of allocating attention in one direction, and not another (Van Patten, 1994). Performance is likely to prioritize fluency, and relegate restructuring and accuracy to lesser importance. A focus on development, on the other hand, is likely to prioritize restructuring, with accuracy and fluency being more secondary. (p. 50)

Although we agree that attentional demand may vary in one direction or another for a given L2 task, we disagree with Skehan's proposal here that an emphasis on *performance* necessarily prioritizes fluency. Such a view of L2 performance issues directly from the assumption that, under certain kinds of task-imposed pressure conditions, communication will become *lexicalized* and will necessarily lose accuracy and complexity in production (and the converse, that a *syntactic* mode of communication will result in attention to accuracy and complexity at the expense of fluency). We see this interpretation of these three performance variables as characteristic of only certain tasks. Indeed, it may be that such tasks can be effectively alternated and manipulated within an L2 syllabus in order to *push* the learner's interlanguage development. However, it is improbable that all L2 tasks can be taken to conform to this restricted interpretation. By extension, *performance* on L2 tasks does not necessarily prioritize fluency at the expense of anything. Quite the contrary, numerous examples of tasks can be cited wherein success might result from a prioritization of complexity in performance (e.g., formal, written hypothesization of the costs and benefits of a business strategy), a combination of complexity and fluency in performance (e.g., oral hypothesization of the same), or any possible combination of the complexity/accuracy/fluency variables. Thus, we see Skehan's definition of performance and task success as unnecessarily limited for the purposes of L2 performance assessment.

Although we suggest a broader view on evaluation of task performance, we do see a practical benefit to Skehan's three task performance variables. That is, such aspects of performance may be utilized in the rating of task success. However, such rating would not approach task success from the assumptions suggested by Skehan above. Rather, each of these variables would be rated in terms of the task-specific requirements for their involvement in success. Based on this L2 performance perspective:

1. Accuracy would involve the minimum level of precision in code usage necessary for successful communication.

2. Complexity would involve the minimum range of grammatical/structural code required for successful completion of a given communication task.

3. Fluency would involve the minimum on-line *flow* required by a given task for successful (acceptable) communication.

With respect to each of these variables, the minimum level would necessarily be determined according to real-world criteria as identified by a needs analysis. Such standards for task accomplishment would not be based on a learner's belief in L2 norms, nor on native-like performance standards, as Skehan suggests (p. 46). Norms or standards for performance would simply be referenced to levels of each variable that are pre-determined as providing minimal criteria for success.

In summary, for the purposes of the current project, and we would contend for assessment of real-world L2 performance in general, task-based performance can be evaluated from two perspectives. The first of these perspectives involves initial determination of real-world criteria for the judgment of task success; this is best accomplished, we suggest, by means of a thorough needs analysis (we return to this point in establishing criteria for success on our prototypical tasks in the current project). Such criteria will vary from task to task, although they will likely include variables such as accuracy, complexity, and fluency of the L2 used in task accomplishment. These and related criteria will only emerge from the real-world requirements for task success that are directly identified with respect to specific tasks. Judgments based on these criteria will also offer an interesting concrete point of reference for comparisons with the influence of task difficulty, the second perspective for evaluation.

Task difficulty, then, will be based on assessment of the variable contributions of the processing components suggested by Skehan (1996): code complexity, cognitive complexity, and communicative demand. Such difficulty components seem to offer a principled means for categorizing *ability requirements* and *task characteristics* that are inherent in L2 tasks. By identifying these components within a given task, variable sources of difficulty can be estimated. With such a system for estimation of task difficulty, learner performances on carefully sampled tasks can be used to predict future performances on tasks that are constituted by related difficulty components. Empirical support for a system like this could lead to much improved generalizability for task-based L2 performance assessments. Furthermore, comparison of the variable contribution of identifiable sources of task difficulty with the rating of examinee performances according to real-world criteria should provide valuable information regarding the contribution of task difficulty to perceived task success.

Of course, this framework is still speculative. As with any assessment, however, the best we can hope for is a reasonably accurate estimation of the construct of interest, in this case L2 performance on real-world tasks. Our hope in conducting the current research project is to further explore factors that figure prominently in such estimation. Ideally, through careful observation of large numbers of L2 examinees accomplishing real-world language tasks, and through follow-up analysis of various aspects of task performances, we will be able to better identify sources of task difficulty and better understand their contribution to successful performance in real-world language tasks.

WHAT ARE THE FACTORS THAT AFFECT
TASK-BASED ASSESSMENT RELIABILITY?

Brindley (1994) refers to task-based assessment as task-centered assessment (TCA). He points out that the reliability of ratings is a major problem in task-centered assessment for the classroom:

> TCA relies heavily on teachers' subjective judgments of language performance. In the interests of fairness to learners, it is important that these judgments are seen to be reliable. As more and more rating tools are developed to assess productive task performance, teachers will need to be trained to interpret and apply assessment instruments in a consistent way. Rater training involving familiarization with the rating criteria and practice in applying them to samples of performances across a range of ability levels has long been standard practice with proficiency rating scales and it has been claimed that high levels of inter-rater agreement can be obtained in this way (e.g., Dandonoli and Henning, 1991). (p. 84)

Although rater training may be the procedure usually followed to insure reliability, there appears to be a chink in the armor. According to various citations in Brindley's article, a rater's tendency for severity or leniency in judgments seems to remain unchanged despite having rater training. Since this factor cannot be easily accounted for or eliminated from the judgments, it introduces a worrisome element in the calculations that could affect interrater reliability. Luckily, new measurement technology offers new hope. According to Brindley (1994), one such tool is item-response theory:

> The Rasch model is one of a family of techniques known as latent trait theory or item response theory (IRT) which have been developed by psychometricians over the last three decades or so. One of the strengths of the theory is that it allows candidate ability and item difficulty to be estimated independently and reported on a common scale, thus avoiding many of the problems associated with sample-dependent classical measurement techniques (Henning 1987). The multi-faceted Rasch model extends previous Rasch models to include rater characteristics... The program adjusts candidate ability estimates to take account of raters' tendency to rate either harshly or leniently. (p. 85)

Brindley also discusses another tool, FACETS, a software application, that not only performs the above multi-faceted, adjustable Rasch analysis but also has the added benefit of informing the raters of how they are rating (i.e., too leniently, too harshly), thus, serving in a way as a rating self-awareness program. Although such new measurement tools are quite useful, they may unfortunately be out of reach to many people due to costs or availability.

Fulcher (1996) raises another reliability problem: the potential lack of generalizability from one task performance to another. However, he notes that this lack of generalizability may be due more to the scoring system employed (especially if it does not refer to test method facets in its descriptors) than to the design of the task. In fact, such a lack of generalizability of one task to another is not only related to the consistency or reliability across tasks but also to the validity of those tasks, a topic which we take up in the following section.

In terms of the current L2 performance assessment design framework, the following areas of task-based reliability also necessitate consideration:

1. To what extent is task selection based on a reliable analysis of population needs in terms of future L2 tasks? Is the needs analysis auditable? Does it include triangulation of decisions for task sampling?

2. To what extent are the real-world criteria for rating task success based on a reliable analysis of actual judgments of task success in real-world situations? Whose judgments are used as the basis for task success criteria? Are these judgments triangulated with input from multiple stake-holders in the task judgment process?

3. Are raters able to consistently apply these real-world criteria as they vary according to individual parameters for task success?

4. Using task descriptors, can multiple raters reliably identify various difficulty components in real-world tasks?

5. Can inherent components of task difficulty be reliably separated from individual differences in task performance evaluation?

Particular techniques will be employed for addressing each of these reliability questions, as well as those mentioned above, in the current project. Results for all reliability estimates and procedures will be reported in the relevant sections describing the particular point in L2 performance assessment design (in this and future volumes).

WHAT ARE THE FACTORS THAT AFFECT TASK-BASED ASSESSMENT VALIDITY?

According to Brindley (1994), one of the assumptions made about task-centered assessment is that, since the communicative tasks used for assessment are based on authentic language use, they are automatically valid. This assumption has been criticized for a number of reasons [see also critique of "alternative assessments" in chapter 1 of this volume].

First, there is a misinterpretation in terms of authenticity; that is, an assessment situation, although possibly employing authentic language, is still an artificial situation, not an authentic one. Second, there is the issue of sufficiency. Even though an assessment task may be authentic (reflecting a real-life situation), it does not mean that the sampling of language involved is of a sufficient amount for assessment purposes and that it can be generalized to other language use situations. In other words, a task may be authentic but may be impoverished in terms of what it reveals about the learner's language. Authenticity is not a panacea for validity. What Brindley suggests instead is moving away from loose authenticity/validity-based assertions to a more theory-based construction of validity.

Fulcher (1996) points to the artificiality in oral tests when he says, "Claims that test tasks replicate natural contexts and real-life situations which encourage natural language use remain the cornerstone of the claim to validity in oral test design." (p. 26). Although interview task types have long been utilized in oral tests, Fulcher cites current research (i.e., in conversational analysis, second language acquisition, etc.) which suggests that "the one-to-one oral interview generates a special genre of language different from normal conversational speech" (p. 26) and as such, might not be as useful a task type by which to compare students' oral abilities (for more on this issue, see Ross & Berwick, 1992). Based on the literature, "interview talk" does not promote an equal exchange of questions, answers, topic-broachings, and topic-discontinuings (the interviewer having the main control over the course of the conversation, inadvertently creating a "test-type" discourse instead of a natural one). Interview talk may also introduce features of "teacher talk" into the discourse (considering that the interviewers tend to be teachers) and can create longer pauses between turns than would normally be tolerated in a regular conversation. [It should be noted that this is what current theory suggests, but much of it still needs more empirical backing.] Many of the student comments in Fulcher's questionnaires and interviews mirror these concerns. Nonetheless, "half of the students who took part in this study very clearly expressed the view that, for them, a group oral task is a much more natural situation in which to engage in conversation than in a one-to-one oral interview" (p. 29). This student preference for a group oral task might have been particularly true because the students felt more at ease in the groups and conversed more like they normally do.

Fulcher (1996) also discusses what he calls perceptions of validity, which others might refer to as face validity. The students in his study generally considered Task 1 too easy and not a good indicator of what they were capable of doing with the language. Interestingly enough, those students who had lower ability levels viewed this task as valid, but as ability level increased, perceptions of validity decreased. Task 2, however, was judged by all to be challenging and valid. Only a few claimed that the task was too difficult, and they were from the lower ability group. As Fulcher notes, "there is a potential relationship among perceptions of validity, task difficulty, and learner ability, which needs to be further investigated." (p. 33) "However, task 3 does appear, from these results, to overcome any affective disadvantage which students may feel they have when being tested by other one-to-one task types" (pp. 33–34), and all but two students considered the task a valid measure of their oral abilities.

In addition to the authenticity issue, Brindley (1994) points to another problem area in the validity of task-centered assessment: how to define the criteria for assessment, upon which student performances will be ranked or scored. According to Brindley, a variety of approaches have been tried in the past, but none of them has been particularly satisfactory.

One of the most common approaches is to rely on expert judgments, namely those of the test developers and/or teachers, to pinpoint key elements for assessment, distinguish differing levels of student performance, and provide descriptors, evaluative ratings, and so on. Part of the problem with such a method is that these "experts" often disagree, based on their own background and personal construct of language ability, resulting more in going around in circles than in achieving consensus. A study of a "bottom up consultative approach" used in Australian primary and secondary ESL education and reported by Griffin and McKay (1992, p. 20) is revealing:

> Limitations of this approach include the difficulties involved in obtaining appropriate descriptions of language behavior from practitioners. It is often the case that practitioners' observations are limited by a lack of knowledge of theoretical models, by inadequate observation skills and/or an inability to articulate descriptions of independent student language behaviour. The developer of the scales has to make decisions about the need to use the imprecise language of the practitioner, and perhaps lose some of the definitive nature of the theoretical model, or to use a specialist terminology and run the risk of practitioner misinterpretation and rejection. (p. 78)

Brindley (1994) further points out that disagreement is not only between test developers and teachers. Even a group of teachers themselves may be lost in terms of assessment criteria:

> Studies aimed at investigating how expert judgments are made, however, cast some doubt on the ability of expert judges to agree on any of these issues. Alderson and Lukmani (1989), for example, in an examination of item content in EFL reading tests, found that judges were unable to agree not only on what particular items they were testing but also on the level of difficulty of items or skills and the assignment of these to a particular level. (pp. 78–79)

Such a list of assessment criteria might end up being quite arbitrary, again stressing the need to consult theoretical research and improve communication. Several methods for developing valid assessment criteria and for checking the validity of the criteria will be discussed in subsequent chapters.

Another, perhaps easier, way to define assessment criteria is to utilize rating scales which already exist and are readily available (such as the ACTFL [American Council on the Teaching of Foreign Languages] or IELTS [International English Language Testing System] scales). However, numerous problems exist with these scales as well, such as lack of empirical support and difficulty in distinguishing clearly between levels (often because of poorly-worded or poorly-specified descriptors), the scales being too general to be applied to the task on hand, and so forth (also see empirical evidence in Norris, 1996, which challenges the validity of inferring second language proficiency based on such holistic descriptors).

Brindley's third approach for defining assessment criteria is the genre-based approach, which has the slight advantage of being driven by theory:

> One way of obtaining detailed assessment information at the level of the individual task is represented by genre-based approaches to assessment which derive from the analysis of spoken and written genres within the framework of systemic-functional linguistic theory (Halliday, 1985). Within this approach, the genres (such as argument, describing a procedure, etc.) are carefully described in terms of their structural organization and linguistic features. These features are then used as the basis for the implementation of a teaching-learning cycle and also serve as the criteria for assessment of overall task performance. (Brindley, 1994, p. 80)

The main problem with this approach, however, is that comprehensive descriptions of the different genres or structures are as yet unavailable, making the development of such an approach quite difficult. Measurement of many of these features also constitutes a tedious process that renders them unwieldy at best and highly unsuitable for classroom assessment.

Brindley's fourth and final approach, not surprisingly, calls for data-based assessment criteria that are consistent with current theories of second language acquisition and use. Research into discourse analysis, consideration of processing dimensions such as analysis of linguistic knowledge and control of processing, and documenting real-world language use, for example, could produce better constructed, better justified, and more satisfying assessment tasks than previous approaches. More research on validity clearly needs to be done, but at least Brindley seems to have illuminated the path for future research. As we explain in the next section, in addition to reliability and validity concerns, task-based assessment faces a number of practical concerns as well.

WHAT ARE THE FACTORS THAT AFFECT TASK-BASED ASSESSMENT PRACTICALITY?

Brindley (1994) points to a number of practical issues that task-centered assessment designers must face:

1. It is a time-consuming method of assessment because it involves eliciting, evaluating, and scoring student performances one at a time over a long period of time instead of all at once like paper-and-pencil tests. As a result, task-centered testing is necessarily more expensive than traditional forms of assessment.

2. A large amount of time must also be spent to train teachers so they can carry out task-centered assessment competently and confidently.

3. Public acceptability may also be a problem because many people might consider such an assessment system to be less than rigorous.

Obviously, these arguments sound quite similar to several listed in chapter 2 in the section on problems for performance assessment implementation, and, although they pose important concerns, such problems can certainly be handled. With careful planning and organization, with careful explanation of the goals, merits, and procedures to all appropriate parties, and with continued research to improve the validity, reliability, and practicality of task-centered assessments, testers might be able to adequately deal with all three of these concerns. This volume describes how we have begun to address these vital concerns in our project.

WHAT ARE THE STEPS INVOLVED IN DEVELOPING TASK-BASED ASSESSMENT?

Though it is not specifically designed for language teachers, *A Practical Guide to Alternative Assessment* by Herman, Aschbacher, and Winters (1992) offers a comprehensive guide for teachers and curriculum planners interested in developing a system of alternative assessment in the schools. It not only delineates the many important factors that must be considered in the development and decision-making process (i.e., instructional goals, task selection, rating scales, reliability, etc.) but also provides numerous samples of actual systems or rubrics that have been created and implemented, mainly in K–12 content classes. For the purposes of this review, chapters 4 ("Selecting Assessment Tasks"), 5 ("Setting Criteria"), and 6 ("Ensuring Reliable Scoring") are of particular interest.

In chapter 4, Herman, Aschbacher, and Winters (1992) lay out a five-step plan for selecting assessment tasks:

1. Establish what the teacher's specific instructional goals are because it is important that the chosen assessment task actually matches the instructional outcome(s) it is designed to measure.

2. Identify the specific, discipline-based content and skills that students are expected to attain and determine whether the task adequately represents or utilizes them.

3. Insure that the task is fair and free of bias, allowing students to demonstrate their true progress and abilities without being disadvantaged by some extraneous element in the task, lack of prior knowledge, unequal access to resources or materials, and so forth.

4. Decide which of the three possible forms the tasks will take (the choice should depend mainly on the type of skills and content that needs to be covered):
   a. authentic, real-world tasks (which have the advantage of generating greater motivation and offering greater transferability than traditional tasks),

b. interdisciplinary tasks (which economically combine and utilize the content and skills from various disciplines in performing the task, i.e., math, science, and reporting skills), or

c. multi-dimensional tasks (which consist of a "mega-task" composed of smaller tasks that need to be tackled to complete the larger task).

5. Describe the assessment task so that others can understand and use it in other settings. Such a description should detail the intended outcomes, the content covered, the work and roles in the task, the materials and instructions involved, the rating system, and so on. Other areas of consideration in task selection include determining whether the task is teachable, feasible, credible, meaningful, and so on.

In addition to task selection and design, Herman, Aschbacher, and Winters (1992) discuss the development of scoring criteria (chapter 5) for evaluating student performance on a task, which function to:

1. Help teachers define excellence and plan how to help students achieve it
2. Communicate to students what constitutes excellence and how to evaluate their own work
3. Communicate goals and results to parents and others
4. Help teachers or other raters be accurate, unbiased, and consistent in scoring
5. Document the procedures used in making important judgments about students (p. 48)

According to Herman, Aschbacher, and Winters (1992), such scoring criteria will often have four elements:

1. Include dimensions used to judge the students' work, which will generally express the qualities or characteristics essential in the performance of a given task. Such dimensions should reflect the instructional goals of the task and reflect what the teacher expects to see in terms of behavior or characteristics if the task is done well, satisfactorily, or poorly;

2. Provide definitions, models, examples, or questions which will help to clarify more explicitly just what those dimensions are;

3. Offer a rating scale of some type, be it a yes-no checklist, a numerical scale, a qualitative scale (either descriptive or evaluative), or a combination numerical-qualitative scale, to help assess student performance of the dimensions; and

4. Standards of excellence (criterion-referenced, norm-referenced, or both) should be specified along with models or examples of each level.

This final step seems to bring together all the previous elements and completes the construction of a rating scale or rubric.

At this point, the authors provide a guide to help teachers begin developing their own scoring criteria:

1. Investigate how the assessed discipline defines quality performance
2. Gather sample rubrics for assessing writing, speech, the arts, and so on as models to adapt for your purposes
3. Gather samples of students' and experts' work that demonstrate the range of performance from ineffective to very effective
4. Discuss with others the characteristics of these models that distinguish the effective ones from the ineffective ones
5. Write descriptors for the important characteristics
6. Gather another sample of students' work
7. Try out criteria to see if they help you make accurate judgments about students
8. Revise your criteria
9. Try it again until the rubric score captures the 'quality' of the work (p. 75)

Once scoring criteria have been developed using the guidelines mentioned above, the last step according to Herman, Aschbacher, and Winters (1992) is to evaluate the scoring criteria. The authors suggest checking to make sure the scoring criteria are:

1. Keyed to important outcomes
2. Sensitive to purpose
3. Meaningful, clear, and credible
4. Fair and unbiased
5. Feasible and
6. Generalizable (pp. 76–79)

Although not covered in any detail here, chapter 6 of Herman, Aschbacher, and Winters (1992) is also important because it pursues the next step, insuring reliable and consistent scoring through rater training and education, sample runs, and reliability studies performed on the actual tests.

In our view, Herman, Aschbacher, and Winters (1992) provides an easy-to-understand, thorough, recipe-book style guide on developing alternative assessment systems. One of its best features is the wealth of examples of actual scoring rubrics that it includes. However, two important things are missing from their book: (a) a discussion of the necessary factors to consider in task development (e.g., see previous discussion in this document of Skehan, 1996 and Nunan, 1989) and (b) any empirical justifications for the claims they make.

This chapter reviewed the issues involved in the reliability, validity, and practicality of task-based assessment as well as crucial steps in the design of such assessment procedures. In chapter 5, we will show how we dealt with several of these issues in designing our own test and item specifications.

chapter five

TEST AND ITEM SPECIFICATIONS

The remainder of this book will lay out the design of a prototypical instrument for assessing second or foreign language performance. The focus of assessment will be L2 performance on a set of real-world English language tasks, following the definition and parameters of task that we set out in chapter 3. The tasks employed in this assessment instrument are not related to any particular curriculum or population of students; instead, they have been selected as possible real-world tasks representative of a wide range of content domains, a wide range of integrative communication elements, and a wide range of estimated difficulties. Task selection for the current instrument was therefore motivated by the necessity of coverage, but not by the particular needs of students. Such coverage was in turn deemed essential in order to elicit a corpus of examinee performance data across a wide variety of tasks, such that analysis would produce interpretable results (e.g., in terms of actual versus predicted task difficulty, etc.). We do not recommend the adoption of the current assessment instrument in its entirety for any classroom or program decision-making purposes; quite the contrary, we reiterate that a thorough needs analysis must be the primary source for task selection that is relevant to a given population of students with directly identifiable L2 goals. This instrument should be taken, therefore, as an example of one assessment alternative that could be used in L2 classrooms and programs for purposes of assessing student performances according to real-world criteria and for predicting likely examinee abilities to perform on related real-world language tasks in the future. Such an instrument, based on a needs analysis and operationalized within a particular curriculum, would ideally be used in conjunction with a number of other assessment alternatives in order to facilitate the range of required decision-making purposes.

In order to operationalize our assessment or decision-making purposes, we will first describe the set of test and item specifications that comprise the current instrument. These specifications will develop the approach to task difficulty that was outlined in the previous two chapters, and the resulting framework will be applied to a set of real-world tasks in order to identify relevant components of task difficulty (i.e., the relevant ability requirements and task characteristics that are found in each task). The purpose of test and item specifications is to minimize ambiguity in assessment procedures. In this chapter, we will provide test and item specifications for the *Assessment of Language Performance* (ALP) prototype procedures. Given this prototypical framework and set of procedures, second language assessment practitioners should be able to generate program- and language-specific tests and items involving those tasks that are determined to be particularly relevant to the given pedagogic context. The chapter is divided into two main sections: one providing test specifications and the other giving item specifications.

TEST SPECIFICATIONS

In order to help minimize ambiguity in assessment procedures, *test specifications* should provide guidelines that explain what the test is designed to measure and what content or skills it will encompass. Test designers should then be able to use the test specifications to select specific test content and design the test. Later, test specifications may also prove useful for thinking about and defending the content validity of the test and communicating the test designer's intentions to future test users. One useful way to organize test specifications is to include an overall descriptor of the assessment procedure and then give specific test descriptors.

Overall test descriptor

As mentioned above, an *overall test descriptor* should explain what the test designers intend the test to do. To that end, they should state the general goals of the assessment procedure and describe the test format, at least in general terms. In a sense, the overall test descriptor serves as an abstract of what the assessment procedures are designed for and how they will look. In addition, the overall test descriptor should include a listing of the components that are of interest in the particular assessment procedure. For instance, if a test is to have a section that measures the ability to use a specific set of vocabulary, that information should be included in the test descriptor. If the test is to contain a functional language section, then that information should be included, too.

The Assessment of Language Performance (ALP) prototype procedures have the overall goal of assessing the performances of university-level second or foreign language students on various language tasks in the L2. Fundamentally, the test attempts to tie classroom L2 instruction to real-world L2 use. The test follows a performance-based approach in focusing only on an examinee's ability to successfully meet the communicative requirements of the task. Although the *process* of learning an L2 obviously plays an important role in preparing an examinee to successfully perform when confronted with a language task, this is not the focus of the current test. Nor does this instrument purport to measure a learner's development within a given L2 or towards a target L2 proficiency norm. Finally, the current test does not focus on the learner's mastery of specific language skills or content areas. Although all of these factors certainly contribute to the L2 learner's ability to perform on given L2 tasks, this test does not presume to measure them. What is of singular interest for this test is measuring the capacity of an examinee to successfully handle real-world language events as evidenced by the examinee's L2 performance.

But just what does it mean for an examinee to successfully handle a real-world language event? For each language task that is utilized within this test, minimum criteria will be established for determining an examinee's successful or unsuccessful performance. These criteria will generally be based on surveys of expert judgments regarding the particular task content and corresponding language genre necessary for successful communication. Obviously, the characteristics of successful

---

performance on various language tasks can be wide-ranging; therefore, the test does not presume to designate examinee levels that include *mastery, excellence, superiority,* or the like (although these descriptors may be used by a rater to indicate impressions of an examinee's L2 use). Rather, it is assumed that certain attributes characterize successful performance on a task, and that if an examinee is able to demonstrate these attributes, then the examinee is *minimally* capable of handling the task under real-world conditions. The attributes of successful task performance will be determined by expert judgments regarding the tasks. Three different types of experts will be used in the current project (for example, one high proficiency non-native speaker of the L2, one university-level teacher of the L2, and one assessment practitioner of the L2). By combining these multiple expert judgments regarding successful task performance, we feel that a more authentic and defensible set of criteria can be generated for describing overall task performance as well as task-specific L2 performance idiosyncrasies. (The criteria for rating task success will be described in detail in a subsequent volume in this series).

The prototypical tasks utilized in the ALP are intended to represent real-world tasks that might face university students studying a second or foreign language. Although quite broad, the examinee population of interest nevertheless represents a certain homogeneity in terms of demographic characteristics. Likewise, the tasks themselves tend to reflect real-world language tasks that international students would likely be faced with in transitional settings. Although the test is based on a particular set of tasks relevant to EFL/ESL for US contexts, the format of the test is intended to be applicable to any foreign or second language (F/SL) context. It should be apparent that in adapting the test format to any other F/SL context and population of learners, the corresponding tasks would have to be adapted to maintain authenticity and generalizability for the given language and the given population. Recommendations from the task-based language testing literature concerning the importance of appropriate needs analysis should be kept in mind at this task selection stage.

The tasks used in the current test are also not intended to cover the entire spectrum of language uses that issue from various F/SL learning situations. They are, rather, representative tasks that involve common language functions and generic content areas. They are intended to be nothing more than prototypes. It is our intention that these prototypes should necessarily be adapted according to specific classroom-level and program-level goals and objectives. Without such adaptation, the test retains little program-related generalizability and can therefore only aid decision making regarding examinee abilities with respect to the specific tasks in the test. In contrast, with adaptation of the language tasks based on needs analysis and implemented within a specific curriculum, the test framework can offer valuable and generalizable information regarding an examinee's capacity to perform a variety of relevant L2 tasks.

As the prototypical tasks utilized in the current test attempt to replicate real-world language events to a high degree, they also integrate language skill areas to varying degrees. Tasks have been selected which represent all four language skill areas;

however, representation is not necessarily equivalent. The foremost concern in task selection was maintenance of authenticity across the several levels of difficulty that are outlined in the specific test descriptors below.

Finally, mention should be made of the type of feedback that is given on the various test tasks. It is assumed that the purpose of feedback on this L2 performance assessment instrument is two-fold. First, feedback should provide task-specific information (to examinees, teachers, and any other interested parties) that *describes* an examinee's performance and a rater's judgment of that performance according to the criteria mentioned above. For such descriptive feedback, rater protocols are utilized for each task. Second, feedback should provide evidence of an examinee's minimal capacity to deal with L2 tasks at various levels of difficulty (ideally reflective of a given syllabus based on graded L2 tasks). Such evidence is essential for the decision-making purposes of teachers and administrators, and it is therefore reported according to a straightforward task performance scale (ALP feedback and rating protocols will be described in detail in a subsequent volume in this series).

Specific test descriptors

General descriptors are helpful in outlining the aims and parameters of a test, but they must also be supplemented by specific descriptors. *Specific test descriptors* should explain the components of the test and what will be included in each item type. For example, if the assessment procedures are to include grammar, reading, and writing, the specific test descriptors should explain in detail what each part — grammar, reading, and writing in this case — will include. We approached this issue with one overarching question: What are the important components of task performance?

Based on the performance assessment and TBLT literatures we found a convenient and practical breakdown of L2 task performance into two major components: examinee L2 manipulation or use, and inherent task difficulty. For the purposes of the ALP, the first of these components is handled sufficiently by the creation of rating criteria and protocols regarding examinee L2 use and based on expert judgments of task success.

However, while conducting the literature reviews in the previous two chapters, we recognized that our biggest problem was going to be determining task difficulty. Based primarily on Skehan (1996) and our own experiences with university-level L2 education, we devised an initial task difficulty matrix to help us explore ways to differentiate and sequence assessment tasks according to their difficulty levels. The task difficulty matrix (shown in Table 2) provides a visual representation of the variable sources of difficulty faced by examinees in attempting to successfully perform the tasks on the current test. Although a broad range of task-difficulty components, features, and characteristics are represented in the current matrix, this version should not be taken as a comprehensive explanation of the universe of possible contributors to task difficulty. That is, the different characteristics of a language event will themselves render a given task more or less difficult according to a variety of possible parameters. The corresponding constituents of a task

Table 2: Initial task difficulty matrix

	easy ⇒ difficult			easy ⇒ difficult			easy ⇒ difficult		
	range			*number of input sources*			*delivery of input*		
code	restricted	constant	amplified	1	2	3+	restricted	constant	amplified
	amount of info. to be processed			*organization of input*			*availability of input*		
cognitive complexity	restricted	constant	amplified	supportive	unrelated	contradictory	present & constant	present & additive	must be assessed
	mode			*channel*			*response level*		
communicative demand	receptive	productive	mixed	written	oral	mixed	planned	mixed	immediate
	number of action levels			*examinee responsibility for task difficulty*			*examinee familiarity*		
overlapping variables	1	2	3+	none	mixed	total	both	genre	content

difficulty matrix will consequently metamorphose according to particular characteristics inherent in a given task type. Naturally, these task types are themselves drawn in turn from classroom syllabuses and program-level curriculums which issue ostensibly form thorough needs analyses. Various features of task difficulty will thus accrete to or detach from the matrix depending on the corresponding program-level or classroom-level decision making that is to be facilitated.

The matrix represents a possible set of components, features, and characteristics that contribute to the difficulty of the generic task prototypes used in the current test. Each major task difficulty *component* is represented in the far left-hand column. *Code* indicates the complexity of the vocabulary, grammar, text structure, pragmatics, pronunciation, and so forth that is involved in the information that must be both processed and produced in a given task. The relative difficulty of the code that is inherent in the current set of tasks can vary according to the three *features* in the same row. These features include the range of the code, the number of sources of code input, and the manner in which the input is delivered. Each of these features can vary independently according to certain *characteristics*; thus, for example, the range of the code that is provided in a reading passage might be restricted to certain basic vocabulary items and grammatical structures, maintained at a level that is authentically consistent with the given writing genre, or amplified to include certain low-frequency vocabulary items and complex grammatical structures.

Moving down the matrix, *cognitive complexity* indicates the relative difficulty of the mental processes that are involved in completion of certain language tasks. Cognitive complexity as described here can vary according to three features: amount of information involved, organization of the input, and availability of the input. Once again, each of these features can vary independently according to certain characteristics.

Communicative demand indicates the extent to which examinees are faced with more or less stress in completing the given task. Such stress can vary according to the following features: language mode, language channel, and the level of immediacy in responding to the task. Each of these features varies independently according to rather obvious characteristics. Finally, the fourth component in the difficulty matrix involves *overlapping variables*, or those aspects of the language task that tend to influence task difficulty across the other components. The features of this component include: the number of discrete actions that must be undertaken in order to successfully complete a task, the extent to which an examinee is responsible for displaying ability by stepping up the complexity of a task response, and the familiarity that an examinee exhibits with respect to the language genre and content inherent in a given task.

It should be obvious that, even though the components, features, and characteristics in the difficulty matrix were selected for relevancy to the task prototypes in the current study, various components and characteristics will contribute more or less to the difficulty in execution of individual tasks. The task difficulty matrix might be conceived of, then, as something akin to the old-fashioned telephone-operator's switchboard, with the corresponding difficulty characteristic cells lighting up in conjunction with the nature of a given language event. It should not be assumed, therefore, that all of the cells in the matrix contribute equally to the difficulty of a given task. For example, a test item that asks an examinee to summarize, compare, and contrast the main ideas given in three different editorials to the newspaper would involve different cells to a greater degree than a test item that asks an examinee to order a pizza based on the preferences of friends who will be sharing the pizza.

In addition, different tasks have varying difficulty levels independent of the characteristics in the matrix. Expanding on the previous example, although the pizza task may involve an amplified range of code complexity (in terms of individuals' preferred ingredients, amount of pizza, etc.), numerous sources of input (menus, coupons, and notes), and amplified delivery of input (a fast-talking expediter on the other end of the phone), the task itself is still likely to present less difficulty than the more formal task of writing an essay comparing the three editorials. Hence, careful attention must be given not only to variations in difficulty within a given task but also to variability in difficulty between tasks.

Given the sources of variable task difficulty represented in the task difficulty matrix and given the fact that tasks seem to vary in what might be termed a *holistic difficulty level*, how is test item selection to proceed in a systematic and valid manner? For the purposes of authenticity, it is absolutely necessary to draw test items from a set of real-world performance instances like those represented in the item bank that we are creating in this project. However, in operationalizing these types of real-world tasks, two sources of real-world variability in task difficulty must be taken into consideration: between-task variability and within-task variability. Since the elimination or control of any particular manifestations of such difficulty would necessarily detract from the authenticity of the task, some other method for gauging actual task difficulty as it exerts an influence on the population of interest must be sought. One obvious means of determining such difficulty is through the investigation of task effect on examinees as they perform. Although this offers important input in terms of a description of the relationship between an examinee and a performance on a given task (and is therefore included as a component in the current investigation), it only offers one idiosyncratic perspective. It also constitutes an *ex post facto* method for decision making. To what extent, however, can we go about *predicting* task difficulty in a valid manner for a given population of examinees? More specifically, how can test creators pre-select a range of test items that cover a variety of performance domains as well as the desired range of performance difficulty?

REVISED TASK DIFFICULTY MATRIX

One possible pre-selection strategy is to begin by basing task difficulty estimates on our original representation of sources of difficulty, or the original task difficulty matrix (in Table 2). Unfortunately, although the matrix offers a good description of the possible sources and variations of difficulty for a wide variety of prototype tasks, its usefulness for task difficulty estimation (in order to facilitate item selection) is somewhat limited. Taking a single characteristic and the variable features of that characteristic as an example, if we consider the *range* cell within *code complexity*, three general features, extending from easier to more difficult, can be seen: restricted, constant, and amplified. Although each of these features most likely does contribute differentially to task difficulty, applying them to item selection is not so straightforward. That is, the separation of tasks into those with restricted, constant, and amplified ranges of code complexity would certainly be possible, but it might not take us much closer to the resulting differences in difficulty for various examinees (which is what is needed for item selection). The differences between the three features are simply too subtle for such differentiation (at least in an *a priori* approach). It is likely that, after a variety of tasks have been administered to representative groups of examinees, the multiple features in the original matrix may indeed illuminate obvious differences in difficulty, but again, their use as *predictors* seems premature.

What is needed for *a priori* task difficulty estimation is a much more general representation of difficulty characteristics and features, as unsound as this might initially seem. In order to make general estimations of task difficulty that are nevertheless grounded in an analysis of the co-contribution of the various components and characteristics, the original 4 x 3 x 3 matrix (which would result in hundreds of possible combinations) can be effectively reduced to the 3 x 3 x 2 matrix shown in Table 3. The first alteration in this new matrix that must be addressed involves the elimination of the fourth component, *overlapping variables*, from the expanded difficulty matrix. Recall that this component included task characteristics that exert overarching influence on the other task difficulty components. These characteristics are therefore extremely important to a final decision regarding task difficulty for various examinees in a given population. However, due to their comprehensive influence, they are not easily invoked for the purposes of estimating the probable difficulty level of various tasks. Furthermore, the presence of these characteristics tends to diffuse the probable contribution of the other components to such a difficulty estimate. For the purpose of initial difficulty estimation, they will therefore be eliminated. Nevertheless, we do not want to ignore the importance of these characteristics/variables in final task selection. We will return to this point, therefore, in the section on item selection.

The second alteration in the new matrix involves the reduction of the *features* cells from three to two. Each feature cell now represents a statement regarding a given task: either the task is considered relatively more easy or more difficult for the particular characteristic. In the revised matrix, then, difficulty estimation decisions are pared down to simple plus or minus choices for three characteristics of the three components. For a given task, a set of corresponding plus and minus decisions will constitute a general estimate of task difficulty. By applying this new matrix to a set of real-world tasks that have already been selected (again, based on a specific syllabus and curriculum), tasks can be assigned an overall task difficulty index (equal to the total number of plusses). Furthermore, the contribution of particular difficulty characteristics to overall task difficulty can be highlighted and studied after examinee performances are collected and examined *ex post facto*.

Table 3: Revised assessment of language performance task difficulty matrix

	easy ⇒ difficult		easy ⇒ difficult		easy ⇒ difficult	
	range		*number of input sources*		*delivery of input*	
code	−	+	−	+	−	+
	amount of info. to be processed		*organization of input*		*availability of input*	
cognitive complexity	−	+	−	+	−	+
	mode		*channel*		*response level*	
communicative demand	−	+	−	+	−	+

Note: In the reduced task difficulty matrix, a *minus* sign always indicates less difficulty with respect to the component and characteristic relative to the given task, whereas a *plus* sign always indicates greater relative difficulty.

For the purposes of focusing on performance difficulty characteristics that are of specific interest to the current L2 performance assessment instrument, six variables were drawn from the revised task difficulty matrix (shown in Table 3). In order to represent the *code complexity* involved in a given task, the two variables selected were: (a) code range and (b) the number of different input sources involved in the task. The third code complexity variable in the revised task difficulty matrix, delivery of input, was subsumed under (a) code range for the current set of tasks. That is, we decided that the manner in which task-essential information is delivered to the examinees was a subset of the overall range of the code involved. In other words, we felt that other input delivery aspects that might play a role in complicating a task would best controlled from the outset (e.g., elimination of overt distortion of aural input, exclusion of excessively rapid speech, etc.).

In order to represent the *cognitive complexity* of a given task, the two variables selected were: (a) the organization of the input or output involved in a task and (b) the availability of input for informing the language act involved in a task. It was decided that the third cognitive complexity variable from the revised task difficulty matrix, amount of information to be processed, would be controlled for at the item level across all tasks presented to examinees. That is, given the potentially vast range in amount of information related to various tasks, it was deemed expedient to first control the amount of information to be processed for individual items and then to counterbalance the presentation of items with varying amounts of information such that all examinees would process approximately the same amount of information during a single testing session.

Finally, in order to represent the *communicative demand* inherent in a given task, the two variables selected were: (a) the language mode(s) within which examinee performance would take place and (b) the immediacy required in response to information presented in a given task. The third communicative demand variable in the revised task difficulty matrix, the channel within which information would be communicated by the examinee, was subsumed under the productive aspect of the mode variable (for the purposes of the current instrument). That is, differences between the communicative demands of written versus oral production were deemed minimal with respect to any differences between relatively receptive versus relatively productive tasks in the current assessment procedures.

The descriptions in the following section provide the parameters of each of the six variables as we currently envision them, especially in light of the set of tasks we outline below and exemplify in chapter 6. We also examine the ambiguities inherent in the application of each of these task difficulty variables and give examples of particular decision problem areas. Remember that, in using these variables to describe potential task difficulty, we do not presume to exhaustively account for the actual difficulty that will be faced by an examinee in the performance assessment setting. Our intent in applying these variables to a set of real-world language tasks is to attempt an *a priori* estimation of relative task difficulty and, furthermore, to enable the investigation of the role that particular aspects of task difficulty play as they manifest themselves in examinee performance with the language.

TASK DIFFICULTY VARIABLE DESCRIPTIONS

Recall that the three variables of central interest at this point are code complexity, cognitive complexity, and communicative demand. Each of these variables will be defined here in detail.

Code complexity

The code complexity of a given task depends on the kind of language and information that is involved in successful task performance (i.e., the linguistic code). The determining factor for this difficulty component is the level of the language that must be understood and/or produced by an examinee. Obviously, this component attempts to account for a great variety of potential sources of task difficulty, and as such, it may represent the most elusive source of variance. For the current set of tasks, the total possible variance attributable to task code complexity will be reduced somewhat by the elimination from tasks of any undue complexity due to the delivery of input (e.g., excessively rapid, obscure, or distorted speech). The primary variables salient for estimating code complexity in the current set of tasks are: (a) range and (b) number of input sources. We will discuss each of these in turn.

Range

Range addresses the extent to which the code that is inherent in the language of a given task represents a greater or lesser degree of *spread*. Particular characteristics of the language code that might exhibit such spread would include vocabulary items, grammatical structures, pragmatic features of the task, structure of the information that is presented or produced, and so forth. Code complexity range is reflected in both any input that must be comprehended and incorporated by the examinee and any output that the examinee is expected to produce. Essential in estimating the contribution of this variable to the relative difficulty or ease of a given task is the determination of whether or not a broad range of low-frequency and high-frequency code characteristics are involved (receptively and/or productively) in successful task completion (lack of such range reduces the effect of the variable). To apply this variable, a subjective decision must be made regarding the task-related difficulty of, for example, the vocabulary used, the grammar needed, the pragmatic sensitivities required, and so forth. Obviously, depending on the types of real-world tasks selected for a given assessment, this variable could prove to be very influential in determining overall task difficulty and may, in many circumstances, override the remaining sources of task difficulty. For this reason, care should be taken when selecting and designing items, such that excesses in code range are either controlled or eliminated (to the extent that this is possible without affecting task authenticity).

Number of different input sources

Number of different input sources addresses whether or not the examinee must *decode* multiple sources of information input, each source representing inherent code differences. A task is not considered to be more difficult simply based on the use of multiple input sources (e.g., a stack of bank deposit slips would not represent different input sources as all slips present the same quality of information within the same code format). Rather, in order for a task to be considered more difficult based on this variable, it must involve a minimum of two independent sources of input, each including some individual variation in terms of the code (most basically, the presentation of new information, but also including differing formats for presentation, e.g., the stack of bank deposit slips and a monthly bank statement). Furthermore, information provided in all sources of input must be essential for successful task performance if this variable is to contribute to task difficulty; that is, each input source must involve a differing code aspect which must be processed by the examinee in order to successfully complete the task. Although often associated with the input/output organization variable, these two should not be confused (see discussion below).

Cognitive complexity

The cognitive complexity of a given task essentially turns on the amount and kind of information processing that an examinee must engage in to successfully perform the task (mental gymnastics, in a sense). Overall amount of information presented to examinees is controlled on the current instrument, as mentioned above, such that each examinee is faced with a set of tasks that represent approximately the same amount of information to be processed. The estimated cognitive complexity of the current tasks is therefore reduced to the following two variables: (a) input/output organization and (b) input availability.

Input/output organization

Input/output organization addresses the extent to which information must be significantly organized, re-organized, or just plain shifted about with respect to parameters of task success. Such information might come in the form of various input sources, from which an organized set of selections must be made according to some external criteria. Alternatively, the information to be organized might come in the form of examinee output on a given task, with successful task performance depending to a certain extent on the ability of the examinee to organize a productive response with respect to some external criteria. The development of organizational criteria themselves would also constitute a higher level of difficulty for this variable. Although often closely associated with multiple input sources that must be compared and contrasted, such association is not a prerequisite for organizational difficulty. The organization might be in response to a single source of input that needs to be rearranged, for example, or a number of input sources might be used to inform a response, but would not necessarily involve organizational demand (and as such would receive a minus on this variable). In estimating the influence of the organization variable, focus should be on whether or not an examinee has to execute extensive manipulations with respect to some type of imposed order (although such imposition may come from the examinees themselves).

Input availability

Input availability addresses whether or not an examinee is required in some significant way to search for the information upon which a task performance is to be based. It is the substantial searching process that is at issue for this variable (i.e., the input is not readily available). One form such searching might take would involve the examinee in actively accessing the appropriate information from a particular source or set of sources. In such a task, the examinee must be able to make decisions regarding the route to take to best encounter input relevant to a given task. This accessing process might include the identification of an appropriate source, the selection of relevant areas within a given source, and the further utilization of information after it has been accessed. A second form that the search for input might take would involve the examinee in generating the information to be processed and utilized in task completion. That is, input would not be provided in such tasks (except in the form of an item prompt); the examinee would instead have to create the information upon which the task performance would be based. Obviously, this second type of task is most easily identified by its creative characteristics. A task that would receive a plus difficulty rating based on this aspect of the variable would require that the examinee actively provide information essential to task completion without the benefit of overt contextual input. The input availability variable is not necessarily more closely associated with any of the other variables. Estimation of its influence on the cognitive complexity of a task should focus on the extent to which examinees must actively engage in the accessing of task-essential information.

Communicative demand

The communicative demand involved in a given task is determined by the type of communicative language activity that is required as well as by a number of moderator variables that can drastically influence the relative difficulty of a particular communicative act. This subset of moderator variables can be extensive, unpredictable, and can present very salient individual variation from examinee to examinee (thus, for example, stress, examinee control over a situation, the stakes involved in a task, time pressure, etc., can all exert independent and highly variable influences on communication). For the current set of tasks, such moderator variables are, where possible, controlled (by providing ample planning time, for example). Regardless of the extent to which such control is attempted, however, examinee interaction with a particular task should always be observed, and apparent undue communicative demand due to such moderator variables should be noted (for future reference in making decisions about examinees, in item analysis, in test revision, etc.). Barring the effect of such moderator variables, the variables deemed most salient for estimating the communicative demand of the current set of tasks are: (a) mode and (b) response level.

Mode

Mode addresses whether or not a task is construed to have a productive element that is inherently connected to task performance success. Thus, in its most basic formulation, this variable is determined by whether or not speaking or writing must be executed within the task performance. However, it should not be taken as a given that any task that involves some manner of speaking or writing on the part of the examinee is therefore more difficult according to the mode variable. A variety of real-world communicative tasks involve what appear to be communicatively productive activities at first glance, but which do not in fact require extensive productive communication on the part of the examinee. For example, very often task performances may involve incidental writing or speaking (filling in basic forms, answering yes-no questions, repeating basic information, etc.). For such tasks, the productive element of the communication is not that aspect which determines performance difficulty (and as such, the task would receive a minus for the mode variable). Only if productive communication issuing from the examinee plays a central role in the successful performance of the task should the mode variable be considered more difficult.

Response level

Response level addresses the extent to which an examinee must interact with input in an *on-line* or *real time* sense. In order for response level to be considered as playing a central role in the difficulty of a given task, successful task performance must require the examinee to process task-essential information in a relatively immediate manner. Thus, tasks that involve a substantial amount of planning time for the central communicative act would be considered less difficult according to this variable (and would therefore receive a minus). However, any task that requires relatively immediate production in response to any form of input or stimulus would be considered more difficult. Furthermore, virtually all tasks that involve listening comprehension to an extensive degree as a central communicative act must be considered more difficult according to the response level variable. Although such difficulty could be authentically reduced in certain tasks (e.g., where repeated listening is a possibility), the reality of most listening tasks is that they require *on-linedness* from the listener. Listening comprehension in authentic communicative situations often poses an immediate demand.

The usefulness of these test specifications and task difficulty descriptions may still seem somewhat ambiguous. We turn now, therefore, to their practical application for actual test item specification and selection for the ALP prototype instrument.

ITEM SPECIFICATIONS

The first step in developing item specifications here involves assignment of difficulty rating estimates to potential tasks using the reduced matrix above. Initial assignment would most profitably be introduced directly following the generation/collection of a set of relevant tasks. All tasks should then be subjected to difficulty ratings, the result being a set of task difficulty indices to be implemented in test item selection. The results of the process of task collection and task difficulty rating in the present project are shown in Table 4.

Two qualifications for the current set of task difficulty indices should be noted here. First, in order to insure a high degree of accuracy in estimating task difficulty, validation procedures must be incorporated into the difficulty rating process. Such validation for the current set of prototypes will involve the independent estimation of the contribution of the different task difficulty components by two trained raters. By working independently through the set of tasks and subjectively estimating the contribution of each difficulty variable, interrater agreement can be calculated, ambiguous tasks and difficulty components can be identified, and any overly problematic tasks can be eliminated. Given the intended use of the tasks in the ALP for developing a systematic approach to generalizability based on these difficulty estimations, we consider such validation of task difficulty indices to be an essential design component. We will report on the validation of the current set of prototypes, in addition to other reliability and validity investigations, at later stages of the test design and implementation process (in future volumes). Second, the current set of prototypes should be taken as representative of the range of tasks that will be selected as items for the ALP. However, in order to operationalize the instrument, it may be necessary to eliminate certain items or to generate new items. Thus, the current set of tasks should be taken as an example item pool, but not necessarily as the final set of prototypes that will be utilized within the ALP. .

ITEM SELECTION

After the assignment of difficulty ratings to all tasks in a pre-selected set, item selection can be effectively undertaken. First of all, the results of difficulty rating assignments should be surveyed, and questions like the following should be considered. How does the set of likely tasks seem to vary in difficulty? Is there a wide range of difficulty, stretching from the relatively easy to the relatively difficult, or is the difficulty range somewhat truncated or bi-modal? Do the different components of task difficulty seem to contribute equivalently to the difficulty of various tasks, or are there certain characteristics and components that seem much more prevalent contributors to task difficulty? What is the source for any such identifiable variations? Is it that the syllabus or curriculum from which the tasks are drawn stresses these particular areas of task difficulty?

Based on answers to these and similar questions, and following the spread of task difficulties, test items can be selected. Thus, if the objective for item selection is to cover all possible combinations of difficulty contributors from the matrix (in order to investigate the eventual difficulty that is actually posed for examinees by the universe of possible variations), then items could be selected such that each possible combination of plusses and minuses would be accounted for. If the test only requires focus on the different components, but not the characteristics within these components, then tasks could be selected based on the relative contribution of each component level, without particular attention being paid to the characteristic cells. Another possibility would simply involve the inclusion of tasks covering a specified range of difficulties, regardless of which components contribute to a greater or lesser degree. One final possibility might see test item selection based on the distribution of task difficulties as it is represented across the entire set of pre-selected tasks (and hence as it is likely represented within the relevant syllabus).

Within the item-selection process, the overlapping nature of the difficulty components should not be forgotten. By this stage, tasks have already been attributed a difficulty estimate based on the total contribution of various difficulty components. The item-selector can now decide the extent to which the overlapping variables should play a role in additional determination of item difficulty. For example, two items might be chosen for the test, one representing a content domain and language function with which the examinees are familiar and a second representing unfamiliar domain and function. All other difficulty characteristics of the tasks being rated equal, the contribution of examinee familiarity to task difficulty might be more easily discerned (and for that matter, the examinee's ability to deal with unfamiliar domains and functions).

The item selection process in this project focuses on the task difficulty components (code complexity, cognitive complexity, and communicative demand) that were discussed in detail above. They are systematically included in our assessment procedures to help us plan, select, and sequence tasks for students to perform, and in order to facilitate the generalizability of ALP scores. These three components and their subparts were examined across a variety of what we are calling task themes.

The task themes that we used (e.g., deciding on a movie, choosing the appropriate film, planning the weekend, getting directions to the party, etc.) were themes that the authors of a variety of different language teaching textbooks found important enough to include in their language teaching materials. In some cases, we have also included ideas from our own classroom L2 experiences in order to generate a wide variety of tasks across many difficulty levels. We then analyzed the difficulty level of the task that we envisioned for each theme in terms of code complexity (including both range and number of input sources), cognitive complexity (including both input/output organization and input availability), and communicative demand (including both mode and response level). From our analysis, we predicted whether the task would be high (+) or low (−) in terms of the difficulty of each factor. In other word, a plus (+) sign indicates generally higher estimated difficulty based on the corresponding characteristic for the particular task, and a minus (−) sign indicates generally lower estimated difficulty based on the characteristic. The results of these tentative analyses are shown in Table 4.

Notice in Table 4 that the label in the first column on the left is for the task themes; next, one column each to the right is provided for range and number of input sources under code complexity, input/output organization and input availability under cognitive complexity, and mode and response level under communicative demand; the second column from the left shows the tentative difficulty levels, which are based on the sum of the + signs.

Notice also that the task themes are organized into what we are calling areas and that each theme is listed with a letter and number in front of it. The letters indicate which area is involved and the number just shows which task theme it is sequentially within the area. The following areas are represented: (A) Health and recreation/entertainment; (B) Travel; (C) Food and dining; (D) At work; (E) At the university; (F) Domesticity; and (G) Environment/politics.

Table 4: Task difficulty matrix for prototypical tasks:
Assessment of language performance

tasks (by theme)	diff. index	component					
		code		cognitive complexity		commun. demand	
		characteristic					
		range	#input sources	in/out organiz.	input available	mode	resp. level
A.1 Deciding on a movie	5	+	+	−	+	+	+

A.2 Choosing the appropriate film	4	+	+	−	+	+	−
A.3 Planning the weekend	2	−	+	+	−	−	−
A.4 Getting directions to the party	2	−	−	+	−	−	+
A.5 Using the dating service	5	+	+	+	+	−	+
A.6 Giving medical advice	4	+	−	−	+	+	+
A.7 Be careful with medicine	1	−	+	−	−	−	−
A.8 Quit smoking cigars!	4	+	+	+	−	+	−
A.9 Getting advice from TEL-MED	6	+	+	+	+	+	+
A.10 Soccer game ejection	4	−	+	+	−	+	+
A.11 Windsurfing advisory	4	+	+	−	+	−	+
A.12 Cable TV survey	4	−	+	+	+	−	+
A.13 Talk radio	3	+	+	−	−	+	−
A.14 Finding the dentist's phone #	1	−	−	−	−	−	+
A.15 Movie show times	3	−	+	−	+	−	+
A.16 Sports nutrition	3	−	−	+	−	+	+
A.17 Restaurant selection	2	−	+	−	−	+	−

continued...

Table 4: Task difficulty matrix for prototypical tasks: Assessment of language performance (cont.)

tasks (by theme)	diff. index	component code range	#input sources	cognitive complexity in/out organiz.	input available	commun. demand mode	resp. level
A.18 Picking the right hikes	3	+	−	+	+	−	−
B.1 Using your 'Advantage Miles'	2	+	+	−	−	−	−
B.2 Booking a flight	3	−	+	−	−	+	+
B.3 Choosing a hotel	2	−	+	−	+	−	−
B.4 Booking a room	3	−	+	−	−	+	+
B.5 Finding your flight	0	−	−	−	−	−	−
B.6 Solving ticket problems	5	+	+	+	+	+	−
B.7 Checking in	2	−	−	−	−	+	+
B.8 Boarding	2	+	−	−	−	−	+
B.9 Finding your lost bag	1	−	−	+	−	−	−
B.10 The bus	3	−	−	−	+	+	+
B.11 Radio weather info.	5	+	+	−	+	+	+
B.12 Spring break plans	4	+	+	−	−	+	+
B.13 Chicago museums	4	+	−	+	+	−	+

B.14 Calling Hawaiian Air	2	–	–	–	+	–	+
B.15 Barbados video travel	3	+	–	–	–	+	+
B.16 'Advantage Miles' listening	3	+	–	–	+	–	+
C.1 Reserving a table	1	–	–	–	–	+	–
C.2 Ordering drinks and appetizers	4	+	–	+	–	+	+
C.3 Ordering the main course	3	+	–	–	+	+	–
C.4 Sending back a dish	2	+	–	–	–	+	–
C.5 Ordering coffee & dessert	3	–	+	–	–	+	+
C.6 Comparing menus	4	+	+	+	–	+	–
C.7 Leaving a message	2	–	–	+	–	+	–
C.8 Getting everyone's order	2	–	+	–	–	–	+
C.9 Deciding on ingredients and #	3	–	+	+	+	–	–
C.10 Ordering pizzas	5	–	+	+	+	+	+
C.11 Comparing items and prices	4	–	+	+	+	+	–
C.12 Investigating nutritional info.	2	+	+	–	–	–	–

continued...

Table 4: Task difficulty matrix for prototypical tasks: Assessment of language performance (cont.)

tasks (by theme)	diff. index	code		cognitive complexity		commun. demand	
		range	#input sources	in/out organiz.	input available	mode	resp. level
C.13 Planning the meeting menu	4	+	+	+	−	−	+
D.1 Writing a job ad	4	+	+	+	−	+	−
D.2 Sorting through candidates	3	+	+	+	−	−	−
D.3 Writing a form letter of rejection	5	+	+	+	+	+	−
D.4 Making a hiring decision	5	+	+	+	+	−	+
D.5 Offering a job	4	+	+	+	−	+	−
D.6 Filling in an application form	2	+	−	−	−	+	−
D.7 Writing a cover letter	4	+	−	+	+	+	−
D.8 Answering phone interview	5	+	−	+	+	+	+
D.9 Creating a rolodex	1	−	−	+	−	−	−
D.10 Taking messages	3	−	+	+	−	−	+
D.11 Transcribing a business letter	2	+	−	−	−	+	−

D.12 Matching a job candidate with a job	4	+	+	–	+	–	+
D.13 Creating two resumes	5	+	+	+	–	+	+
D.14 Sending a fax	4	–	–	+	+	+	+
D.15 Editing a letter	3	+	–	+	–	–	+
D.16 Choosing a city for a conference	4	+	+	+	+	–	–
D.17 Job rankings	2	–	–	+	+	–	–
E.1 Applying to a university	2	–	–	–	+	+	–
E.2 Corresponding with the dept. chair	4	+	–	+	+	+	–
E.3 Phone call with the admissions officer	4	+	–	+	+	+	–
E.4 Inquire about financial support	3	+	–	+	–	+	–
E.5 Select your courses	2	–	+	+	–	–	–
E.6 Calculating and paying your fees	3	+	+	+	–	–	–
E.7 Planning your presentation	4	+	–	+	+	+	–
E.8 Creating a handout	2	+	–	+	–	–	–
E.9 Delivering a presentation	3	+	–	+	–	+	–

continued…

Table 4: Task difficulty matrix for prototypical tasks:
Assessment of language performance (cont.)

tasks (by theme)	diff. index	component					
		code		cognitive complexity		commun. demand	
		characteristic					
		range	#input sources	in/out organiz.	input available	mode	resp. level
E.10 Summarizing a lecture	4	+	–	+	–	+	+
E.11 Find relevant literature	4	+	+	–	+	+	–
E.12 Comparing lit. with lecture	5	+	+	+	+	+	–
E.13 WWW real audio essay	6	+	+	+	+	+	+
E.14 E-mailing schedule	4	–	+	–	+	+	+
E.15 APA search	2	+	–	–	+	–	–
E.16 Highlighting main ideas	1	+	–	–	–	–	–
E.17 APA tables	3	+	–	+	+	–	–
E.18 University rankings	2	–	–	+	–	–	+
E.19 NICE information	3	–	–	+	+	+	–
F.1 Looking for a house	3	+	+	+	–	–	–
F.2 Using a rental agency	4	+	+	+	–	–	+

F.3 Filling out a rental application	3	−	+	+	−	−	+
F.4 Advertising for a housemate	4	−	+	+	+	+	−
F.5 Filling out change of address form	2	−	−	+	−	−	+
F.6 Ordering things from a catalogue	3	−	+	+	+	−	−
F.7 Paying your monthly bills	3	+	+	+	−	−	−
F.8 Depositing money in the bank	3	+	+	+	−	−	−
F.9 Comparing credit card offers	5	+	+	+	+	+	−
F.10 Applying for emergency loan	4	+	−	+	+	+	−
F.11 Bank over-draft	4	+	+	−	+	+	−
F.12 Listing emergency phone numbers	1	−	−	−	+	−	−
F.13 Ordered chores	2	−	−	+	−	+	−
F.14 Talk about your schedule	2	−	−	−	+	+	−
F.15 Deciding on a car to buy	3	+	+	−	+	−	−
G.1 Comparing environmental orgs.	3	−	−	+	+	−	+
G.2 Gun crimes around the globe	3	+	+	−	−	−	+

continued...

Table 4: Task difficulty matrix for prototypical tasks:
Assessment of language performance (cont.)

tasks (by theme)	diff. index	component code		cognitive complexity		commun. demand	
		characteristic					
		range	#input sources	in/out organiz.	input available	mode	resp. level
G.3 Expressing environmental views	3	–	+	–	+	+	–
G.4 Product packaging ranks	3	–	–	+	+	+	–
G.5 Organizing the ads	3	–	+	+	–	+	–
G.6 Rainforest deforestation	2	–	+	–	–	–	+

In examining the results reported in Table 4, you may have noticed there are only seven possible difficulty scores (0, 1, 2, 3, 4, 5, and 6) and there are different ways to arrive at each of the scores. In fact, as shown in Table 5, there are a total of 64 different possible combinations of + and – for the six factors being examined in that table. Table 6 summarizes the number of possible combinations that result in each score between 0 and 6.

Table 5: Matrix of item difficulty and all possible combinations of code complexity, cognitive complexity and communicative demand

diff. index	component code		cognitive complexity		commun. demand	
	characteristic					
	range	#input sources	in/out organiz.	input available	mode	resp. level
6	+	+	+	+	+	+
5	+	+	+	+	+	–
5	+	+	+	+	–	+
5	+	+	+	–	+	+

5	+	+	−	+	+	+
5	+	−	+	+	+	+
5	−	+	+	+	+	+
4	+	+	+	+	−	−
4	+	+	+	−	−	+
4	+	+	−	−	+	+
4	+	−	−	+	+	+
4	−	−	+	+	+	+
4	+	+	+	−	+	−
4	+	+	−	+	+	−
4	+	−	+	+	+	−
4	−	+	+	+	+	−
4	+	+	−	+	−	+
4	+	−	+	+	−	+
4	−	+	+	+	−	+
4	+	−	+	−	+	+
4	−	+	+	−	+	+
4	−	+	−	+	+	+
3	−	−	−	+	+	+
3	−	−	+	+	+	−
3	−	+	+	+	−	−
3	+	+	+	−	−	−
3	−	−	+	+	−	+
3	−	+	+	−	−	+
3	+	+	−	−	−	+
3	−	−	+	−	+	+
3	−	+	−	−	+	+
3	+	−	−	−	+	+
3	+	−	−	+	−	+
3	−	+	−	+	−	+
3	−	+	−	+	+	−
3	+	−	−	+	+	−
3	−	+	+	−	+	−
3	+	−	+	−	+	−
3	+	+	−	−	+	−
3	+	+	−	+	−	−
3	+	−	+	+	−	−
3	+	−	+	−	−	+
2	−	−	−	−	+	+
2	−	−	−	+	+	−
2	−	−	+	+	−	−
2	−	+	+	−	−	−
2	+	+	−	−	−	−
2	−	−	−	+	−	+
2	−	−	+	−	−	+
2	−	+	−	−	−	+

continued…

Table 5: Matrix of item difficulty and all possible combinations of code complexity, cognitive complexity and communicative demand (cont.)

diff. index	component					
	code		cognitive complexity		commun. demand	
	characteristic					
	range	#input sources	in/out organiz.	input available	mode	resp. level
2	+	−	−	−	−	+
2	−	−	+	−	+	−
2	−	+	−	−	+	−
2	+	−	−	−	+	−
2	−	+	−	+	−	−
2	+	−	−	+	−	−
2	+	−	+	−	−	−
1	−	−	−	−	−	+
1	−	−	−	−	+	−
1	−	−	−	+	−	−
1	−	−	+	−	−	−
1	−	+	−	−	−	−
1	+	−	−	−	−	−
0	−	−	−	−	−	−

Table 6: Possible combinations of plusses and minuses across the seven difficulty levels

difficulty index	n
6	1
5	6
4	15
3	20
2	15
1	6
0	1

We then reorganized the information in Table 4 so that each of the possible combinations of plusses and minuses is represented only once across the seven difficulty levels. Notice also that the information is sorted from high to low based on the difficulty levels. Otherwise, the information shown in Table 7 is presented in much the same manner as in Table 5, except that multiple representative tasks are shown in the left-most column for each difficulty level. Thus, Table 7 shows our set of pre-selected tasks (by task identification number) and where they fall in terms of task-difficulty components.

Table 7: Combinations matrix

tasks	diff. index	code		cognitive complexity		commun. demand	
		range	#input sources	in/out organiz.	input available	mode	resp. level
E13, A9	6	+	+	+	+	+	+
B6, D3, E12, F9	5	+	+	+	+	+	−
A5, D4	5	+	+	+	+	−	+
D13	5	+	+	+	−	+	+
B11, A1	5	+	+	−	+	+	+
D8	5	+	−	+	+	+	+
C10	5	−	+	+	+	+	+
D16	4	+	+	+	+	−	−
F2, C13	4	+	+	+	−	−	+
B12	4	+	+	−	−	+	+
A6	4	+	−	−	+	+	+
D14	4	−	−	+	+	+	+
A8, C6, D1, D5	4	+	+	+	−	+	−
A2, E11, F11	4	+	+	−	+	+	−
D7, E2, E3, E7, F10	4	+	−	+	+	+	+
F4, C11	4	−	+	+	+	+	−
A11, D12	4	+	+	−	+	−	+
B13	4	+	−	+	+	−	+
A12	4	−	+	+	+	−	+
C2, E10	4	+	−	+	−	+	+
A10	4	−	+	+	−	+	+
E14	4	−	+	−	+	+	+
B10	3	−	−	−	+	+	+
E19, G4	3	−	−	+	+	+	−

continued...

Table 7: Combinations matrix (cont.)

tasks	diff. index	code		cognitive complexity		commun. demand	
		range	#input sources	in/out organiz.	input available	mode	resp. level
C9, F6	3	–	+	+	+	–	–
D2, E6, F1, F7, F8	3	+	+	+	–	–	–
G1	3	–	–	+	+	–	+
D10, F3	3	–	+	+	–	–	+
G2	3	+	+	–	–	–	+
A16	3	–	–	+	–	+	+
B2, B4, C5	3	–	+	–	–	+	+
B15	3	+	–	–	–	+	+
B16	3	+	–	–	+	–	+
A15	3	–	+	–	+	–	+
G3	3	–	+	–	+	+	–
C3	3	+	–	–	+	+	–
G5	3	–	+	+	–	+	–
E4, E9	3	+	–	+	–	+	–
A13	3	+	+	–	–	+	–
F15	3	+	+	–	+	–	–
A18	3	+	–	+	+	–	–
D15	3	+	–	+	–	–	+
B7	2	–	–	–	–	+	+
E1, F14	2	–	–	–	+	+	–
D17	2	–	–	+	+	–	–
A3, E5	2	–	+	+	–	–	–
C12, B1	2	+	+	–	–	–	–
B14	2	–	–	–	+	–	+
E18, A4, F5	2	–	–	+	–	–	+
G6, C8	2	–	+	–	–	–	+
B8	2	+	–	–	–	–	+

F13, C7	2	–	–	+	–	+	–
A17	2	–	+	–	–	+	–
D11, C4, D6	2	+	–	–	–	+	–
B3	2	–	+	–	+	–	–
E15	2	+	–	–	+	–	–
E8	2	+	–	+	–	–	–
A14	1	–	–	–	–	–	+
C1	1	–	–	–	–	+	–
F12	1	–	–	–	+	–	–
B9, D9	1	–	–	+	–	–	–
A7	1	–	+	–	–	–	–
E16	1	+	–	–	–	–	–
B5	0	–	–	–	–	–	–

Based on Table 7, the Assessment of Language Performance procedures can now be designed to systematically represent these 64 possible task difficulty combinations with a view to empirically testing the accuracy of our *a priori* estimations of the difficulty of the six categories as well as the adequacy of using them in combination for distinguishing task difficulty in an assessment environment.

Chapter 6 will provide complete descriptions of the item prompts for all of the items listed in Tables 5.3 and 5.6. The appendix will show example items within several content areas in their generative form. The forms exemplified in the appendix were utilized in the task generation process and should offer examples of how to begin to assign difficulty ratings to given language tasks in different content areas. Chapter 6 and the appendix will therefore add to and complete the prototypical item specifications begun in this chapter.

chapter six

ITEM PROMPTS

This chapter provides item/task prompts for all of the areas and themes listed in Table 4 in the previous chapter. Each description provides a general prompt as well as a list of any realia or materials that will be necessary to administer the prompt. The areas and themes are organized just as they were in Table 4. It should be noted that this sample set of item prompts is in progress, which is to say that the item pool should not be taken as the final set of ALP tasks to be utilized for assessment purposes. Furthermore, the item prompts and realia descriptions included here are intended for the use of test designers; this is not the form that the final items will take when being utilized with examinees.

Area A: Health and recreation/entertainment

Task A.1:   Deciding on a movie
difficulty index: 5

prompt:
Read your friend's note describing when he can go to the movies and what kind of film he would like to see. Then listen to the list of movies from your local movie theater. Pay careful attention to the show-times and the brief movie descriptions. Note titles and times that seem appropriate. Now match up your friend's times and preferences with any of the films that fit both. Call your friend and leave a message on his answering machine giving pertinent information about your choices. Finally, suggest one film that seems preferable to you (be sure to state a reason for your preference).

realia/materials:
Note from the friend (high-code description; logical organization); tape-recorded list of (multiple, varied) movies and times like you get from US theaters ("Welcome to Varsity theater…), with movie-jargon descriptions of different films and possible show-times, well-organized (parallel to friend's note); telephone; answering machine message from the friend (standard — easy code).

Task A.2:   Choose the most appropriate film
difficulty index: 4

prompt:
Your friend did not like any of the movies you suggested for tonight, and he has changed his mind about the type of film he wants to see. Read his e-mail message to you (noting any important information). Then look through the movie reviews section of the Sunday paper to identify any films that he might enjoy. Write an

e-mail back to him, describing the one film that you think best fits his requirements. Be sure to mention the show times and location of the film you choose. .

realia/materials:
Computer with e-mail connection (post-login, don't want technology to get in the way of success on this task) and e-mail from friend (standard, non-complex e-mail style); entertainment section of the local paper (Honolulu Advertiser).

Task A.3:   Planning the weekend
difficulty index: 2
prompt:
Several friends are coming to visit you (e.g., in Honolulu) this weekend. Look through the three following lists: arrival and departure times and pre-determined schedule of activities for your visitors, the things they would like to do while in town, and the weekend entertainment section of the newspaper. After comparing these three sets of information, write out a weekend activity schedule that includes all activities that can be matched up from the three sources of information. Start by including all activities that have already been scheduled.

realia/materials:
Written notes (e.g., from a previous phone conversation) that have arrival and departure times and pre-determined activities (whale-watching at 5:00 p.m. on Sunday); further written notes about their desired activities (what they heard/read about Oahu ahead of time); entertainment section of local newspaper, isolating only highlighted activities for this weekend (don't want this to be a task of searching for information, rather just organizing it); daily planner type schedule pages with days and times from Friday through Monday.

Task A.4:   Getting directions to the party
difficulty index: 2
prompt:
You have to drive several friends to a party tonight. Although you have a map of the general area where the party is going to be held, you are unsure of exactly where the party is going to be. Listen to the directions that the party's host has left on your answering machine. On the map, trace the route to the party as it is described by the host.

realia/materials:
Map of portion of a city, with roads clearly labeled, landmarks highlighted, and compass directions obviously displayed; pen for marking route; answering machine message from host, giving careful directions utilizing street names, simple landmark names (post office, stoplight, etc. — don't want too high a code); directions (N/S/E/W, as well as left and right).

Task A.5:   Making the most of a dating service

difficulty index: 5

prompt:

A friend of yours is too embarrassed to follow up on her first trip to the dating service. Watch the video of herself that she left at the dating service. Then go through the set of possible dates that the service came up with, taking notes from the video information as you see fit. Now create three lists: one for those possible dates that match her requirements, one for those possible dates whose requirements your friend matches, and a final list that includes only the dates that both match her requirements and whose requirements she matches.

realia/materials:

One video segment beginning with the friend's video and followed by 5 to 10 videos of other people (thirty-second spots each giving brief personal descriptions and stating what they are looking for in a date), physical characteristics differ in obvious ways from person to person (this will play a role in the matching exercise); examinee has control over the video, can stop and rewind with remote, and so forth; three list sections with obvious headings.

Task A.6:   Giving medical advice

difficulty index: 4

prompt:

Familiarize yourself with the chart (from the *Time Life Home Medical Guide*) covering symptoms of various common illnesses. Then listen to your neighbor describing the symptoms that her child is exhibiting. Use the chart to check off the corresponding symptoms for your neighbor (who can speak but not read English). What is the probable sickness? What should your neighbor do (refer to the advice section on the chart)? Call you neighbor and explain the probable illness and what steps the neighbor should take.

realia/materials:

Chart of symptoms, illnesses, and advice (not too much, just common symptoms); tape recording of neighbor describing the child's symptoms (several flu-like symptoms), tape player; telephone and answering machine with message from friend.

Task A.7:   Be careful with medicine

difficulty index: 1

prompt:

Compare the four different medicines that your friend brought home from the pharmacy for her daughter. Can all of the medicines be taken at the same time? If not, which one(s) should not be taken together?

realia/materials:

Four medicine labels, two of which are contra-indicated (aspirin and x).

Task A.8: Convince your friend to quit smoking those nasty cigars

difficulty index: 4

prompt:
Read the following article about the health risks involved in smoking cigars. Then read the brief e-mail message from your friend extolling the virtues of cigar smoking. Now write an e-mail response, arguing for your friend to quit smoking cigars. Try to counter the points raised in the message from your friend by using evidence from the article.

realia/materials:
Article from Island information health journal on cigar smoking and the myths attributed to it; e-mail message from friend addressing similar ideas and suggesting why cigars are not as bad as other forms of tobacco (post-login e-mail).

Task A.9: Getting advice from TEL-MED

difficulty index: 6

prompt:
You are worried about the health condition of several colleagues in your office. Using the TEL-MED health information service, find out as much as you can about the relationship between diet/exercise and heart disease. After you have gathered enough information, write up a brief office memo (no more than one page) describing the most important points to keep in mind with respect to this issue.

realia/materials:
Telephone and the TEL-MED guide from the Island Scene HMO magazine (up to the examinee to access the appropriate information — a number of sources are available); paper or computer document for office memo write-up.

Task A.10: Making a decision on the soccer game ejection

difficulty index: 4

prompt:
Watch the video from the soccer match. The player who was ejected from the game is protesting the decision, and you have been assigned to review the incident. Now listen to the taped explanations about what happened by: 1) the referee, 2) the player who was ejected, and 3) a newspaper reporter who was at the game. Based on the different reports of the incident, was the referee correct in his decision? Briefly explain your opinion.

realia/materials:
Short video segment (30 seconds) showing the incident in question (player is struck by another player from behind and seems to be retaliating just as the referee is turning to see the play — referee shows red card to first player and does nothing to the original fouling player); three taped explanations of three points of view (short, thirty seconds each, with player and reporter expressing basically the same point of view that the referee did not act justly and that the player was not really retaliating); tape-recorder for the decision.

Task A.11: Windsurfing advisories

difficulty index: 4

prompt:

Tune in to one of the 24-hour weather reports on television to find out about current surf and wind conditions. Then cross-reference today's conditions with the windsurfers' advisory chart. Is it a good day to take your novice friends windsurfing off Diamond Head? Show why or why not, using the information that you have gathered.

realia/materials:

Television with 24-hour weather reports (perhaps just a taped version of one report would be sufficient); windsurfer's advisory chart (shows wind-speeds, optimal conditions for different classes of windsurfer).

Task A.12: Cable TV survey

difficulty index: 4

prompt:

As part of a team researching cable television providers and what they have to offer, your job today is to find out the following information: How many of the following types of stations are offered by your local cable provider (Categories include foreign language, sports, 24-hour news/weather, and PPV/pay movie channels). Use the television with cable access for conducting your research.

realia/materials:

Chart containing the categories to be investigated and space for recording channel names; television with cable access.

Task A.13: Choosing a talk radio program

difficulty index: 3

prompt:

Read through the three transcripts from three different talk radio programs. Which of these would you probably listen to and which would you probably ignore? Write a short e-mail convincing your friend jnorris to do the same.

realia/materials:

Three transcripts (short, 1 page each) of three programs that differ along a political spectrum from radical conservative to middle of the road to radical liberal (according to a US context); e-mail setup for letter writing (post-login).

Task A.14: Find the dentist's phone number

difficulty index: 1

prompt:

Your tooth is very painful, and you need to contact the dentist right away. Unfortunately, you do not have a phone book in your new apartment. Listen through the following phone messages as quickly as possible to find the phone number that the dental assistant left on your machine. Write down the dentist's number.

realia/materials:
Answering machine (or tape-recorded simulation) with 5 to 10 messages, each from a different source and addressing a different subject (identified quickly by the introduction of each message: "Hi, this is the yard man..."); a single message is from the dental assistant reminding examinee about an appointment and leaving a phone number.

Task A.15: When's the movie and how much will it cost?
difficulty index: 3

prompt:
Find out the show-times and prices for the following movie at the three different theaters where it is showing. Use the advertisements in the newspaper to locate the phone numbers for the theaters. Note relevant information.

realia/materials:
Newspaper page with movie and theater information (but not with show times: "Now showing at Cineplex 2000, call for more information...;" audio-recordings of show-times and movie prices (matinee vs. regular admission, etc.).

Task A.16: Sports nutrition
difficulty index: 3

prompt:
Listen to the figures taken from a radio program about sports nutrition and the longevity of athletes. Take notes as necessary. After listening, create two lists based on the information provided. One list should rank the sports mentioned in the show according to the average number of calories burned (from most to least) in ten minutes of playing. The other list should rank the sports according to the likelihood of injury (from least to most) when participating in the particular sport.

realia/materials:
Short tape-recorded summaries of 5 to 10 different sports with different calorie-burning and injury potentials (both figures given at the same time for each sport); chart for filling in information on the rank orders for two categories.

Task A.17: Choose an appropriate restaurant
difficulty index: 2

prompt:
First read through the advertisements for two new restaurants. Then read through the two reviews of the restaurants. Finally, write a message to your housemates explaining why you want to go to one but not the other this evening for dinner.

Two advertisements (e.g., from dining section of newspaper) extolling the virtues of each restaurant (both in very positive light, if different); two newspaper reviews (brief, not complex), one very positive, one slightly negative, with a few positive comments (both with plenty to say about each place).

Task A.18: Picking the right hikes

difficulty index: 3

prompt:

You are planning several hikes for some visiting friends. Look through the book, *The Hikers Guide to O'ahu*. Find the section on the hikes in the windward Ko'olau range. Within this section, identify all of the hikes that include waterfalls and that are recommended for novices. List all possible hikes in this category, and rank them in order from shortest to longest. If mosquitoes are present on any of the hikes, note this beside the hike name.

realia/materials:

Book, *The Hikers Guide to O'ahu*; table set up for listing hikes (no pre-defined number of blanks, though), and including space for name of the hike, distance of the hike, and mosquito factor.

Area B: Travel

Task B.1: Decide where you can go based on your 'Advantage Miles'

difficulty index: 2

prompt:

You are planning a vacation with one traveling companion for the month of (x) and you have volunteered to arrange and pay for the airline tickets. You would like to use the Advantage Miles that you have been earning over the past several years. Read through the list of travel destinations that you and your companion would like to visit. Now read through your Advantage Miles statement and the conditions that apply. Circle all of the vacation spots on your list that you would be able to pay for with Advantage Miles.

realia/materials:

Handwritten list of travel destination cities and countries (at least ten); world atlas (just in case the cities are obscure — we don't want this to be a geography test); Advantage Miles statement (listing miles earned and with conditions of awards on the back — to where from where and how many miles are needed, and any blackout dates for specific destinations).

Task B.2: Booking a flight

difficulty index: 3

prompt:

Now that you have decided on a travel destination, you need to make airline reservations. Familiarize yourself with the travel plans that you have agreed upon with your companion (see Travel Calendar). Then listen to the following questions from the airline reservations agent. After each question, provide the requested information. Refer to the Advantage Miles information and to the Travel Calendar for specific details.

realia/materials:

Travel Calendar (listing on specific dates the departure and return times, the destination, other specifics); Advantage Miles form with pertinent information for making airline reservations; set of question prompts (taped or delivered by examiner) from the travel agent (covering basic information with easy code: "When will you be leaving…", etc.).

Task B.3: Choosing a hotel

difficulty index: 2

prompt:

Read the e-mail message from your companion listing his hotel needs. Note any information that will affect your choice of hotel accommodations in the vacation city. Now locate your city in the travel guide book that is provided. Select the hotel that best suits the information provided by your travel companion.

realia/materials:

E-mail from friend (listing his needs/preferences in a very straightforward manner: "View of the ocean, two king-size beds, bathroom and shower in the room, less than forty dollars a night, etc.); travel guide book like *Lonely Planet* series (with lists of multiple hotels in given cities, recommendations regarding the various accommodations, prices, etc.).

Task B.4: Booking a room

difficulty index: 3

prompt:

Now you need to book a room in the hotel for yourself and your companion. Refer to the Travel Calendar for travel dates and to the information provided by your companion in his list of accommodation requirements. For purposes of payment, refer to the VISA card provided. Now listen to the following questions from the hotel desk clerk. After each question, provide the requested information.

realia/materials:

Travel Calendar (with overnights at the hotel highlighted); list of accommodation information from the friend (how many beds, what kind of view, etc.); VISA card (with account number, expiration date, name as on the card); set of question prompts (taped or delivered by examiner) covering mundane hotel information (easy delivery).

Task B.5: Find your flight
difficulty index: 0

prompt:
At the airport, you want to find out where and when your flight is boarding. Refer to your ticket. Then look at the flight departure screens and try to identify your flight. Write down the important information regarding your flight.

realia/materials:
Standard airline ticket, with destination, airline, time of departure; set of screens (3 to 6) with departure and arrival information (including departures and arrivals for the destination city, as well as different departures on different airlines to the same city).

Task B.6: Solving airline ticket problems
difficulty index: 5

prompt:
At the airport, thirty minutes before your flight, you have discovered a conflict between the ticket you were issued by mail and the flight schedule that is currently being posted on the departure screen. Read through the departure screen and ticket information to find the discrepancy. Then explain the problem to the clerk at the ticket counter, using specific details from the airline ticket and the departure screens.

realia/materials:
Airline ticket with flight departure information, airline, time of departure; flight schedule screens with departure and arrival information (with apparently conflicting information: passenger has already missed the flight due to a change in flight departure time; passenger forgot to reconfirm).

Task B.7: Checking in
difficulty index: 2

prompt:
Now that you have resolved your flight information, you need to check in at the gate. Listen to the questions asked by the stewardess at the gate. After each question, provide the requested information.

realia/materials:
Set of question prompts (taped or delivered by examiner) asking standard gate questions (how many traveling, how many bags, what is your destination, did you pack your own bags, etc.).

Task B.8: Boarding
difficulty index: 2

prompt:
Listen to the following boarding calls and other information provided over the loudspeakers at the departure gate for you flight. Indicate which of the

announcements is your boarding call. Refer to your ticket for relevant information.

realia/materials:
Airline ticket with departure gate, travel class, and seat number information; set of audio prompts with variety of information (Mr. Mohammed Jones, please come to the American Airlines ticket counter, etc. — buried somewhere in the middle is a set of boarding calls for various flights, then examinee's flight, class, and set number, with other boarding calls following).

Task B.9: Trying to find your lost bag
difficulty index: 1

prompt:
You have arrived at your vacation destination. Unfortunately, it seems that the bag that you checked is not in the baggage claim area. Fill out the lost baggage form in order to claim your bag. Refer to the notes about your luggage that you keep in your briefcase for just such emergencies.

realia/materials:
Set of notes regarding the type of bag and the contents of the bag (color, make, value and nature of contents, etc.); standard lost bag claim form (asking for the information in the notes, as well as name, flight info., etc.)

Task B.10: Catching the bus
difficulty index: 3

prompt:
You would like to visit Sea Life Park today. Call the bus (phone number provided) and write down the directions for the next bus from your location, as well as any transfers you will need, to get to Sea Life Park.

realia/materials:
The bus phone number (either use the real interlocutor on the other end, or examiner can provide the information in response to appropriate questions); note paper.

Task B.11: Radio weather information
difficulty index: 5

prompt:
Use the radio guide to find a station for 24-hour local weather information. Access the station and check out the weather patterns for the next four days in Honolulu. Call your friend who is planning a visit, and leave a message detailing what the weather is going to do in Honolulu and on Oahu in general.

realia/materials:
Radio guide (listing the various accessible stations for Honolulu and the types of programming they have); weather report (taped, offering some extraneous information, public service announcements, and then the weather report covering

the next week — including wind, water temperature, air temperature, rainfall, cloud cover, wave action, and regional variations like windward, leeward, north shore, etc.); telephone and answering machine at friend's place.

Task B.12: Spring break plans
difficulty index: 4

prompt:
Listen to the two travel advertisements on the radio about the two different popular American spring break destinations (South Padre Island and Aspen). After listening to both, send an e-mail to your friend suggesting which city you would like to visit during spring break and why that city is more appealing to you than the other option.

realia/materials:
Two short advertisements addressing location, activities, weather, cost, expected crowds for upcoming spring break, etc.; e-mail access (post-login set up for writing message to friend).

Task B.13: Chicago museums
difficulty index: 4

prompt:
The following video gives tips for tourists who are planning a visit to Chicago. You will be visiting Chicago for three days and would like to focus on the museums while you are there. Note the museums available, and the days and times they are open. Following the recommendations in the video for how long to spend in each (to see all of the exhibits), what possible combinations of museums could you visit during this trip? List all possible combinations, assuming you will spend the suggested amount of time in each.

realia/materials:
Video of Chicago — five minutes (giving some mundane information, but focusing on the variety of museums, with a brief synopsis of what each has to offer, when they are open, and how much time one needs to enjoy all of the exhibits).

Task B.14: Call Hawaiian Air/last flight out
difficulty index: 2

prompt:
Your friend needs to be picked up from the airport this evening. Call Hawaiian Airlines and find out what time the last plane from Hilo arrives today in Honolulu. Write down the flight arrival time and any other pertinent information provided.

realia/materials:
Hawaiian Airlines automated flight information number (touch-tone access to flight schedules); telephone with touch tone capabilities.

Task B.15: Barbados travel video

difficulty index: 3

prompt:
You and your friend are planning a trip to Barbados. Watch the travel video on Barbados and take notes regarding any important points as you feel necessary. Then answer the following questions from your friend regarding the place as a vacation destination.

realia/materials:
Travel video on Barbados (showing major tourist attractions, hotels, activities, prices, etc.); set of question prompts from friend (taped or delivered by examiner) and covering the general information in the video (not necessarily in the same order).

Task B.16: 'Advantage Miles' listening

difficulty index: 3

prompt:
You need to find out some information about the possibility of free flights on United Airlines. For each of the two ' accounts, access relevant information by calling the Advantage Miles 800-number (using the account cards provided). Note all pertinent information about the two accounts. Then answer the following questions regarding the accounts: (current miles, miles toward premier, last two flights). Fill in the answers in the spaces provided on the account form.

realia/materials:
Two Advantage Miles account cards (with account numbers and the toll-free phone number); account information (based on authentic provision of information from the service); account form with question prompts (how many current Advantage Miles, how many miles toward premier, what were the last two flights).

Area C: Food and dining

Task C.1: Reserving a table

difficulty index: 1

prompt:
You would like to try out the fancy new Italian bistro "Il Gondoliero" tonight. Unfortunately, no one is free to accompany you to dinner. Look up the phone number of the restaurant in the phone book and call to reserve a table for one at an appropriate time this evening. You will have to speak with the answering machine, as the staff do not come in until around 5:00 p.m.

realia/materials:
Phone book with phone number for Il Gondoliero (or whatever 'x' restaurant); telephone and answering machine apparatus (giving 20 to 30 seconds to leave a message.

Task C.2:   Ordering drinks and appetizers

difficulty index: 4

prompt:

You have just arrived at a fancy Italian restaurant for a nice evening dinner (alone again!). Listen to the waiter's explanation of the various options for the following: appetizers, salad, salad dressing, and beverage. When the waiter asks for your order, select one of each of the categories and order for yourself.

realia/materials:

Set of waiter explanations of the different categories (four, including multiple options in each category — taped); four waiter question prompts (one each for appetizer, salad, dressing, and beverage — taped or delivered by examiner).

Task C.3:   Ordering the main course

difficulty index: 3

prompt:

All of the dinners in this restaurant must be ordered 'a la carte'; that is, you have to select what you would like to eat from the lists of available choices on the menu. Study the menu and the various selections that are available for this evening. Choose a main dish (meat or vegetarian), a pasta, and a vegetable from the different options. When the waiter requests your order, tell him what you have decided.

realia/materials:

Menu (with sections for main courses, pastas, and vegetables, all with multiple choices); prompt from waiter (taped or delivered by examiner).

Task C.4:   Sending back the fish (or whatever x main dish) that tastes like a shoe

difficulty index: 2

prompt:

After waiting for forty-five minutes, your dinner has finally been served. Unfortunately, the fish (x) that you ordered is excessively overcooked. When the waiter returns to your table, request that he return the fish to the kitchen. Give him your reasons for sending it back, and request a new serving.

realia/materials:

Prompt from the waiter asking what the problem seems to be; perhaps a photographic representation of the particular offending food item(s) (clumped pasta, black steak, etc.).

Task C.5:   Ordering coffee and dessert

difficulty index: 3

prompt:

After finishing your meal, the waiter brings a dessert menu. Study the different options. When the waiter returns, order your choice of dessert. Listen to the available after-dinner beverage options that the waiter recites. Choose a beverage to accompany your dessert choice.

realia/materials:
Dessert menu (showing basic set of 5 to 10 different options); waiter's set of after-dinner drinks (including coffees, teas, as well as liqueurs, and suggesting what drinks go with what desserts — taped); prompts by waiter (would you like any after dinner drink?).

Task C.6: Comparing food types on menus and making a recommendation
difficulty index: 4

prompt:
Your friend, who has recently had surgery, has some major restrictions on what she can and cannot eat. Compare the three menus from three different restaurants with the list of your friend's dietary restrictions. Decide which restaurant offers the most dinner options for your friend. Now call her and leave a message on the answering machine, explaining your choice of restaurant and detailing the options that are available.

realia/materials:
List of dietary restrictions (say, for post-angioplasty surgery — basically, no cholesterol, alcohol, caffeine, etc.) from the doctor; three menus with varying degrees of accord with the restrictions list (one with few options, like a French restaurant, one with a moderate amount, one with many — all menus show ingredients to a sufficient degree for determining membership on the list or not); telephone and answering machine message.

Task C.7: Informing your friend about the evening's arrangements
difficulty index: 2

prompt:
Check your note about the final plans for this evening. Call back your friend and leave a message regarding the dinner reservations. Be sure to mention all relevant information in a logical order.

realia/materials:
Notes about tonight's plans, requiring some reorganization for effective presentation in the message (where are we going, when are the reservations, what to wear, when and where to meet, etc.); telephone and answering machine set-up.

Task C.8: Getting everyone's orders
difficulty index: 2

prompt:
You and your friends have decided to order pizza for dinner tonight (it's finals' week and nobody feels like cooking). Each of your friends has called and left a message on your machine. The messages describe how much pizza each individual

would like and what kinds of ingredients they want. Listen to all of the messages and write down any information necessary for placing an order.

realia/materials:
A number (5 to 10) of messages from different friends with different requests (ingredients that do not necessarily match up with each other, differing number of slices, differing styles — pan, thin, hand-tossed, etc.).

Task C.9: Deciding on ingredients and how many pizzas to order
difficulty index: 3
prompt:
Refer to the notes on individual preferences to decide on the types and number of pizzas to be ordered. Use the coupons provided from different pizza delivery places in order to decide on the best value. Try to order pizzas that will: a) provide everyone with enough to eat, b) have ingredients that will not offend anyone (but you can order more than one pizza), and c) be the best value with the coupons. Write out your final decision on orders, and select the appropriate coupons to go with the order.

realia/materials:
Notes (based on the previous task) regarding individual preferences for ingredients, style, and amount (large variety in requests); set of coupons for several different deals from several different pizza places (different combinations for different prices).

Task C.10: Ordering pizzas for delivery
difficulty index: 5
prompt:
After making your decisions about the kinds and number of pizzas you need to order, look up the phone number of the pizza delivery place that you have chosen, and place your order. The pizza should be delivered to your friend's house, where you have all decided to meet after work. Your friend has given you a map. Refer to the map for necessary information to give the pizza delivery person.

realia/materials:
Final notes on what to order (how many pizzas of what size, what ingredients on each, and what coupons apply); map of the general area where the friend lives (showing phone number, house and address, cross streets, etc. for leaving instructions); set of question prompts from the pizza delivery person (asking for locational information first, phone number, etc., and then prompting the various pizza categories — what kind, how big, what ingredients).

Task C.11: Comparing grocery items and prices
difficulty index: 4

prompt:
 Read through the shopping list that you and your roommate created this morning. Compare these items with the coupon books you have from different stores. Decide where you will do your shopping today (assuming that you only have time to go to one store). Write a note explaining your decision to your roommate and citing specifically why you made this decision.

realia/materials:
 Three different coupon books (with a variety of deals on different food and grocery items); shopping list (detailing exactly what needs to be bought at the store today); calculator (if available).

Task C.12: Investigating nutritional information
difficulty index: 2

prompt:
 Read through the dietary recommendations (involving sodium, fat, cholesterol, and calories) from your family doctor. The set of products that follow are food items that you generally buy at the grocery store. Compare the nutritional information for the different options within each category. Based on the nutritional information provided and the doctor's recommendations, select one item from each of the product categories that you will buy during your trips to the grocery store.

realia/materials:
 List of dietary recommendations (suggesting levels of sodium, fat, cholesterol, and calories to be avoided in any prepackaged foods); set of product labels for various categories of pre-packaged food items (two or three labels for each food category, each label with different levels of the four recommended elements to be controlled).

Task C.13: Planning the menu for a meeting
difficulty index: 4

prompt:
 You are planning a luncheon for the local Sierra Club meeting, and you know that there are four different groups of members involved, as far as you are concerned, when it comes to ordering food: meat-eaters, and three groups of vegetarians with different dietary restrictions. The meat-eaters don't pose much of a problem for planning, but you want to be sure about the three vegetarian groups. Listen to the three descriptions of three kinds of vegetarians (vegen, lacto-ovo, and lacto-ovo-pesco) that your nutritionist friend has left for you on your voice mail. Then review the following list of possible food items (with ingredients) that the caterer could supply for the meeting. Place each of the food items into the appropriate category on the form provided.

Descriptions on voice mail of the three types of vegetarians (detailing what they can and cannot eat in basic nutritional/ingredient terms); menu of possible food items from the caterer (with multiple possibilities for the four different categories); form for recording the different food items in four different categories (each category shows what can be eaten by those people, thus various items will appear multiple times in different categories).

Area D: At work

Task D.1:   Write a job advertisement
difficulty index: 4

prompt:
Look through the following notes that describe a job at your place of work. As the personnel manager, it is your responsibility to write a job advertisement for the new position. Refer to the sample advertisements as you create an announcement for the new position. Be sure to consider the level and type of job that you are advertising as you create the announcement.

realia/materials:
Set of notes from a meeting with the boss, describing the aspects of the new position (not in any pre-determined order); set of sample advertisements that the company has used before in advertising for positions at different levels (giving good idea of format and approach to take in writing the ad); computer word processor document (for creating the job advertisement).

Task D.2:   Sorting out possible job candidates
difficulty index: 3

prompt:
Now that the application deadline has passed, it is your responsibility to sort out those candidates who meet the minimum qualifications from those who do not. Using the original position announcement as a guide, review all of the applicants (by looking at their curriculum vitae) and create two separate files, one for those who meet the minimum qualifications and one for those who do not.

realia/materials:
Position announcement (stating clearly what the MQs and DQs are for the position); multiple applicants (6 to 10) with varying degrees of qualification for the job (but with obvious fit our lack of fit with the MQs).

Task D.3:   Write a form letter of rejection
difficulty index: 5

prompt:
Now that you have decided which candidates absolutely do not meet the MQs, you can go ahead and write a form letter rejecting their applications. Go through the file of previous rejection letters that your boss recently reviewed and

commented on. Based on these previous letters, and not forgetting to incorporate the boss's suggestions, write a new and appropriate form letter of rejection to the candidates for this particular position.

realia/materials:
Original job advertisement (listing MQs and DQs); set of previous rejection letters for jobs at different levels (including boss's comments, like: "tone this part down — too abrupt", etc.); computer word processing document for creating form letter (with letterhead from the company, etc.).

Task D.4:   Making a hiring decision
difficulty index: 5

prompt:
The boss has decided to leave the final hiring decision up to you in your capacity as personnel manager. The list of candidates has been reduced to four possibles by the interviewers. Unfortunately, you were out of town for an emergency meeting when the candidates came for their job interviews. Read through the following list of job qualifications (both minimum and desired) once again. Then listen to the taped interviews of the four top candidates. Using the forms provided (which list the MQs and DQs), mark the qualifications of each candidate. Use the scale provided on the form. Which candidate would you hire? Write *hire* on your first choice.

realia/materials:
Job advertisement with MQs and DQs; four tapes of interviews (interviews exploring various levels of qualification for the four different candidates); forms listing the MQs and DQs and showing a rating scale from 0 to 3 (low to high) for each area.

Task D.5:   Offer the job
difficulty index: 4

prompt:
Write a letter offering the new position to your number one candidate. Refer to the file on acceptance letters and to the candidate's CV as you write the new letter. Pattern your letter on previous acceptance letters for positions at a similar level. Be sure to personalize this letter (you're only offering the job to a single candidate!).

realia/materials:
Candidate's CV and the rating form for the candidate (showing scores for MQs and DQs); file of acceptance letters at various position levels (differing tones for differing level positions); computer word processing document (set up for letter writing, company letter head, etc.).

Task D.6:   Fill in the application form
difficulty index: 2

prompt:
Choose a single application form that corresponds to a job for which you find yourself the most qualified (based on the job descriptions attached to each of the available forms). Fill in the application form to the best of your ability, leaving blank any information that you do not have currently available.

realia/materials:
Set of job descriptions and attached job application forms (descriptions cover a wide variety of possible job types in major areas of interest; applications are appropriate to the given area/job type, with general information, work record, educational experience, as well as several open-ended questions for the applicant to answer).

Task D.7:   Writing a cover letter in response to a job advertisement
difficulty index: 4

prompt:
Read through the following job advertisements from the *New York Times*. Based on your personal background and experience, decide which job you would be most qualified for. Then write a (no more than one-page) cover letter to the employer, describing your interest in the job and briefly outlining your relevant job experience or education. Try to address in what way you are a good candidate for the position.

realia/materials:
Help wanted section from the *New York Times*, with all possible job types covered; computer word processing program (opened to a document, but without letter set-up — examinee has to set up letter head, closing, etc.).

Task D.8:   Answer questions in a phone interview
difficulty index: 5

prompt:
As a follow-up to your job application, your potential employers would like for you to answer a few questions. Listen carefully to each question. After each question, answer to the best of your ability, referring to your actual experience and education as a source for your answers.

realia/materials:
Telephone or simulation; set of interview prompt questions (wide range but not too specific, asking for general elaboration on education, experience, career plans, etc. — taped or delivered by examiner, but with specific time limit so that examinee does not ramble, as interviewees tend to do on the phone).

Task D.9: Creating a Rolodex
difficulty index: 1

prompt:

   The secretaries at your place of employment have decided to go on strike for
better working conditions. You must therefore assume some of the duties that are
normally handled by them. Alphabetize the set of business cards from your various
professional contacts. After alphabetizing, fill out a rolodex entry for each so that
your secretary will be able to access the necessary corresponding information
when he returns to the job.

realia/materials:

   Set of loose business cards (each with essential information like telephone,
e-mail, fax, position title, etc.) from numerous contacts; rolodex cards with
alphabetical tabs (and standard entry formula: name, company, position, etc.).

Task D.10: Taking messages
difficulty index: 3

prompt:

   Listen to the voice mail messages left for yourself and for your secretary. Fill out a
pink 'While you were out' form for each message, noting the essential information
from each call. Be sure to keep your forms separate from those that are directed at
your secretary.

realia/materials:

   Several voice mail messages (5 to 10) with different information (numbers,
directions, messages) directed at either the examinee or the secretary (tape-
recorded); pink while you were out forms (with standard message information
entry system).

Task D.11: Transcribing a business letter
difficulty index: 2

prompt:

   Listen to the following letter that has been dictated by your boss. Using the
Dictaphone, transcribe with as much accuracy as possible the exact words of the
letter. The header and closing have already been created for you, thus you should
only concern yourself with an exact transcription of the letter.

realia/materials:

   Taped or Dictaphone version of short business from the boss (less than one page
with no exceptionally difficult vocabulary); computer word processing document
with header and closing already prepared (multiple listenings okay — accuracy is
the key).

Task D.12: Matching a job candidate with a job

difficulty index: 4

prompt:

Listen to John's taped monologue on his job priorities and job skills. Take notes as you listen. Now read through the list of want ads below and find the three jobs that best match both John's desires and qualifications.

realia/materials:

Taped monologue from John (explaining briefly the kind of job he is looking for, what he is best suited for, etc. — no longer than one minute); set of want ads (with multiple sections and multiple possibilities within each section — likely from a large city); John's skills and desires match up to more than three, but three of the jobs are obviously best suited for him.

Task D.13: Create two resumes for specific purposes

difficulty index: 5

prompt:

Listen to the following description of your client's qualifications on the interview tape. Take notes about important information that would belong on a resume. Then construct two different resumes based on the data. Each resume should be designed to match one of the two different job announcements provided.

realia/materials:

Interview tape of client (giving his experience and education in two divergent fields — e.g., soccer coaching and language teaching); resume format with fill in the blank style set up (blanks for each entry on the resume: name, address, etc., as well as position sought, relevant experience, education, etc.).

Task D.14: Send a fax

difficulty index: 4

prompt:

Listen to the following steps for sending a fax using the present fax machine. Take notes sufficient for you to recall the steps. Write up the steps in a logical order, and then fax them to the following fax number.

realia/materials:

Set of clear steps for sending a fax using the present fax machine (but not necessarily in a logical order, that is, the person giving the steps could mention towards the end: "oh yeah, I almost forgot, you have to turn on the..."); fax number for sending the fax; fax machine.

Task D.15: Edit your boss's letter

difficulty index: 3

prompt:

Listen to the following editorial comments from your boss about how she wants to change the letter you typed for her. Make editorial marks on the letter to correspond with the changes she wants to insert. Then go back and re-organize the letter according to your editorial marks.

realia/materials:
Comments from the boss on voice mail (tape-recorded, involving rearrangement of paragraphs, sentences, words, etc.); copy of original letter (on paper, one page in length, double-spaced for editing); computer document opened to a word processing document.

Task D.16: Choose a city for a conference site
difficulty index: 4
prompt:
You are on the committee to pick your organization's next annual conference. Read the e-mail from your colleague about the requirements for a conference site. Look on the World Wide Web for information regarding the following possible cities (x, y, z). Which city most fits the profile?

realia/materials:
E-mail message from friend delineating the requirements for a conference site (needs to be near a beach, have cheap hotels, lots of sunlight, etc.); access to the WWW for the three cities to be investigated (three cities are widely divergent, and only one city obviously fits; information being sought must be specific enough that examinee will not likely know it outright already).

Task D.17: Ranking available jobs
difficulty index: 2
prompt:
Part of your job at the employment agency is to locate work for clients. In the Help Wanted section of the newspaper, find all jobs being advertised for construction workers. Then create two lists. The first list shows all full-time positions being offered. The second list shows all part-time positions being offered. Within both list, rank order the jobs from highest to lowest paid.

realia/materials:
Help Wanted section of the local paper (has to be from a large enough city to include multiple construction worker positions at various pay rates, full- and part-time); chart with sections and blanks for full-time and part-time construction worker position (number from 1 to x, with obvious high end and low end designation, e.g., 1 = highest paid).

Area E: At the university

Task E.1: Applying to the university
difficulty index: 2
prompt:
You have received the following application form in the mail from the university. Fill in the form to the best of your ability. Keep in mind that these forms are used

---

by the university to screen potential candidates for admission, so try to be as complete as possible with your responses.

realia/materials:
Application form (containing only the first half of a standard form, that is, *not* requiring open-ended responses to essay type questions, e.g., "Why do you want to attend the University of X?", rather only fill in the blank providing personal information of various sorts).

Task E.2:   Corresponding with the department chair
difficulty index: 4

prompt:
The chair of the department to which you have applied has received your application and has a few questions that require further explanation. Respond to the follow-up questions in writing. Each question is followed by ample space to write an appropriate response (that is, do not try to write beyond the space provided).

realia/materials:
Set of questions from the department chair (three maximum), asking general short answer type questions (e.g., why do you want to study in X department?; what are your educational objectives?; what are your career objectives?, etc.); questions should be personalized by inserting the individual examinee's major field of study into the variable slot within each question.

Task E.3:   Phone interview with the department chair (making a case for yourself)
difficulty index: 4

prompt:
After receiving more information regarding your application to the department, the department chair would like to follow up on a few other issues by telephone. She has sent you the following instructions by e-mail, and has asked that you call when ready to discuss them. In her e-mail she has asked that you choose a single concept or issue that you consider central to your proposed field of study (see e-mail instructions). You will be given 3 to 5 minutes during the telephone interview to explain the concept or issue and to explain why you think it is of central importance to your field. When the question is posed, deliver your planned response, remembering to keep it within the five minutes allotted to you.

realia/materials:
E-mail printout from the department chair (giving the parameters for the phone interview, what will be asked, what the examinee should talk about, and why this question is being asked); possibility for taking notes and using them during the interview; telephone or intercom system (simulated); prompt from the department chair (greeting, asking the question, closing — taped or delivered by examiner).

Task E.4: Inquiring about financial support

difficulty index: 3

prompt:

Congratulations! Your application was successful and you are now accepted to the university. In the acceptance letter, you read that financial assistance is available from a number of different sources within the department and at the university. However, the acceptance letter provides no specific information regarding types of assistance, amount of assistance, or the application process. Write a brief e-mail to the department chair, requesting more information regarding different types of assistance, amount of assistance from different sources, and what you need to do to apply for financial assistance.

realia/materials:

Acceptance letter giving possibilities for financial assistance, but not providing information about how to go about accessing such assistance; e-mail access (post-login setup for sending a message to the department chair).

Task E.5: Selecting the courses you want and are eligible to take

difficulty index: 2

prompt:

Familiarize yourself with the following list of courses. Pay close attention to which courses you are eligible to take as a new student and which courses require pre-requisites. Now read the comments in an e-mail from your adviser. Note which courses your adviser suggests as well as any other pertinent information in the message. Finally, fill in the weekly calendar with the course name, instructor, and room number for all of the courses for which you will register this semester.

realia/materials:

List of courses available for next semester in the department (with pre-requisites listed when applicable, times, instructors, meeting rooms, etc.); e-mail message from adviser (detailing what a first semester student should take) in list form with little extranea — just the recommended courses and instructors; weekly planner type calendar with slots for course numbers, instructors, times, and meeting places.

Task E.6: Calculating and paying your fees

difficulty index: 3

prompt:

After registering, you have received a payment form in the mail. Fill in the requested information regarding your courses, your residency status, and any other necessary fees (you will need to refer to the fee schedule on the reverse side of the payment form). Total the fees in the blanks provided. Then pay your tuition and fees using the VISA card provided. Be sure to record all pertinent information in order for your fees to be processed correctly.

realia/materials:
> Payment form listing courses that you registered for (blanks for credit hours, extra fees, residency status, other miscellaneous fees to be charged for certain classes, etc. followed by payment blanks for subtotals, totals, method of payment, etc.); VISA card (with account number, expiration date, etc.).

> (N.B.: Tasks E.7 through E.9 work ideally if they follow one another in the order given, and are probably best not sampled independently or randomly. If sampled independently, each subsequent task much contain the product of the previous task(s). They may also be combined into a single 'mega-task' that would probably have a difficulty index of 4.)

Task E.7:   Plan your presentation

difficulty index: 4

prompt:
> You have been asked to give a presentation in one of your classes. The topic for your presentation will be an explanation for pursuing your current degree (see presentation assignment). It should be between 3 and 5 minutes in duration. The audience for your presentation will be your classmates (and the teacher of the class); hence, you should develop your presentation accordingly. The first step you need to accomplish is the planning of your presentation. The final product of this stage should be a set of note cards, each of which highlights a point that you will make in your presentation.

realia/materials:
> Presentation assignment (detailing the idea of the presentation, that it should be an expression of reasons for pursuing the current degree, the objectives in pursuing the degree, what will be accomplished by obtaining the degree, and that it is all to be explained from an individual point of view); brief explanation of the classmates and teacher (included in the assignment); blank 3x5 inch note cards.

Task E.8:   Create a handout

difficulty index: 2

prompt:
> The next stage in the development of your presentation is to create a handout with pertinent information for your audience. Your handout should be based on the major points that will be raised in your presentation (see stack of note cards) and it should note any extra information that needs to be given in a visual format. The handout organizes your presentation for your audience, so it should reflect the logical presentation order of various points that you will be raising.

realia/materials:
> Presentation note cards (showing an explicit points that will be raised in the presentation, but not in any particular order); blank paper for drafting the handout (with no hints as to content or structure).

Task E.9: Deliver your presentation

difficulty index: 3

prompt:

Now deliver your formal, in-class presentation, based on the note cards for specific points you want to raise. You should also try to stick to the logical order given in the presentation handout (in order for your audience to be able to follow you). This is the real thing, so try to do your best and to stay within the time limit (five minutes maximum). Break a leg!

realia/materials:

Presentation note cards (giving brief description of each point to be raised in the presentation); presentation handout (showing order of the points to be raised); tape-recording device (for recording the presentation).

Task E.10: Summarize the lecture

difficulty index: 4

prompt:

Look through the following four lecture titles. Pick the one that seems the most interesting to you. Listen to the lecture and take notes as necessary. After the lecture has been completed, write a brief (one page) summary of the main points of the lecture.

realia/materials:

Four taped lectures on four different topics of general interest (one social sciences, one humanities, one computer sciences, one hard sciences — each taped lecture around four minutes); blank note paper.

Task E.11: Find relevant literature

difficulty index: 4

prompt:

Based on the lecture summary provided, find at least five bibliographic references (in the library) for articles that deal with some aspect of the lecture content. All of the references should deal with generally the same aspect of the lecture, although they may take a variety of points of view. Record these references in APA style, as you would in the reference or bibliography section of a term paper.

realia/materials:

Lecture summary (giving a paragraph or two detailing the main points from a previously heard lecture, with explicit theme, e.g., the effect of massive handgun sales on murder rates in the US); access to library bibliographic sources (ideally computer terminal link to a search system like UHCARL, UNCOVER, etc.); APA manual on hand for reference style.

Task E.12:   Compare/contrast two sources with the lecture

difficulty index: 5

prompt:
Now select two of the reference sources and read the articles. After reading and noting relevant information, write a short paper comparing or contrasting the two sources and the lecture summary. This paper may take the perspective of a critique of the topic from multiple points of view, or it may critique one of the points of view using the other two as evidence. Include the lecture summary (noting who gave the original lecture) and the two sources in a reference section at the end of the paper, and be sure to cite each, where appropriate, in the body of the paper.

realia/materials:
Lecture summary (giving main points of lecture as well as bibliographic information); articles (multiple, covering different aspects of the lecture theme, brief — several pages maximum for time constraints); APA manual on hand for reference style.

Task E.13:   World Wide Web real audio essay

difficulty index: 6

prompt:
Using the WWW, access the National Public Radio 'real audio' service. Download two reports given within the past two years on one of the following themes: (w, x, y, z). Write a brief (no more than two pages) critical essay about the theme, using and citing the two reports as sources.

realia/materials:
Access to the World Wide Web (computer set up with NetScape, search engines, and audio capabilities); choice of themes (based on availability of relevant reports over the last two years on particular subjects) from four general areas (social sciences, humanities, computers, hard sciences).

Task E.14:   Sorting out your schedule on e-mail

difficulty index: 4

prompt:
Read through the three e-mails from your departmental colleagues. Each e-mail addresses an upcoming event that you have promised to attend. After reading all three messages, respond to each as quickly as possible (you have a class to teach within the next 5 minutes). In each response you should accept, decline, or modify your acceptance, and you should explain why (noting any unavoidable conflicts).

realia/materials:
Three e-mail messages with simple statements of upcoming events (don't forget the office party from 5:30 until midnight on Friday, etc. — two of the messages contain conflicting agendas, one of these events taking obvious precedence over

the other, e.g., job interview); e-mail access for responding (set up in pine or similar program for facilitating sending of messages).

Task E.15: Searching the APA
difficulty index: 2

prompt:
Use the APA manual to find on what page you would look for the answers to the following questions: how does one cite multiple authors within the text of a paper?; how does one use quotes given in a secondary source when citing in a paper?; how should footnotes be created in an APA-formatted document?; how should numerical plurals be written (e.g., with dates)? how should unpublished dissertations and theses be cited in the reference section?

realia/materials:
Most recent edition of the APA manual for publication; form with each question listed and a blank for the corresponding APA page numbers.

Task E.16: Highlighting main ideas
difficulty index: 1

prompt:
You are preparing for an in-class discussion by reading the following short article. Underline the main idea in each paragraph (being careful to underline *only* that sentence or portion of a sentence that you think best demonstrates the main idea, or most closely approaches it).

realia/materials:
One brief article (2 to 3 pages, 5 to 7 paragraphs) with more or less obvious main ideas for each paragraph (that depend, nonetheless, on an understanding of the text content).

Task E.17: Formatting APA tables
difficulty index: 3

prompt:
Using the APA manual, rearrange the following information into an APA-formatted table.

realia/materials:
APA manual for publications; set of data with each component of the data clearly labeled (*N*-size, mean, *Note*, row headings, title, etc.), however, not in APA table format; blank paper for sketching out table format or computer table software (e.g., MS Word).

Task E.18: University rankings

difficulty index: 2

prompt:
Listen to the following segments from a report on the quality of university education in the US. Record the data provided in the report. You will hear rankings for the same ten universities for three different categories. The three categories are (social sciences, science and engineering, and the humanities). Create three lists, one for each category, showing the orders for each university.

realia/materials:
Segments of taped radio report on the quality of higher education in the US (segments giving only the rankings for each university across the three categories, with no extra information); page for list creation (with three categories, social sciences, science and engineering, and the humanities), each category with numbers one through ten and blanks for the names of corresponding universities.

Task E.19: NICE information

difficulty index: 3

prompt:
Your friend in Japan is interested in taking a conversational English course for a few weeks this summer. Look in the summer programs catalogue for the University of Hawaiʻi. Try to find a course that matches your friend's needs. Call your friend and leave message that reports any important information about possibilities that you find.

realia/materials:
Summer course offerings catalogue from UH Mānoa (with information on various English language programs in the summer, the only one of which would fit the friend's needs and schedule being the NICE program; telephone and answering machine set-up (simulated).

Area F: Domesticity

Task F.1: Look for a place in the housing advertisements

difficulty index: 3

prompt:
Look through the following notes about the housing needs that you and your future housemates share. Using the information from these notes, go through the housing advertisements of the newspaper and try to find any suitable options that fit within the parameters created by you and your housemates. Circle all of the possibilities as you identify them. Be sure to pay close attention to the details in each advertisement.

realia/materials:
Notes about housing parameters (based on agreement between the future housemates) including such aspects as: cost, down payment, security deposit, number of bedrooms, bathrooms, kitchen furnishings, furnished or not, yard

space, garage space, parking, and so forth; housing advertisements section of the local newspaper (good size city for plenty of options).

Task F.2: Using information from a rental agency
difficulty index: 4
prompt:

Another possible method for finding appropriate accommodations is by using a rental agency. Listen to the descriptions from the rental agency about the different houses and apartments (on their rental hotline). Select the category of housing that most closely fits what you and your roommates will need (from the list of options given at the beginning of the message). As you listen to the descriptions within this category, take down all pertinent information. Now match this information with the list of further parameters that you have. Circle all of the possible rentals that meet your requirements.

realia/materials:

Notes on the rental parameters for the housemates (see previous task); rental agency hotline (with options based on cost or on housing type, e.g., one-bedroom, two-bedroom, three-bedroom, etc. — tape-recorded); within the appropriate category, taped segments describing characteristics of different available rental units (detailing information like that found in the list of parameters that the housemates have).

Task F.3: Filling in the rental application
difficulty index: 3
prompt:

Listen to the messages from your future housemates on your answering machine. Pay careful attention to the information given, and take notes as needed. Then fill out the rental application, including information for yourself and for all of your roommates.

realia/materials:

Messages on answering machine (three different messages from three housemates, giving pertinent information regarding application: occupation, income, name, other address, etc. — taped, information provided in different orders for each and with respect to the application form); rental application form requesting general information about the future occupants.

Task F.4: Advertising for a housemate
difficulty index: 4
prompt:

It seems that one of your housemates decided to move to another city at the last minute, just before signing the lease to your new place. Look through the sample 'Housemate wanted' advertisements. Then create an ad of your own, advertising for a new housemate. Use the information from the rental application to supplement your ad.

realia/materials:
Set of Housemate wanted advertisements from the newspaper (numerous ads with different formats, to serve as potential models for the new ad); rental application (including relevant information about other housemates, about the apartment, etc.).

Task F.5:   Filling out a change of address form
difficulty index: 2

prompt:
Your housemate has broken a bone in his writing hand. You have promised to help him when he needs to have written work completed. He has just called and left a message on your answering machine. Listen to the message about his old and new addresses. Then fill out the change of address forms that he left with you.

realia/materials:
Message from roommate (giving old address, telephone, some extraneous information, and same for new address, adding apartment number, new zip code, etc.); change of address forms (several, from VISA, the post office, a magazine, etc., each with different format).

Task F.6:   Using a catalogue to order things for your new apartment
difficulty index: 3

prompt:
You and your housemates have compiled two lists each, one containing household items that each of you already has and one containing household items that each of you thinks are needed for the new apartment. First compare the different lists and create a single list of things that are needed but that none of you have. Then look through the catalogue provided. Identify any of the things that you should order from the catalogue, based on your needs list. Fill out the order form for any corresponding items that you find, including the prices.

realia/materials:
Set of four lists (each showing two columns, one with things that the individual will contribute and one with things that the individual thinks are necessary for the apartment — varying items, some are duplicated, some not); master list with two blank columns (one for haves, one for needs); catalogue from household goods store (e.g., Crate and Barrel, etc.), must have order form.

Task F.7:   Calculating and paying your monthly bills
difficulty index: 3

prompt:
It is nearing the end of the month, and the responsibility for paying the household bills happens to be yours. Read through the following stack of bills. Using the checks and envelopes provided, pay any bills that are due within the next thirty days. Pay careful attention to the information provided. If a bill is past due, be sure to include the overdue fee.

realia/materials:
Set of common household bills (water, gas, electric, rent, phone, long distance, cable, yard service, etc. — different formats, different requirements, due dates, etc.); envelopes (without addresses — examinee has to identify where to send bill and fill in on envelope); enough checks for paying all bills (standard check format).

Task F.8:   Depositing money into the bank

difficulty index: 3

prompt:
You have just been paid for your two jobs, and you have received some other checks in the mail. Based on the recent bank statement providing your current balance, and making sure to cover the total amount of money that will be paid out in bills over the next month, fill out a deposit form for your checking account. Make sure that you have covered any checks that might be drawn on your account over the next month. Fill out a second deposit form to deposit the remainder of your money into your savings account, except for fifty dollars cash received.

realia/materials:
Paychecks and other checks (from grandmother, etc. — each check different amount); bank statement from previous day (showing current balance); list of bills that examinee paid today (with dollar amounts) and which will be coming to bank within the next month; two deposit slips (one for checking, to cover all checks; one for savings, with space for signature and cash received).

Task F.9:   Comparing credit card offers and arguing for the best choice

difficulty index: 5

prompt:
Compare the information from three different student credit card offers. Decide which credit card is best for you (there is not necessarily one right answer — which card you choose will depend in large part on what seems the most important reason for you to have a credit card). Now summarize (in writing) what you consider to be the differences between the three, and then defend your choice of which card is the best offer for a student like yourself.

realia/materials:
Three credit card offers (typically received in the mail, lots of extra stuff, at least one page with fine print terms and conditions — each offer has different possible benefits for different students, e.g., higher credit limit, lower APR, no annual fee, etc.).

Task F.10:   Applying for an emergency student loan

difficulty index: 4

prompt:
   Look over the list of predicted semester expenses for an international student at your university. Based on these calculations, and assuming that you have x dollars saved up for this first year, how much money will you need in order to make ends meet for two semesters at the university? Fill in the following emergency student loan application. Be sure to provide accurate information and to fill in the open-ended questions (regarding the nature of your immediate financial needs) in a convincing manner.

realia/materials:
   List of predicted semester expenses (provided typically in student application materials, giving dollar amounts for tuition, books, housing, food, etc. — total savings in bank account are not sufficient to cover expenses); calculator; emergency student loan application form (asking for amount, when and how money will be paid back, personal information regarding course being taken, student standing, etc., open-ended questions asking why the money is needed and what it will be spent on).

Task F.11:   Bank overdraft

difficulty index: 4

prompt:
   Look through your bank statement and the overdraft statement. Why was your checking account overdrawn this month? Check through the stack of bank deposits, and access the mistake that caused your bank account to be overdrawn. Now, call the bank and leave a message explaining what the problem was.

realia/materials:
   Bank statement (showing deposits and withdrawals into checking and saving accounts over the past month); overdraft statement (showing that the bank covered a check when the checking account had insufficient funds); bank deposit slips for checking and savings accounts (herein lies the problem — that the wrong account number was used, causing money to be deposited into savings instead of checking, even thought the checking account box was checked).

Task F.12:   Listing necessary phone numbers

difficulty index: 1

prompt:
   List who you would call and their phone numbers for the following problems (the neighbor's child has just swallowed poison; your Saab has an oil leak in the engine; you are not receiving mail; you want to register to vote; you want to order a pizza from the local Pizza Hut delivery restaurant; your Bankoh bank card won't work; you need to talk to an immigration officer, etc.).

realia/materials:
  Local telephone directory (with state and local office listings, white pages, and yellow pages); form with each question and a blank for the corresponding appropriate phone number.

Task F.13:   Ordered chores around town
difficulty index: 2
prompt:
  Read through the list of things you have to do today. Look at the accompanying map to see where you have to go for each one. Now plan the route you will take. Call your housemate and leave a message telling where you will go and in what order.

realia/materials:
  List of randomly ordered chores to be completed today (bank, post office, veterinarian, grocery store, library, department office, hardware store, cleaners, etc.); map that shows the location of each destination and clearly marks the roads that can be used to get around town (should be able to draw a logical order for the trip from destination to destination); telephone and answering machine set up.

Task F.14:   Talking about your typical evening schedule
difficulty index: 1
prompt:
  A future housemate has asked about your evening schedule. Explain your typical evening activities and what kind of schedule you usually keep on weeknights.

realia/materials:
  No realia — although picture prompts showing typical evening activities could be substituted (showing television watching, reading, studying, sports, eating dinner, etc.) if deemed necessary, this would necessarily reduce the authenticity of the task for the examinees; authentically, no realia is needed beyond that which must be accessed by the individual examinee based on individual experience.

Task F.15:   Deciding on a car to buy
difficulty index: 3
prompt:
  You and your housemates have decided to share the cost of buying a used car. First you would like to determine the make and model of any reliable possibilities. Read through the description that the three of you wrote about the kind of car you want to buy. Now look through the *Consumer Reports* special issue on cars of this type. Which of the cars (may be more than one) reviewed in the magazine seems to best fit your description?

realia/materials:
  Written description of aspects of the car (size, fuel economy, handling, maintenance, expense, foreign/domestic, etc. — not all aspects will be a perfect fit with any of the listed cars, but should approach one or several of those

reviewed); multiple *Consumer Reports* issues on a variety of types of automobiles (e.g., four-wheel-drive vehicles, compacts, trucks, minivans, etc. — examinee has to narrow down choice to general type, then search within the type for best options).

Area G: Environment/politics

Task G.1:   Comparing environmental organizations
difficulty index: 3

prompt:
Find the section in *Save Our Planet* that compares different environmental organizations and their efforts. Familiarize yourself with the charts in this section. Then answer the questions about environmental organizations as they are posed.

realia/materials:
Save Our Planet book (recent survey of environmental issues and efforts that are being taken on behalf of environmental preservation/protection — final section in the book is composed of a chart that compares major environmental organizations and the types of issues that they address); set of questions not to be seen by the examinee, rather first exposed through the test prompts (questions ask examinee to identify different organizations that address different issues, how much membership costs, etc.).

Task G.2:   Gun crimes around the globe
difficulty index: 3

prompt:
Watch the three short video segments regarding gun-related crimes in three different countries. Take notes as necessary, paying special attention to figures cited. After watching the videos, use your notes to fill in the chart comparing the three different countries.

realia/materials:
Three short (2- or 3-minute) video segments discussing gun production and importation, gun control legislation, and gun related crimes (especially homicides) in three countries (e.g., Japan, Germany, and the US); table set up to compare the figures cited for each country across each category (fill in the blanks).

Task G.3:   Expressing views on the environment and pollution
difficulty index: 3

prompt:
Read the two short views told by people from different countries about the environment and human pollution. Then compare, using your own words, the two views to the typical point of view in your country. Do people in your country think more like one of the two views, or do they have very different views from those expressed in the two readings?

realia/materials:
Two short points of view, told by the 'man on the street' (written as a person would speak, simple vocabulary and structures, common and accessible ideas — one point of view represents the individual as responsible for maintaining a clean environment, the other represents the innocence of the individual and the responsibility of the government and big industry to take care of things).

Task G.4:   Product packaging ranks
difficulty index: 3

prompt:
Examine the set of products from your local grocery store. Pay special attention to their packaging. Now create a list of the products, ranking them from the most environmentally safe packaging to the least. After creating your list, explain your top two and bottom two choices. Why did you place these products at the top and the bottom of the list?

realia/materials:
Set of products (photographs or actual products, if possible) numbering around ten (with obvious differences in degree of environmental consciousness, from the small and completely recyclable/organic to the large, superfluous packaging that is typical with many products); list with blanks for the ranking of products (from best packaging to worst packaging).

Task G.5:   Organize the advertisements
difficulty index: 3

prompt:
Look through the stack of advertisements from magazines. Separate the advertisements into two files. One file should have ads that show products which seem to be friendly to the environment. The other file should have ads that do not address the environment or seem unfriendly to the environment. For each ad, write a brief sentence explaining why you chose to put it in a particular file.

realia/materials:
Set of advertisements for different products (selected from different magazines — each ad either keys on some kind of environmental conscience, e.g., our product is dolphin safe, or does not, e.g., smoking is fun, with inclusion in one or the other category fairly obvious) totaling no more than 15; two file folders; page within each folder for short explanation of why the ad is included.

Task G.6:   Rain forest destruction
difficulty index: 2

prompt
Listen to the first segment from a recent radio broadcast about rain forest destruction. Record the figures presented in the chart provided, paying careful attention to the figures for total rain forest acreage and rate of destruction in each country. Then listen to part of a similar radio broadcast from ten years ago.

Record again the important figures given for the different countries. How much has total acreage of rain forest and the rate of destruction changed for all of the countries combined?

realia/materials

Portions of two radio broadcasts separated by ten years (identical format, simply giving the salient figures for a number of rain forest areas, the total acreage at the time of the report, and the rate of deforestation at the time of the report — taped, no extraneous information, simple presentation of figures); chart with blanks for categories of total acreage and rate of destruction (each country listed as a row, with four columns, two each for each end of the decade); final blanks for total change in each category for all countries represented across the ten years.

chapter seven

CONCLUSIONS

In the first chapter, we began by exploring the general topic of so-called "alternative assessments" and how they contrast with our notion of alternatives in assessment. Then, in chapter 2, we turned to the issues involved in performance assessment as it is covered in general education circles as well as in the language testing literature. Next, in chapter 3, we outlined salient elements from the task-based language teaching literature which seemed directly applicable to L2 performance assessment: task definitions, needs analysis, and approaches to task difficulty. In chapter 4, we further explored several recommendations for task-based testing and the issues involved in assessment of L2 task performance. In chapter 5, we provided test and item specifications that showed how our performance task items were selected and how they might be sequenced based on task difficulty. In chapter 6, we provided detailed listings of the corresponding item prompts for the Assessment of Language Performance instrument. Examples of the task generation process from which test and item specifications later issued are found in the appendix. Finally, in this chapter, we are summarizing the project, discussing our immediate plans for research, and providing suggestions for other future research.

IMMEDIATE PLANS FOR RESEARCH

At this stage in the current project, we have searched relevant literature and identified what we consider to be issues central to designing L2 performance assessments. We have also proceeded from these general issues to the development of a large set of prototypical English language items based on a number of real-world tasks. Our immediate plans are to operationalize these and similar prototypes (covering a wide range of predicted difficulty levels) in order to develop a full-fledged version of the Assessment of Language Performance instrument. Our hope is that this ALP instrument will serve as an appropriate framework for the implementation of L2 performance assessments in relation to specific L2 classrooms, programs, and curriculums. Accordingly, we will administer the English language prototype forms of the ALP to a large number of L2 English users representing a wide range of proficiency levels. Performances and ratings that result from this broad-based pilot testing program will be analyzed from a variety of perspectives. Based on findings from these analyses (outlined briefly below), program-specific ALP instruments will be developed for several university-level foreign language departments. We turn now to a brief discussion of our research agenda and corresponding analyses.

Real-world rating criteria

One of our foremost concerns in designing the ALP will be the use of real-world criteria for the rating of L2 task accomplishment. We are working under the assumption that the use of such criteria will enhance the predictive and face validity of the instrument, and, more importantly, will provide for essential feedback regarding success or failure in terms of the task performance. Such feedback should prove valuable for L2 students and teachers in addressing the relationship between L2 learning and task performance, as well as in reflecting on the appropriateness and effectiveness of instruction. We will report on the specific rating scales and criteria relevant for the ALP prototype in a subsequent volume in this series. Essentially, the creation of such scales and criteria will likely involve the following steps:

1. Two groups of task success assessors will be formed. Each group will consist of three members representing three different stake-holders in the assessment process (e.g., advanced L2 learner, L2 teacher, domain expert, etc.). Both groups will be made up of the same types of stake-holders.

2. Each member of each group will work independently through all ALP tasks, considering the elements that are minimally required for each task to be *successfully accomplished*. They will be asked to describe these elements in their own words.

3. Each group will meet to establish criteria and rating rubrics for each task. Discrepancies will be resolved through within-group negotiation, with the deciding factor being an agreed-upon answer to the question: Is this an essential component of task success?

4. The resulting rating rubrics and criteria will be submitted by both groups to an arbiter (e.g., a language tester), who will combine both sets into one formal set of rating guidelines relevant to each test task.

5. The resulting rating guidelines will be piloted by raters judging small samples of examinee (from a variety of different language ability levels) performances on prototype tasks. On the basis of what is learned during the piloting, the rating guidelines will be revised.

6. The rating guidelines that result from this process will then be used in providing feedback and in making decisions regarding task accomplishment for individual task performances. Such ratings will also be compared with task difficulty predictions in order to further investigate the role of task difficulty in affecting L2 performance.

A priori task difficulty

A second major concern and research interest will thus be how to check on the degree to which estimations of task difficulty prove to be reliable. The present rating process (like any rating process) of task difficulty levels involves the subjective application of certain standards. As such, task difficulty rating can be rendered much more reliable by employing multiple raters in the process. We will use at least two raters to independently estimate the difficulty of the prototype tasks (and any future L2 tasks when they become available). We will then calculate reliability estimates, and any discrepancies will be discussed and resolved. Rating subjectivity notwithstanding, we recognize that this entire endeavor is exploratory in nature, and we enter into it in order to improve our performance assessment procedures and ultimately our decision-making capabilities.

Beyond checking the reliability of the ratings, we will investigate the validity of our task difficulty estimates by minimally including the following steps:

1. Select representative raters from those groups with a stake in testing outcomes. For example, for the current set of prototype English language tasks, we might select three ESL teachers, three ESL students, and three content area teachers, all from the university where the items will be piloted. The three content area teachers, or experts, could be selected from three different disciplines that represent likely areas of eventual university-level study for our population of examinees. The three ESL teachers could either represent three different levels of instruction or they could all represent the highest level of instruction. As the current test prototypes take as the level of ultimate performance an international student who can successfully function with real-world tasks in the day-to-day university environment (and in related surroundings), selecting teachers from the highest level of ESL instruction might provide for the most relevant perspective (as they should be able to envision the entire range of L2 English learners and their potential difficulties with various tasks). Finally, the same case could be made regarding the three ESL student raters. The most relevant perspectives might be garnered from three students at the highest level of instruction or those who have just been exited into the mainstream university environment.

2. Present the three groups of raters with the set of tasks that have been selected to serve as eventual test items. The tasks should be presented in the form of simple item prompts and instructions, just as they will be seen by students in the final form of the test. It should also be stressed to the raters that the tasks are in no particular order of difficulty or presentation, and the order of presentation might further be randomized to counterbalance for possible rater norming effects.

3. Explain to the raters that they should use a quasi-pilesort technique in rating the difficulty of the different tasks. First, they should envision a 'typical' international student who is prepared (and able) to engage in university-level academic work as well as other day-to-day real-world activities. This student should function as their norm for difficulty

decisions regarding the tasks. Second, they should create three piles of tasks, each pile corresponding to one of the three following categories:

a. This task would be easy for the student to perform

b. The student would be able to perform this task, but it would pose difficulties

c. This task would pose considerable difficulties for the student and would therefore be at the boundaries of the student's abilities.

Depending on the depth of information required for this stage of validation, it might prove beneficial to have raters take notes as they assign tasks to the three categories. These notes could take the form of a simple answer to the question, "Why did you place the task in this category?" Finally, raters should be given the option to withhold judgment on a task if there is any aspect that renders it unclear or suspect in their perception. Reasons for withholding these tasks should definitely be recorded for further reference.

4. After ratings have been assigned by the various rater groups, results can be tallied and statistical comparisons can be made. These analyses should provide insight into the extent to which individual tasks will indeed be perceived as relatively easy or difficult by the population of examinees. Any discrepancies between the predicted item difficulty and the rated (or perceived) item difficulty can then be investigated and resolved prior to item pilot testing. Finally, the *a priori* data can later be compared with actual performance data in order to check the functioning of the item selection system.

A *posteriori* task difficulty

Given an item pool based on a broad range of tasks (with related difficulty estimates) and corresponding real-world rating criteria, the next step will be to select and adapt the prototype L2 tasks to the levels and purposes of assessment in a range of English L2 classrooms (and eventually in other L2 programs). The adapted versions of the Assessment of Language Performance procedures will then be administered to as wide a range of ability levels as makes sense in each of the testing situations. Then, the results of that pilot administration will be analyzed.

Investigation of actual examinee performance difficulty at the time of administering the assessment procedures will obviously generate valuable information that can contribute to decisions regarding the difficulty level and validity of given items for a particular population (and for score inferencing based on these performances). Such investigation will be based on recording and observation of all task performances as well as on retrospective interviews with the L2 examinees. A third source of information will come from the use of trained raters to judge task performances using the real-world task-success guidelines.

Further analyses

Following collection of test performance data, the scores that result from the rating process will be analyzed for item characteristics, descriptive statistics, reliability, validity, and practicality using classical test theory item and reliability analysis, generalizability theory dependability analysis, item response theory, standard setting theory as well as ordinary parametric and non-parametric statistics. The purpose of these analyses will be to improve the Assessment of Language Performance procedures and analyze their reliability and validity. We will also be examining the degree to which combinations of code complexity, cognitive complexity, and communicative demand and their separate parts are effective predictors of task difficulty.

In brief, in this analytic stage of the research, we will be addressing the following research questions:

1. What are the difficulty levels of the tasks in terms of human performance?

2. How well do items discriminate between low level students and high level students?

3. What kinds of distributions of scores do the items (taken together) produce?

4. How reliable are the scores in terms of internal consistency (using Cronbach alpha)?

5. How reliable are the scores in terms of interrater reliability?

6. How many raters are necessary to achieve acceptable reliability levels?

7. To what degree are these procedures content valid in the sense that the actual difficulty levels match our theoretically motivated predictions of difficulty levels?

8. To what degree are these procedures valid in the sense that they distinguish between independently established high and low proficiency groups in a differential groups construct validity study?

9. To what degree does the factor structure of the items support the construct validity of the items that make up these procedures?

10. To what extent do results from observational, interview, and other qualitative techniques corroborate or contradict other findings?

SUGGESTIONS FOR FUTURE RESEARCH

Naturally, more questions may be raised than answered by this project. Already, some questions have come up that we will probably not be able to immediately answer:

1. Will similar results be obtained at other institutions and in other languages?

2. Are the procedures for test development and validation adaptable to other alternatives in assessment?

3. What specific factors most affect the reliability of performance assessments? Raters? Item types? Item content? Item difficulty?

4. What is the most effective and practical combination of the factors listed in #3 above?

5. What is the criterion-related validity of these procedures when compared to various other alternatives in assessment of language proficiency?

6. What is the criterion-related validity of these procedures when compared to other performance assessment procedures?

7. How can these procedures be adapted to classroom criterion-referenced assessment settings? How effective are they for those purposes?

8. Once applied operationally in classrooms, to what degree are these procedures content valid in the sense that the tasks sampled adequately represent the domain of interest?

While we may not be able to immediately answer such questions, our hope is that, through the current research project and through similar future investigations of these central issues, the capabilities of teachers and students, program administrators, language testers, and language researchers to make valid decisions regarding real-world L2 performances will be greatly enhanced.

REFERENCES

Alderson, J., & Lukmani, Y. (1989). Cognition and reading: Cognitive levels as embodied in test questions. *Reading in a Foreign Language, 5*(2), 253–270.

Allaei, S. K., & Connor, U. (1991). Using performative assessment instruments with ESL student writers. In L. Hamp-Lyons (Ed.), *Assessing second language writing in academic contexts* (pp. 227–240). Norwood, NJ: Ablex.

American Psychological Association. (1985). *Standards for educational and psychological testing.* Washington, DC: American Psychological Association.

American Psychological Association. (1986). *Guidelines for computer-based tests and interpretations.* Washington, DC: American Psychological Association.

Aschbacher, P. A. (1991). Performance assessment: State activity, interest, and concerns. *Applied Measurement in Education, 4*(4), 275–288.

Bachman, L. F. (1989). The development and use of criterion-referenced tests of language proficiency in language program evaluation. In K. Johnson (Ed.), *Program design and evaluation in language teaching.* London: Cambridge University.

Bachman, L. F. (1990). *Fundamental considerations in language testing.* Oxford: Oxford University Press.

Bachman, L. F. (1991). What does language testing have to offer? *TESOL Quarterly, 25,* 671–704.

Bachman, L. F., & Palmer, A. S. (1996). *Language testing in practice.* Oxford: Oxford University.

Bailey, K. M. (1985). If I had known then what I know now: Performance testing of foreign teaching assistants. In P. C. Hauptman, R. LeBlanc, & M. B. Wesche (Eds.), *Second language performance testing* (pp. 153–180). Ottawa: University of Ottawa.

Baker, D. (1990). *A guide to language testing.* London: Edward Arnold.

Benson, J. (1989). The academic listening task: A case study. *TESOL Quarterly, 23*(3), 421–445.

Berk, R. A. (Ed.). (1980). *Criterion-referenced measurement: The state of the art.* Baltimore: Johns Hopkins University Press.

Berk, R. A. (Ed.). (1984). *A guide to criterion-referenced test construction.* Baltimore: Johns Hopkins University Press.

Berwick, R. (1989). Needs assessment in language programming: From theory to practice. In R. K. Johnson (Ed.), *The second language curriculum* (pp. 48–62). Cambridge: Cambridge University.

Brindley, G. (1984). *Needs analysis and objectives setting in the adult migrant project.* Sydney: AMES.

Brindley, G. (1994). Task-centered assessment in language learning: The promise and the challenge. In N. Bird (Ed.), *Language and learning*. Papers presented at the Annual International Language in Education Conference (Hong Kong, 1993). (ERIC Document 386 045).

Brown, J. D. (1984). Criterion-referenced language tests: What, how and why? *Gulf Area TESOL Bi-annual, 1*, 32–34.

Brown, J. D. (1988). *Understanding research in second language learning*. Cambridge: Cambridge University Press.

Brown, J. D. (1989a). Improving ESL placement tests using two perspectives. *TESOL Quarterly, 23*(1).

Brown, J. D. (1989b). Language program evaluation: A synthesis of existing possibilities. In K. Johnson (Ed.), *Program design and evaluation in language teaching*. London: Cambridge University.

Brown, J. D. (1989c). Criterion-referenced test reliability. *University of Hawai'i Working Papers in ESL, 8*(1), 79–113.

Brown, J. D. (1990a). Short-cut estimates of criterion-referenced test consistency. *Language Testing, 7*, 77–97.

Brown, J. D. (1990b). Where do tests fit into language programs? *JALT Journal, 12*(1), 121–140.

Brown, J. D. (1992). Classroom-centered language testing. *TESOL Journal, 1*(4), 12–15.

Brown, J. D. (1993). A comprehensive criterion-referenced testing project. In D. Douglas & C. Chapelle (Eds.), *A new decade of language testing: Collaboration and cooperation* (pp. 163–184). Ann Arbor, MI: University of Michigan.

Brown, J. D. (1995a). *The elements of language curriculum: A systematic approach to program development*. Boston, MA: Heinle & Heinle.

Brown, J. D. (1995b). Differences between norm-referenced and criterion-referenced tests. In J. D. Brown & S. O. Yamashita (Eds.), *Language testing in Japan* (pp. 12–19). Tokyo: Japanese Association for Language Teaching.

Brown, J. D. (1996). *Testing in language programs*. Upper Saddle River, NJ: Prentice Hall.

Brown, R. W. (1973). *A first language: The early stages*. Cambridge, MA: Harvard University.

Candlin, C. N. (1987). Towards task-based language learning. In C. N. Candlin & D. Murphy (Eds.), *Lancaster Practical Papers in English Language Education: Vol. 7. Language learning tasks* (pp. 5–22). Englewood Cliffs, NJ: Prentice Hall.

Cartier, F. (1968). Criterion-referenced testing of language skills. *TESOL Quarterly, 2*, 27–32.

Cathcart, R. L. (1989). Authentic discourse and the survival English curriculum. *TESOL Quarterly, 23*(1), 105–126.

Clark, J. L. D., & Grognet, A. G. (1985). Development and validation of a performance-based test of ESL "survival skills." In P. C. Hauptman, R. LeBlanc,

& M. B. Wesche (Eds.), *Second language performance testing* (pp. 89–110). Ottawa: University of Ottawa Press.

Cook, H. G. (1990). Tailoring ESL reading placement tests with criterion-referenced items. Unpublished M.A. theses. Honolulu, HI: University of Hawai'i at Mānoa.

Crookes, G. V. (1986). *Task classification: A cross-disciplinary review.* Technical Report No. 4. Honolulu, Center for Second Language Research, Social Science Research Institute, University of Hawai'i at Mānoa.

Cziko, G. A. (1982). Improving the psychometric, criterion-referenced, and practical qualities of integrative language tests. *TESOL Quarterly, 16*, 367–379.

Cziko, G. A. (1983). Psychometric and edumetric approaches to language testing. In J. W. Oller, Jr. (Ed.), *Issues in language testing research.* Cambridge, MA: Newbury House.

Dandonoli, P., & Henning, G. (1991). An investigation of the construct validity of the ACTFL proficiency guidelines and oral interview procedure. *Foreign Language Annals 23*(1), 11–22.

Doyle, W. (1983). Academic work. *Review of Educational Research, 53*(2), 159–199.

Dunbar, S. B., Koretz, D. M., & Hoover, H. D. (1991). Quality control in the development and use of performance assessments. *Applied Measurement in Education, 4*(4), 289–303.

Eisenberg, A. R. (1985). Learning to describe past experiences in conversation. *Discourse Processes, 8,* 177–204.

Ferris, D., & Tagg, T. (1996). Academic oral communication needs of EAP learners: What subject-matter instructors actually require. *TESOL Quarterly, 30*(1), 31–58.

Fleishman, E. A. (1978). Relating individual differences to the dimensions of human tasks. *Ergonomics, 21*(12), 1007–1019.

Fulcher, G. (1996). Testing tasks: Issues in task design and the group oral. *Language Testing, 13*(1), 23–51.

Givón, T. (1979). *On understanding grammar.* New York: Academic Press.

Givón, T. (1985). Function, structure, and language acquisition. In D. I. Slobin (Ed.), *The crosslinguistic study of language acquisition: Vol. 1* (pp. 1008–1025). Hillsdale, NJ: Lawrence Erlbaum.

Givón, T. (1989). *Mind, code and context: Essays in pragmatics.* Hillsdale, NJ: Lawrence Erlbaum.

Glaser, R. (1963). Instructional technology and the measurement of learning outcomes: Some questions. *American Psychologist, 18,* 519–521.

Glaser, R., & Klaus, D. J. (1962). Proficiency measurement: Assessing human performances. In R. M. Gagné (Ed.), *Psychological principles in systems development* (pp. 419–474). New York: Holt, Rinehart, & Winston.

Griffee, D. T. (1995). Criterion-referenced test construction and evaluation. In J. D. Brown & S. O. Yamashita (Eds.), *Language testing in Japan* (pp. 20–28). Tokyo: Japanese Association for Language Teaching.

Griffin, P., & McKay, P. (1992). Assessment and reporting in ESL Language and Literacy in Schools project. In P. McKay (Ed.), *ESL development: Language and literacy in schools. Volume II: Documents on bandscale development and language acquisition.* Melbourne: National Languages and Literacy Institute of Australia.

Gruber, J. (1967). Topicalization in child language. *Foundations of Language, 3,* 36–65.

Hale, G., Taylor, C., Bridgeman, B., Carson, J., Kroll, B., & Kantor, R. (1996). A *study of writing tasks assigned in academic degree programs.* TOEFL Research Report # 54. Princeton, NJ: Educational Testing Service.

Halliday, M. (1985). *An introduction to functional grammar.* London: Edward Arnold.

Hauptman, P. C., LeBlanc, R., & Wesche, M. (1985). *Second language performance testing.* Ottawa: University of Ottawa Press.

Henning, G. (1987). *A guide to language testing: Development, evaluation, research.* Cambridge, MA: Newbury House.

Henning, G. (1996). Accounting for nonsystematic error in performance ratings. *Language Testing, 13*(1), 53–61

Herman, J. L., Aschbacher, P. R., & Winters, L. (1992). *A practical guide to alternative assessment.* Alexandria, VA: Association for Supervision and Curriculum Development.

Honeyfield, J. (1993). Responding to task difficulty: What is involved in adjusting the relationship between learners and learning experiences? In M. L. Tickoo (Ed.), *Simplification: Theory and application* (pp. 127–138). Singapore: SEAMEO Regional Language Centre.

Horowitz, D. M. (1986). What professors actually require: Academic tasks for the ESL classroom. *TESOL Quarterly, 20*(3), 445–462.

Hudson, T. D. (1989a). Mastery decisions in program evaluation. In K. Johnson (Ed.), *Program design and evaluation in language teaching* (259–269). London: Cambridge University.

Hudson, T. D. (1989b). Measurement approaches in the development of functional ability level language tests: Norm-referenced, criterion-referenced, and item response theory decisions. Unpublished Ph.D. dissertation. University of California at Los Angeles.

Hudson, T. D. (1991). Relationships among IRT item discrimination and item fit indices in criterion-referenced language testing. *Language Testing, 8,* 160–181.

Hudson, T. & Lynch, B. (1984). A criterion-referenced approach to ESL achievement testing. *Language Testing, 1,* 171–201.

Huerta-Macías, A. (1995). Alternative assessment: Responses to commonly asked questions. *TESOL Journal, 5*(1), 8–11.

Jacobson, W. H. (1986). An assessment of the communication needs of non-native speakers of English in an undergraduate physics lab. *English for Specific Purposes, 5*(2), 189–195.

Jasso-Aguilar, R. (forthcoming). Sources, methods, and triangulation in needs analysis: A critical perspective in a case study of Waikiki hotel needs. To appear in *English for Specific Purposes*.

Jones, R. L. (1985). Second language performance testing: An overview. In P. C. Hauptman, R. LeBlanc, & M. B. Wesche (Eds.), *Second language performance testing* (pp. 15–24). Ottawa: University of Ottawa Press.

Kimzin, G., & Proctor, S. (1986). An ELI academic listening comprehension needs assessment: Establishing goals, objectives, and microskills. Unpublished manuscript Honolulu, HI: University of Hawai'i at Mānoa.

Lee, James F. (1995). Using task-based activities to restructure class discussions. *Foreign Language Annals, 28*(3), 437–446.

Long, M. H. (1985). A role for instruction in second language acquisition: Task-based language teaching. In K. Hyltenstam & M. Pienemann (Eds.), *Modelling and assessing second language acquisition* (pp. 77–99). Clevedon, England: Multilingual Matters.

Long, M. H. (1989). Task, group, and task-group interactions. *University of Hawai'i Working Papers in ESL, 8*(2), 1–26.

Long, M. H. (forthcoming). *Task-based language teaching*. Oxford: Blackwell.

Long, M. H., & Crookes, G. V. (1992). Three approaches to task-based syllabus design. *TESOL Quarterly, 26*(1), 27–56.

Long, M. H., & Crookes, G. V. (1993). Units of analysis in syllabus design. In G. Crookes & S. Gass (Eds.), *Tasks in a pedagogical context: Integrating theory and practice*. Clevedon: Multilingual Matters.

Lynch, B. (1996). *Language program evaluation: Theory and practice*. Cambridge: Cambridge University.

McNamara, T. F. (1990). Item response theory and the validation of an ESP test for health professionals. *Language Testing, 7*(1), 52–75.

McNamara, T. F. (1995). Modelling performance: Opening Pandora's box. *Applied Linguistics, 16*(2), 159–179.

McNamara, T. (1996). *Measuring second language performance: A new era in language testing*. New York: Longman.

Mehrens, W. A. (1992). Using performance assessment for accountability purposes. *Educational Measurement: Issues and Practice, 11*(1), 3–9, 20.

Messick, S. (1994). The interplay of evidence and consequences in the validation of performance assessments. *Educational Researcher, 23*(2), 13–23.

Messick, S. (1996). Validity and washback in language testing. *Language Testing, 13*, 241–256.

Miller, M. D., & Legg, S. M. (1993). Alternative assessment in a high-stakes environment. *Educational Measurement: Issues and Practice, 12*, 9–15.

Mohan, B. (1986). *Language and content*. Reading, MA: Addison-Wesley.

Moss, P. A. (1992). Shifting conceptions of validity in educational measurement: Implications for performance assessment. *Review of Educational Research, 62*(3), 229–258.

National Standards in Foreign Language Education Project. (1996). *Standards for foreign language learning: Preparing for the 21ˢᵗ century*. Yonkers, NY: Author.

Norris, J. M. (1996). *A validation study of the ACTFL Guidelines and the German Speaking Test*. Unpublished master's thesis. Honolulu, HI: University of Hawai'i at Mānoa.

Nunan, D. (1989). *Designing tasks for the communicative classroom*. Cambridge: Cambridge University.

Nunan, D. (1993). Task-based syllabus design: Selecting, grading, and sequencing tasks. In G. Crookes & S. Gass (Eds.), *Tasks in a pedagogical context: Integrating theory and practice* (pp. 55–68). Clevedon: Multilingual Matters.

Paltridge, B. (1992). EAP placement testing: An integrated approach. *English for Specific Purposes, 11*, 243–268.

Pica, T., Kanagy, R., & Falodun, T. (1993). Choosing and using communicative tasks for second language instruction and research. In G. Crookes & S. Gass (Eds.), *Tasks in a pedagogical context: Integrating theory and practice*. Clevedon: Multilingual Matters.

Popham, W. J. (1978). *Criterion-referenced measurement*. Englewood Cliffs, NJ: Prentice-Hall.

Popham, W. J. (1981). *Modern educational measurement*. Englewood Cliffs, NJ: Prentice-Hall.

Prince, D. (1984). Workplace English: Approach and analysis. *The ESP Journal, 3*, 109–116.

Quellmalz, E. S. (1991). Developing criteria for performance assessments: The missing link. *Applied Measurement in Education, 4*(4), 319–331.

Robinson, P. (1995). Task complexity and second language narrative discourse. *Language Learning, 45*(1), 99–140.

Robinson, P. (1996a). Introduction: Connecting tasks, cognition and syllabus design. *The University of Queensland Working Papers in Language and Linguistics, 1*(1), 1–14.

Robinson, P. (1996b). Task-based testing, performance-referencing and program development. *The University of Queensland Working Papers in Language and Linguistics, 1*(1), 95–117.

Robinson. P., & Ross, S. (1996). The development of task-based testing in English for academic purposes contexts. *Applied Linguistics, 17*(4), 455–476.

Ross, S., & Berwick, R. (1992). The discourse of accommodation in oral proficiency interviews. *SSLA, 14*, 159–176.

Scott, M. L., Stansfield, C. W., & Kenyon, D. M. (1996). Examining validity in a performance test: The listening summary translation exam (LSTE) — Spanish version. *Language Testing, 13*(1), 83–109.

Shohamy, E. (1992). Beyond performance testing: A diagnostic feedback testing model for assessing foreign language learning. *Modern Language Journal, 76*(4), 513–521.

Shohamy, E. (1995). Performance assessment in language testing. *Annual Review of Applied Linguistics, 15*, 188–211.

Short, D. J. (1993). Assessing integrated language and content instruction. *TESOL Quarterly, 27*(4), 627–656.

Skehan, P. (1996). A framework for the implementation of task-based instruction. *Applied Linguistics, 17*(1), 38–62.

Skehan, P. (1998). *A cognitive approach to language learning.* Oxford: Oxford University Press.

Stansfield, C. W., & Kenyon, D. M. (1992). The development and validation of a simulated oral proficiency interview. *Modern Language Journal, 76*(2), 129–141.

Stiggins, R. J. (1987). Design and development of performance assessments. *Educational Measurement: Issues and Practice, 6*(3), 33–42.

Stiggins, R. J. (1988). Revitalizing classroom assessment: The highest instructional priority. *Phi Delta Kappan, 69*, 363–368.

Thompson, C. K. (1992). Learner-centered tasks in the foreign language classroom. *Foreign Language Annals, 25*(6), 523–531.

Tulving, E. (1985). Precis of "Elements of Episodic and Semantic Memory". *Behavioral and Brain Sciences, 7*, 223–238.

Van Patten, B. (1994). Evaluating the role of consciousness in SLA: Terms, linguistic features, and research methodology. *AILA Review, 11*, 27–36.

Wesche, M. B. (1987). Second language performance testing: The Ontario Test of ESL as an example. *Language Testing, 4*, 28–47.

West, R. (1994). Needs analysis in language teaching. *Language Teaching, 27*(1), 1–19.

Wiggins, G. (1989). A true test: Toward more authentic and equitable assessment. *Phi Delta Kappan, 70*, 703–713.

Zessoules, R., & Gardner, H. (1991). Authentic assessment: Beyond the buzzword and into the classroom. In V. Perrone (Ed.), *Expanding student assessment.* Alexandria, VA: Association for Supervision and Curriculum Development.

EXAMPLE ITEMS AND ITEM GENERATION

This appendix displays a set of task notes developed by the task creator. We include these notes to provide insight into the task generation process. By examining the task notes, the reader should develop a much clearer idea of how to go about breaking down (according to ability requirements and task characteristics) the various tasks that have come out of a needs analysis. Furthermore, it will become obvious that the notes were treated as *working* documents, not as final products. Indeed, the note form of many of the tasks included here differs substantially from the item prompt forms presented in chapter 6.

One systematic approach to task classification and development involves delineation by task areas and themes. Long and Crookes (1993) suggest that target tasks should often be collapsed and classified into more general task types. Accordingly, the example tasks in this appendix are organized into the following general *areas*:

1. Food and dining

2. At work

3. At the university

4. Domesticity

5. Travel

6. Health and recreation/entertainment

Within those areas, the example tasks will be further subdivided into *themes* as follows:

1. Food and dining
    a. At the Italian bistro
    b. Planning a dinner engagement with a "special" friend
    c. Ordering a pizza to be delivered
    d. Shopping at the grocery store
    e. Other food and dining tasks

2. At work
   a. Filling the empty position
   b. Applying for a job
   c. Those mundane office chores

3. At the university
   a. Application to a university
   b. Registration at the university
   c. In-class presentation
   d. Responding to a lecture and readings

4. Domesticity
   a. Housing
   b. Paying those pesky monthly bills
   c. Credit

5. Travel
   a. Planning a vacation
   b. At the airport
   c. Other travel tasks

6. Health and recreation/entertainment
   [there are no theme subdivisions for this area]

Individual tasks are then listed under the appropriate *areas* and *themes*. Each task description includes a *prompt* and descriptions of ways to vary the task difficulty by making (linguistic) code, cognitive complexity, and communicative demand high or low.

Area: food and dining
sample themes and tasks

Theme: Dinner at the swanky Italian bistro

This (common) theme could pose effective circumstances for eliciting performances on numerous relatively low-level to intermediate-level tasks that require a certain amount of pragmatic, strategic, and formal knowledge/ability of using the language in situ. [Now that I think about it, these are tasks that I had great difficulty with in my first L2, even after 4 years of college study, but they are also tasks that became automated very quickly — something to think about in terms of desired washback effects and the corresponding syllabus.] During the test, the situations could be quite easily reproduced using either taped speech and visual realia (menus, bills, etc.) or using an interlocutor (obviously, the first choice reduces sources of test-external variance but requires a higher degree of acceptance of authenticity on the part of the examinee). In chronological order, the tasks might be broken down along the following lines. Within the theme, task difficulties could be manipulated to a certain extent by changing the code, the cognitive complexity, or the communicative demand involved.

Task: Reserving a table

prompt

You would like to try out the fancy new Italian bistro "Il Gondoliero" tonight. Unfortunately, no one is free to accompany you to dinner (this can be changed to include a dinner partner). Look up the phone number of the restaurant in the phone book and call to reserve a table for one at an appropriate time this evening. You will have to speak with the answering machine, as the staff do not come in until 5:00 p.m.

code:
low

Phone book layout, where to look (restaurants — could give option of white vs. yellow pages, let them choose, white actually being more efficient, alphabetically); comprehension of the message on answering machine and when to begin talking; forms and necessary information for requesting a reservation ("I would like to reserve a table for one..."); time vocabulary, day of the week, evening; socio-cultural knowledge of when dinners take place, typically in the United States (not 2 a.m.).

high

Could step up the code with difficult message, heavily accented speech; however, success is pretty generically dependent on examinee knowledge of forms and vocabulary for the situation (as well as cultural knowledge of the situation/task itself); could also add the element of a dinner partner (dinner for two).

cognitive complexity:
low

Monologic speech with a machine and planning time make it a pretty easy task; ratings could be based to some extent on *efficiency* of execution.

high

Step up demand by introducing an interlocutor on the other end of the line when reserving; likewise, new information introduced through the message could increase demand ("we will be closed this evening for the cook's birthday, but will re-open tomorrow...," "if you are making a reservation, please indicate smoking preference").

communicative demand:
low

One-way task with near total control in examinee; skimming phone book, calling restaurant, understanding machine, making reservation; low pressure, plenty of time.

high

Varied time pressure introduced through message ("you have twenty seconds to leave a message...") or through situation (you are phoning from work, so you should make it quick); interlocutor makes it two-way.

Task: Ordering drinks and appetizers

prompt

You have just arrived at a fancy Italian restaurant for a nice evening dinner (alone again!). Listen to the waiter's explanation of the various options for the following: appetizers, salad, salad dressing, and beverage. When the waiter asks for your order, select one of each of the categories and order for yourself.

code: low	General vocabulary for appetizers, salads, beverages; understanding formal 'waiter-talk'; pronunciation of selected items (menu available for reference?); forms for basic ordering ("I think I'll have" and "I'd like…", etc.)
high	Varied food types, drink, and salad options; accented/snooty waiter; addition of a dinner partner would require forms for soliciting choices and ordering for a second party.
cognitive complexity: low	If with an interlocutor, opportunity to negotiate meanings, ingredients, etc.? ("what's in the vinaigrette?"); opportunity to request repetition, solicit suggestions?; menu on hand
high	Could add a wine list (increasing cognitive load), although might be more streamlined to have input from waiter only; increase number of options; waiter recalls that that option is no longer available (unexpected information); higher demand if placing order for partner as well, more information to process; imposition of monetary restrictions (how much examinee can spend); menu not on hand (increased memory demand).
communicative demand: low	Simple understanding of options and selection process; control over selections; one-way ordering, if everything is available; low stakes; listening comprehension is heavy, as spoken request forms depend on received information
high	Some time pressure due to immediate nature of task, need to give answer to waiter; introduce a two-way element by having waiter interlocute; add third modality (listening, speaking, reading) with menu and wine list (but does this facilitate or debilitate communication?); pressure to interlocute with optional partner.

Task: Ordering the main course

prompt

All of the dinners in this restaurant must be ordered 'a la carte'; that is, you have to select the different components from the lists of available choices. Study the menu and the various selections that are available for this evening. Choose a main dish (meat or vegetarian), a pasta, and a vegetable from the different options. When the waiter requests your order, tell him what you have decided.

code: low	Code only requires understanding of various menu items, selection of one from each of three categories; forms for ordering from each of the three categories; comprehension of waiter's moves to take order.

high	More variety of items; strategic knowledge of when to state selections; politeness forms (subjunctive).
cognitive complexity: low	Processing during planning time for the ordering of three items; simple menu format, limited number of selections; everything available, no need to interact with waiter, simply state selections in a pragmatically reasonable manner.
high	More or less obvious category membership for items; on-line processing of new information from waiter or possible dinner partner; confusing/extensive menu; lengthy explanations in menu; follow-ups by waiter ("yes, the crab is exquisite tonight, and it is complemented so nicely by the angel hair pasta…"); monetary restrictions.
communicative demand: low	Individual is in near complete control, must only choose any three combination; low stakes; some on-line pressure to produce; reading menu and speaking about choices.
high	Could manipulate planning time (waiter arrives quickly); introduce exchange with a partner or with the waiter (if a dish is not available or if the waiter suggests that a different pasta might go better with the main dish choice, etc.).

Task: Sending back the fish (or whatever x main dish) that tastes like a shoe

prompt

After waiting a good forty-five minutes, your dinner has finally been served. Unfortunately, the fish (x) that you ordered is excessively overcooked. When the waiter returns to your table, request that he return the fish to the kitchen. Give him your reasons for sending it back, and request a new serving.

code: low	Pragmatic functions for registering a complaint, returning the food, requesting something else; forms for returning/ requesting ("I'd really like to send this back…", "it's quite overcooked", "could you bring me another…," etc.).
high	Pragmatic knowledge of how much explanation is necessary, tone to take with waiter; understanding of extent of rights to expect in restaurant.
cognitive complexity: low	Relatively low in terms of amount and processing of information and interaction.
high	Need to maintain control, present request with tact under embarrassing circumstances; monetary restrictions.

communicative demand: low	Control is uni-directional; sufficient planning time makes it easier (e.g., signal the waiter when you wish to make your request); only speaking and understanding of situation are required.
high	Pretty high stress/stakes; face-threatening for all parties involved; need for tact; could reduce planning time to increase demand.

Task: Ordering coffee and dessert

prompt

After finishing your meal, the waiter brings a dessert menu. Study the different options. When the waiter returns, order your choice of dessert. Listen to the available after-dinner beverage options that the waiter recites. Choose a beverage to accompany your dessert choice.

code: low	Limited number of dessert options with obvious components; understanding of beverages available; forms for ordering.
high	Increased variety of possibilities; increased number of variables with desserts ("flaming or á la mode?") and beverages ("cream and sugar with your coffee?", etc.); forms of assent or negation.
cognitive complexity: low	Fewer options; use of visual aids (dessert tray?; photographic representation); little on-line processing; little interaction with waiter required.
high	Greater number of options and more interaction with waiter and variables increases processing demand; monetary restrictions (are you going to be able to pay for all of this and leave an appropriate tip?).
communicative demand: low	Sufficient time for making choices; low stakes; some interaction; high control.
high	Involves reading and listening, interspersed with speaking; reduction of planning time available (partner would make it a multi-way task).

Task: Paying the bill

prompt

Read through the bill that the waiter has left on your table. Compare the prices on the bill with the prices listed in the menu. If the bill is correct, write a check for the appropriate amount. If the bill is incorrect, recalculate the amount that you should have been charged. Then write your check for the appropriate amount. Be sure to examine the bill to see if a service charge has been included. If not, then calculate an appropriate tip for the waiter.

code: low	Understanding of parts of a bill, parts of a menu, tipping system in the US, writing a check; simple mathematics.
high	Depends on system of writing out or printing bill, structure of menu, tip information given, construction and clues for check writing; calculating percentages.
cognitive complexity: low	Bill is correct, composed of easily understood and listed components; easy decimals; service is included; menu prices are obvious and menu states that service is included; calculator available.
high	Bill is incorrect, hence recalculation is required; service is not included; menu prices are listed obscurely (at top of section, with different variations, with or without dessert, etc.); difficult bill to decipher (using abbreviations, drinks on back, 15% listed but not explained, etc.); not within monetary restrictions?
communicative demand: low	Unidirectional, relatively unlimited planning time, only reading and writing; no interaction involved.
high	Need to question waiter for clarification of confusing or unclear entries in the bill, special prices, etc.; restaurant is closing and waiter is hovering around, waiting for the bill; higher stakes if the bill is wrong.

Theme: Planning a dinner engagement with a 'special' friend

This theme is similar to the previous, but it focuses on the planning involved in a dinner situation. The primary cognitive activity involves processing of information from various sources in order to make comparisons, judgments, and decisions. Language is used to gather information (from written and spoken sources), to report on comparisons, and to make requests. This theme generally seems to be cognitively more demanding than the previous theme, although the communicative demand is much lower. Here again, the entire theme could be simulated with a telephone, taped messages, and written realia.

Task: Comparing food types on menus and making a recommendation

prompt

Your friend, who has recently had surgery, has some major restrictions on what she can and cannot eat. Compare the three menus from three different restaurants with the list of your friend's dietary restrictions. Decide which restaurant offers the most dinner options for your friend. Now call her and leave a message on the answering machine, explaining your choice of restaurant and detailing the options that are available.

code: low	Basic food types and ingredients, reading comparison; spoken comparisons, pronunciation of food items. Vocabulary items,

leaving messages on an answering machine. List of restrictions could include specific items. Forms like 'let's go to' and 'they have'.

high   Varied food types, bigger or more complicated food types; knowledge of food groups, ingredients, and so forth; vague list that requires inferencing; menu items that require inferencing. Use of modals for recommendations, 'we should go to' and 'it might be better because'.

cognitive complexity:
low   Limited information; short, basic menus; short message on the machine; less inferencing and more simple comparisons through recognition.

high   More information; higher inferencing; in answering talks directly to person with some new information; on-line processing required for leaving the message ("If that's you John, the doctor just called and said to avoid black forest cake no matter what — so where shall we go?")

communicative demand:
low   Easy, individual task for the most part; stakes are pretty low because there is little that could go really wrong; individual is entirely in control; includes reading, minimal listening, and monologic speaking.

high   Could manipulate the time allowed to read the menus and the time allowed to leave a message, 'you have thirty seconds to leave your message'; could provide more stress by expanding the listening modality in terms of new information on the answering machine.

Task: Re-evaluating a recommendation based on new evidence

prompt

Your friend calls you back regarding the message you left about the different restaurant menus (and her dietary restrictions). She has some specific questions about the ingredients in some of the dishes you mentioned. Listen to and note the important issues in her questions. Then call the restaurant and talk to the manager. Try to find out answers to your friend's questions. Note any clarifications that seem important.

code:
low   Basic listening comprehension issues; understanding main ideas in questions and details for further comparisons; questioning strategies for getting more information about ingredients; ability to explain situation to manager; understanding ingredients/ aspects of foods and categories of ingredients (milk, protein, calories, sodium, saturated fat, etc.); necessary elements of telephone discourse.

| high | Higher variety of food types, components, and the restrictions; asking the specific questions of the manager that are going to elicit the necessary information efficiently; more specific or medical vocabulary. |

| cognitive complexity: low | Easy note-taking from clear message from friend; less inferencing between categories and components of foods served at restaurants; little cross-referencing between lists/menus; less explanation required by manager. |

| high | Message from friend less clear; manager less forthcoming, requiring explanation; lots of movement and transposition/translation of information necessary between evidence that is given about the different food possibilities. |

| communicative demand: low | Multiple listenings with message; all appropriate information on hand; stakes not too high; no need for on-line processing of and reaction to information. |

| high | Two-way interaction with restaurant manager; reading/listening/writing/speaking, all contributing to outcome. |

Task: Making a reservation

prompt

Call back the restaurant and make a reservation for dinner for two this evening. Be sure to mention to the manager any important factors regarding your friend's dietary restrictions.

| code: low | Comprehension of manager or phone message; knowledge of necessary components in a dinner reservation (time, how many people, etc.); forms for polite requests ("I would like to make a reservation for two for this evening…"); vocabulary to explain any special requirements ("we will need to have everything cooked without the use of salt…"). |

| high | More advanced interaction with manager; more difficult problem to explain ("my dinner partner is restricted from having any lactose in her food…"). |

| cognitive complexity: low | Basic ability to make requests, transfer information from one context to another; pretty easy task. |

| high | Step up demand through need to process on-line in interaction with an interlocutor (the manager); new information ("we cannot accommodate you at seven, but we may have something available at eight-thirty…"); inferring and transferring information from restrictions to explanation of what the restaurant needs to know. |

communicative demand: low	Uni-directional control (if talking with answering machine); plenty of planning time and execution time; low stakes; basically only involves speaking and incidental listening.
high	Step up demand with introduction of interlocutor (although adds possibility to negotiate); reduce planning time (calling from work, make it quick); reduce execution time (twenty seconds to leave a message...); on-line processing and reacting to new information; added weight of listening modality.

Task: Informing your friend about the evening's arrangements

prompt

Call back your friend and leave a final message regarding the dinner reservations. Be sure to mention all relevant information.

code: low	Basically, this task assesses the ability to recall/summarize necessary information; requires answering machine skills; vocabulary for time, restaurant, clarity of information reporting; pronunciation.
high	Not much advancement of the code; message on the machine could require knowledge of specific code.
cognitive complexity: low	Pretty easy, involving memory and reporting of facts.
high	Processing of lots of information might increase demand; processing of new information on the answering machine also.
communicative demand: low	High control, unidirectional; plenty of time; uni-modal speaking.
high	Only by introduction of conveyance of new information on answering machine; otherwise quite easy, warm-down type task.

Theme: Ordering a pizza to be delivered

This theme deals with an informal situation that involves all language modalities in a low-stakes use environment. The tasks require simple listening comprehension and note-taking skills, the ability to make comparisons among various food types, strategies for ordering and giving directions. Again, the tasks can be easily simulated using tape-recorded information, real-time tape recording, and written realia. The tasks can be easily manipulated to create greater or lesser degrees of difficulty, based primarily on changing the cognitive complexities involved.

Task: Getting everyone's orders

prompt

You and your friends have decided to order pizza for dinner tonight (it's finals' week and nobody feels like cooking). Each of your friends has called and left a message on your machine. The messages describe how much pizza each individual would like and what kinds of ingredients they want, and it gives the amount of money each person is willing to contribute. Listen to all of the messages and note any necessary information for placing an order.

code: Basic listening comprehension and note-taking of pizza
low ingredients, styles (thin, pan, hand-tossed), and numbers; understanding of answering machine forms; ability to discern salient information from task-extraneous information; money vocabulary.

high Step up by increasing variety of ingredients, styles; change the productive code using multiple voice/speech types, registers, accents, and so forth; add task-extraneous information to complexify code ("by the way, have you heard about the romance between you know which students in the department...").

cognitive Limit the number of people, the amount of input in terms of
complexity: ingredients/types/ and so forth; provide simple input in terms of
low calculating what pizzas to order, how many are needed, and so forth; this task is the foundation for the following task.

high Increase number of people to listen to, amount of information, amount of variation; alter speech rates, styles, accents, forms for talking on machine, types of extraneous information that people provide.

communicative Allow multiple rewinding and listening to messages; pretty easy
demand: as the primary mode is listening and is under control of the
low examinee; low stakes if no time limit is imposed.

high Decrease listening time; impose restrictions (pizza place stops taking orders in five minutes); less control if time is restricted.

Task: Deciding on ingredients and how many pizzas to order

prompt

Now that you have noted everybody's preferences, you need to decide on the types and number of pizzas to be ordered. Use the coupons provided from different pizza delivery places in order to decide on the best value. Try to order pizzas that will a) provide everyone with enough to eat, b) have ingredients that will not offend anyone (but you can order more than one pizza), and c) be the best value for the amount of money that you are able to spend (given what everyone promised to contribute and the amount of money that you can pitch in).

code: low	Comparison/synthesis strategies; simple math; ability to understand what the options are, what the coupons offer.
high	Multiple coupons, variety of deals; more complex preferences/ingredients; more difficult mathematical combinations.
cognitive complexity: low	Small total number of requested ingredients, easily matched preferences; obvious correct choices from small number of people, all contributing similar amounts of money and requesting similar amounts of pizza.
high	Could easily become quite demanding by stepping up the amount and complexity of comparisons/syntheses/calculations (17 different people coming over, requesting five kinds of dough, 10 different ingredients, some allergic to tomato sauce, others vegetarians, others meat lovers, some contributing lots of money but light eaters, others contributing little money but heavy eaters, and five different delivery places to choose from, each with multiple coupon deals...etc.).
communicative demand: low	Very little communicative demand (this is mostly a cognitive process task); logical reading and mathematical reasoning (but don't forget that this is a very real-world task, something that we have to do, so the reasoning is an integral part of task success, even in the L2); one-way, low stakes, ample time.
high	Could step up by constraining time, imposing higher stakes (your boss has put you in charge of the office pizza party, etc.), but this might reduce authenticity (we all are faced with this kind of task under our own circumstances; why not let the individual imagine their most likely pizza-ordering scenario and leave it at that?).

Task: Ordering pizzas for delivery

prompt

After making your decisions about the kinds and number of pizzas you need to order, look up the phone number of the pizza delivery place that you have chosen, and place your order. The pizza should be delivered to your friend's house, where you have all decided to meet after work. Your friend has given you a map. Refer to the map for necessary information to give the pizza delivery person.

code: low	Knowledge of phone book, pizza delivery versus dine-in restaurants, reading a map; ability to comprehend turns and requests on the phone with the pizza order person; ability to produce request forms ("I would like to order a pizza to be delivered...", "We need one..."); ability to explain various sizes, types, combinations; ability to mention coupon (pragmatic knowledge); necessary vocabulary and forms for giving minimal directions.

high	Understanding of wait-time involved in hold, holding process; difficult map.
cognitive complexity: low	Simple/minimal order; no holding; easy prompts from the order person; no new information; easy oral summary of decision that has already been made; acceptance of minimal directions (address and phone number).
high	Complex/extensive orders; must wait on hold; prompts containing new information ("we're all out of thick crust tonight…"); need to revise request; delivery person requires more information (cross-street, north of the highway or south, etc.).
communicative demand: low	Holder of all necessary information; easy if interlocutor gives simple, logically ordered requests for information; should not be much time pressure overall (you're the customer, after all), but it is an immediately interactive situation with little time to plan/prepare responses to queries.
high	Two-way task, interaction essential, understanding of routines involved; on-line processing required; stakes are not too high, but more stressful than other tasks in this theme; not so much control over order of information delivery, new information requested, and balanced need for listening as well as speaking; incidental reading of any notes.

Theme: Shopping at the grocery store

Understanding and becoming functional in a grocery store is one of the most essential of early L2 survival skills (let's face it, we all have to by food, and it takes some L2 ability to do it). These tasks generally involve the lone shopper and are almost exclusively based on a single language modality, reading. Although just about anyone could stumble through a grocery store, find something to eat, and shovel out enough money to cover the cost, efficient and effective shopping requires the refinement of somewhat more specialized language abilities. For most students, budgeting also plays an important role in day to day life. The following tasks involve comprehension and comparison skills as well as the ability to reason in the L2. They can be easily manipulated by altering the code and the cognitive complexity inherent in the task. Communicative demand is generally low.

Task: Comparing grocery items and prices

prompt

Read through the shopping list that you and your roommate created this morning. Compare these items with the coupon books you have from different stores. Decide where you will do your shopping today (assuming that you only have time to go to one store). Explain your decision to your roommate (in person or in a note), citing specifically why you made your mind up the way you did.

| code: | Different vocabulary names for the same product, name-brands |
| low | of common items, money system, counting; knowledge of coupons; easy list with only major items; defending decision, 'let's go to Safeway' and 'it's better today because'. |

| high | More unusual items; different products and different brands; use of varied coupon techniques, '50% off the price of the second one when you buy two or more', 'buy three get two free'. |

| cognitive complexity: low | Straightforward items and common names; price reductions only; easy productive component if monologic/written; reading comprehension of prices, discernment between brand-names and types of goods, simple mathematics; speaking or writing numbers/prices. |

| high | More difficult if mathematics is more involved, if coupons are more varied; production could be impeded by dyadic situation where the roommate resists the decisions already made. |

| communicative demand: low | Pretty easy if examinee has enough time to do thorough comparisons and only has to write a response or deliver it monologically; perceived stakes are very low; examinee is basically in complete control. |

| high | Could manipulate scale and control by introducing a dyadic defense of the decision situation; perceived stakes could be driven up by providing a monthly shopping budget that cannot be exceeded and by suggesting priorities in terms of the items that must be purchased. |

Task: Investigating nutritional information

prompt

Read through the dietary recommendations (involving sodium, fat, cholesterol, and calories) from your family doctor. The set of products that follow are food items that you generally buy at the grocery store. Compare the nutritional information for the different options within each category. Based on the nutritional information provided and the doctor's recommendations, select one item from each of the product categories that you will buy during your trips to the grocery store.

| code: low | Basic understanding of the nutritional categories discussed; vocabulary and abbreviations used in nutrition facts labels (serving size, cups, grams, percents, etc.); reading comprehension of medical advice and lists. |

| high | Step up the code with variety of nutritional categories, expanded types of foods and ingredients; dietary restrictions could be made more complex, expanded to include various ingredients; code used by the doctor might not match up with |

the information available on the labels and will therefore need to be translated into a common language for comparison.

cognitive complexity: low No need to interlocute or to process new information in an on-line or productive fashion, hence pretty low cognitive complexity; low number of nutritional categories and less variety of different types of foods covered would keep the task pretty simple; simple comparison of doctor's recommendations and a few different product labels with obvious information.

high Step up the cognitive complexity by increasing the number and variety of both doctor's recommendations and food types; more categories of varied information would increase the memory required as well as the processing difficulty; doctor's categories might not always match up with the information available on the labels.

communicative demand: low Pretty low in general; individual task, no productive skills required (simple understanding and selection of appropriate items; total control of reading and comparison process; in authentic situation, the time pressure would be pretty limited as well (no one rushes you when you are shopping alone, generally).

high The only communicative demand that would be a little higher would involve the stakes of the task; the doctor's recommendations need to be perfectly understood and the selections need to be well-motivated, as the individual's health is on the line; this aspect could be intensified within the doctor's letter detailing the severity of the health risks, and so forth.

Theme: Other food and dining tasks

Task: Getting and giving directions to the bathroom

prompt

Your friend has just finished her fifth cup of coffee at the museum cafe, and she desperately wants to use the bathroom. Unfortunately, the museum's designer was not very utilitarian with the maze-like floor plan. Furthermore, your friend has laryngitis — she cannot ask directions to the bathroom on her own. Ask the museum guard where the closest bathroom is. Then re-tell the directions to your friend.

code: low Forms for requesting information; comprehension of simple direction terminology in order given; ability to read map; forms for re-telling directions (essentially the same productive side of the same forms that were comprehended); simple politeness forms in requesting.

high	Code is pretty simple and straightforward (museum guards are used to giving bathroom directions, so probably pretty clear); only made more complex by altering the architectural complexity of the location of the bathroom and the explanation of how to get there ("first go halfway through the Bauhaus wing..."); type of museum, art, exhibits, complexity and distance to the bathroom, and so forth.
cognitive complexity: low	If a map or floor-plan is made available, the demand is relatively low, as the examinee can follow the explanation with visual support; only the information requested is supplied in the most efficient manner possible.
high	No map increases cognitive complexity; provision of new information not originally requested causes parsing difficulty for the examinee; more versus less speech required for the explanation due to complexity, distance, verbosity of interlocutor, and so forth; information that is retold must first be understood.
communicative demand: low	If map is involved, memory does not play as big a role; dyadic, first in listening and then in telling, but kept simple by limiting the interaction (e.g., request, listen, retell — no interruptions).
high	Task must be executed post haste, due to the urgency of the situation; time is short and stakes are driven up; stakes are also greater for the listening event in that it must not only be understood, but also retold in an efficient and understandable way.

Task: Planning the menu for a meeting

prompt

You are planning a luncheon for the local Sierra Club meeting, and you know that there are four different groups of members involved, as far as you are concerned when it comes to ordering food: meat-eaters, and three groups of vegetarians with different dietary restrictions. The meat-eaters don't pose much of a problem for planning, but you want to be sure about the three vegetarian groups. Listen to the three descriptions of three kinds of vegetarians (vegen, lacto-ovo, and lacto-ovo-pesco) that your nutritionist friend has left for you on your voice mail. Then review the following list of possible food items (with ingredients) that the caterer could supply for the meeting. Place each of the food items into the appropriate category on the form provided.

code: low	Basic understanding of food types, categories, and individual items; ability to associate different food items with categories; listening and reading skills (transfer of comprehension to orthographic representation); food and nutrition vocabulary.

---

high	Stepped up through the use of greater variety of food types to identify and place into categories, more technical/scientific explanation of three types of vegetarians.
cognitive complexity: low	Limited amount of total food items; simple, efficient explanations; obvious choices meeting the requirements for the three different groups and fitting easily into the three different categories
high	Greater number of food items; mixed explanations from nutritionist ('oh yeah, I almost forgot to tell you something very important to remember about lacto-ovos...'); inclusion of extra information to process (e.g., possible substitute ingredients for different food groups, etc.)
communicative demand: low	Entirely passive/receptive task; one-way requiring no interaction, only comprehension; time could be unlimited (in the natural setting probably no time demands); opportunity to re-listen to the message on voice mail.
high	Stakes are inherently somewhat high, that is, care has to be taken not to order the wrong kinds of food for the group membership; time could be artificially stepped up (orders have to be placed within the next thirty minutes and your boss needs the memo now).

Area: At work
sample themes and tasks

Theme: Filling the empty position

This theme covers a practical range of tasks from the point of view of the employer. It offers, therefore, a valuable learning experience in and of itself by providing insight into the considerations that employers have when hiring new employees. The tasks are largely focused on reading and writing modalities, although some listening and speaking is mixed in as well. Other abilities and knowledge that must be exercised include comparison/contrast, formal letter writing, and meta-level review of the hiring process. Code and cognitive complexity seem to entail the greatest differences between the different tasks, and cognitive complexity is the most easily manipulated within tasks. Generally, the tasks seem to range from intermediate-level to quite advanced-level difficulties.

Task: Write a job advertisement

prompt

Look through the following job description notes from your last meeting with the boss. As the personnel manager, it is your responsibility to write a job advertisement for the new position for which she is hiring. Refer to the sample advertisements as you create an announcement for the new position. Be sure to consider the level and type of job that you are advertising as you create the announcement.

code: low	Job announcement vocabulary and forms; understanding of format of notes; recognition of level of job and the corresponding type of announcement to create (hiring a new copy guy requires a different kind of code than hiring a new account executive); specialized nature of code is somewhat moderated by the inclusion of sample advertisements, whose format can be mimicked.
high	Pretty specialized task; requires broad knowledge of the job announcement genre, hence background in job-seeking or personnel issues is a prerequisite and creates an inherently complex task; ability with formal written code and specific language corresponding to the types of jobs involved is also essential.
cognitive complexity: low	Basic ability to mimic the appropriate job announcements with all necessary information; only one job announcement necessary, so energy can be devoted to the creation of a single product; need to compare information given in the notes with that in the sample advertisements in order to produce an effective announcement; limiting the amount of information and the ambiguity of the notes facilitates the cognitive processing of the task.
high	Multiple announcements would increase the processing demands; in addition, extensive and/or ambiguous notes, as well as unclear or ambiguous examples, would step up the processing difficulty; new information could be added through follow-up by the boss ('I just thought of something to add to that latest job announcement').
communicative demand: low	Involves reading and writing modalities, hence no face-to-face interaction; time pressure is not inherently high; total control in the hands of the examinee, so scale is singular.
high	Stakes are pretty high, as this is job performance; time pressure could be increased by giving a deadline (boss needs it before lunch and it is already 11:30); could input some ambiguous information that would require follow-up from the boss, adding communicative elements of scale and control.

Task: Sorting out possible candidates

prompt

Now that the application deadline has passed, it is your responsibility to sort out those candidates who meet the minimum qualifications from those who do not. Using the original position announcement as a guide, review all of the applicants (by looking at their curriculum vitae) and create two separate files, one for those who meet the minimum qualifications and one for those who do not.

code: low	Requires a basic understanding of resume/vita vocabulary and structure; ability to interpret information provided in applications in terms of the minimum requirements for the position; straightforward language and structure for all of the applications.

high	Less clear information provided in variety of resume formats; addition of cover letters that offer extra and pertinent information; ability to 'read between the lines' for actual minimum qualifications.

cognitive complexity: low	Lower if all of the applications have easily recognizable information in comparable formats; focus of the work will be on simple elimination of those not meeting a minimum of one of the minimum qualifications; limited number of minimum qualifications and greater specificity for each minimum qualification will also simplify task; lower number of applicants.

high	Greater number of minimum qualifications and more general statements increase difficulty of identifying what counts as sufficient for the minimum qualification; larger number of applicants using a variety of formats and structures to present information relevant to the job announcement.

communicative demand: low	Total control, little inherent time pressure, single modality of reading comprehension, and no new information added create low communicative demand; no need to produce any kind of communication except for the two piles of accept and reject.

high	Only increase in communicative demand centers on stakes, which are in fact quite high due to the critical nature of selecting all candidates for the job who actually meet the qualifications; stress is driven up by the fact that this is an occupational setting and that the ramifications of the decision could produce negative outcomes if incorrectly managed; artificial time constraints could easily be imposed without undue acceptance necessary on the part of the examinee (to be expected in a hiring situation).

Task: Write a form letter of rejection

prompt

Now that you have decided which candidates absolutely do not meet the minimum qualifications, you can go ahead and write a form letter rejecting their applications. Go through the file of previous rejection letters that your boss recently reviewed and commented on. Based on these previous letters, and not forgetting to incorporate the boss's suggestions, write a new and appropriate form letter of rejection to the candidates for this particular position.

code: low	Code is simplified by being presented in the sample previous letters, and it could thus be rendered quite obvious (simply a matter of copying and changing a few words); basically the code

involves formal business letter structures and vocabulary as well as a good deal of pragmatic knowledge.

high Code is made more difficult by involving more letter samples of a greater variety with numerous suggestions from the boss (vocabulary, syntax, pragmatics, formatting, etc.); to some extent the code must be assessed with some subtlety by the examinee in choosing which sample after which to pattern the current rejection letter.

cognitive complexity: low Basic ability to judge the level of the job and the type of response that is appropriate; ability to comprehend and incorporate feedback into new letter writing (this is really the crux of the task); easier if there are obvious corresponding examples to base the letter on, with obvious and easily-incorporated comments.

high More difficult to process if the number and variety of examples and comments is greater; could be made much more difficult by the exclusion of example letters all-together (replaced with notes from the boss for how best to handle letters of rejection).

communicative demand: low Individual task involving two modes (reading comprehension and writing) with essentially total control in the hands of the examinee and no possibility of the introduction of new information.

high Time is not necessarily an issue, but could be manipulated; stakes are quite high, given that the task involves incorporation of feedback from the boss on a very sensitive issue, and given that the letter is inherently going to be greeted with negative feelings by the recipients (plays on the communicative abilities of the writer).

Task: Making a hiring decision

prompt

The boss has decided to leave the final hiring decision up to you in your capacity as personnel manager. The list of candidates has been reduced to four possible hires by the interviewers. Unfortunately, you were out of town for an emergency meeting when the candidates came for their job interviews. Read through the following list of job qualifications (both minimum and desired) once again. Then listen to the taped interviews of the four top candidates. Using the forms provided (which list the minimum qualifications and desired qualifications), mark the qualifications of each candidate. Use the scale provided on the form. Which candidate would you hire? Place a check mark at the top of the page of your first choice.

code: low Interview and job-related vocabulary, both spoken and written; key words and ideas representing the presence or absence, as well as the degree, of qualifications for all of the required areas.

high	More difficult code if the interviewees use ambiguous language; necessitates understanding of the code behind the code (what are they really saying about themselves?); individual speakers will affect the difficulty of the spoken code as well (fast vs. slow speech, difficult intonation patterns, etc.).
cognitive complexity: low	Easier if the interviews are short and to the point with explicit delineation of qualifications which match or do not match the qualifications required for the job (but when is it ever this easy?).
high	Heavy listening comprehension of a variety of speakers; necessitates the ability to listen for detail that is identified in a written form; compare/contrast information provided by different speakers and render a decision based on explicit criteria; longer interviews with less obvious explication of qualifications; ability to discern truth value of interviewees (hedging); extend the demand with two categories of minimum qualifications and desirable qualifications.
communicative demand: low	Time pressure is limited (especially if the tapes can be listened to repeatedly); control is in the hands of the examinee, and no production is required.
high	Involves three modalities (reading, listening, and minimal writing) in a very high stakes situation, but no productive response (yet).

Task: Offer the job

prompt

Write a letter offering the new position to your number one candidate. Refer to the file on acceptance letters as you write the new letter. Be sure to incorporate the boss's comments into this letter as well.

code: low	Code is again determined by the letter examples and the feedback provided by the boss; basic format for business letter, pragmatics of offering a job.
high	Requires a good amount of knowledge relevant to writing such letters; more difficult depending on the type and amount of feedback given by the boss as well as the variety of example letters; understanding of the relative prestige of the position being offered.
cognitive complexity: low	Pretty simple task if the format, prestige level, and the boss's comments are all straightforward; involves translation of the correct style of letter into the current position specifics and incorporation of comments.

| high | Increase the demand by including ambiguous examples that do not closely match the type of job being offered, vague comments from the boss that require some interpretation in the current context; elimination all-together of the examples would drastically increase the amount of processing involved. |

| communicative demand: low | Individual task with essentially total control by the examinee; two modes (reading and writing); time pressure is not inherently too high (opportunity to think through and revise before mailing, etc.); stakes are somewhat lower, as the job is being offered (a positive affective variable). |

| high | Time pressure can be imposed through artificial deadline; stakes are perhaps ambiguous due to the fact that this is on-the-job performance and necessitates approval from the boss. |

Task: Review the interviewers' performances

prompt

The boss has decided that the personnel department needs to be down-sized. Specifically, she has suggested that one of the two professional interviewer positions should be eliminated. Review the tapes from the last set of interviews. Based on these performances, which interviewer will you eliminate? Write an office memo to your boss, explaining your reasons for choosing the employee who will be fired. Explain the reasons for your decision based on the notes from your boss and on characteristics of the employee's performance in the interviews.

| code: low | Understanding of language of the job interview situation; what constitutes superior versus inferior performance by the interviewer; language of memos and the pragmatics of a touchy situation. |

| high | As can be seen in the basic requirements for this task, it involves an inherently complex code (and is perhaps only appropriate for ESP business circumstances); ability to rate performances of interviewers and then to write a convincing memo based on evidence is essential. |

| cognitive complexity: low | Lower if the performances are obviously superior and inferior; boss provides explicit criteria which are to be followed in making the decision; taped interviews are brief and to the point. |

| high | Higher if the performances are closer together in quality, if the two interviewers are alternately superior or inferior according to different criteria; criteria from the boss are not straightforward; interviews are lengthy and complex; (this is a highly meta-cognitive task involving reflection on the performance characteristics of other tasks — as such, it seems pretty difficult); movement between different comprehension and expression genres increases the difficulty. |

communicative demand: low	Control is still in the hands of the examinee, and time is not necessarily an issue.
high	Three integrated modalities are involved in a complex fashion; the stakes are extremely high, given the very serious consequences of the task; the communication involved must be very carefully worded, which increases the stress of execution.

Theme: Applying for a job

This theme entails a number of tasks that incorporate the expression of real-world individual details in authentic settings. As such, the required code and cognitive complexities are complex and tend to vary from individual to individual. Rating of performances on these tasks will need to take one of two routes: either a good deal of background knowledge of the examinee will have to be held by the raters (e.g., raters in the form of the examinee's teachers, who should have enough background knowledge to associate appropriate task levels and outcomes with the individual student), or the raters will have to treat the examinees as legitimate job applicants for whichever jobs the candidates happen to choose (and are more or less qualified for). Rating in the second instance would then involve the application of expert criteria that apply to whatever level and type of job the examinee happens to choose. On the one hand this format of task eliminates the random nature of task authenticity by individualizing all of the tasks; on the other hand, it increases the difficulty and most probably the reliability of the rating of relative success or failure for each task. [Any ideas? — should this simply be a pedagogic task, or can it be manipulated as an assessment task as well?]

Task: Write a 'Position Sought' advertisement about yourself

prompt
Review the 'Position Sought' section of the classified advertisements. Now write a similar advertisement about yourself. Base your ad on the skills that you will have and the area that you will most likely be interested in upon completion of the degree that you are currently working towards.

code: low	Most basically, the code here depends on the genre of position sought advertisements, including the corresponding vocabulary, abbreviations, forms, and formatting; given a sufficient range of examples (big newspaper), the code should be obvious enough; dictionary available will facilitate.
high	More complex code would seem to accompany more complex abilities, levels of education and training, more advanced

expectations in terms of jobs; code is pretty variable due to the individualized nature of the task. |

cognitive complexity: low	The crux of success with this task will involve the transfer of individual information into the corresponding format from the example advertisements; to some extent, then, the task is influenced by background (whether or not the examinee has anything to advertise), imagination (whether or not the examinee can successfully project individual qualifications at the end of the pursued degree), and the nature of the example advertisements (how closely do they correspond with the examinee's interests and abilities); cognitive processing is dependent on these factors.
high	Like code, cognitive processing demand will increase or decrease on an individual basis; higher demand could result from both more qualifications and background as well as from very little qualifications and background.
communicative demand: low	Individual is in control of the task and no on-line communication is necessary (reflective task instead); two modalities (reading and writing); inherently no time pressure.
high	Pretty high stakes in the portrayal of self in a format that is somewhat narcissistic (put your best face forward); creative written communication is not necessarily a genre that many lower level examinees will be able to handle with facility.

Task: Fill in the application form

prompt

Choose a single application form that corresponds to a job for which you find yourself the most qualified (based on the job descriptions attached to each of the available forms). Fill in the application form to the best of your ability, leaving blank any information that you do not have currently available.

code: low	Pretty basic task that involves understanding and writing in the code used in application forms, essentially simply the vocabulary and format of the form (name, date of birth, address, etc.).
high	To some extent, the code could be made more complex throughout the form, each section involving more complexity than the previous (moving from general personal information to job qualifications and experience to more ambiguous questions that elicit other kinds of writing — e.g., why do you think you are a good candidate for this job?; what would you say are your best attributes as a candidate for this type of work?); might run into trouble with this task due to the unavailability of certain types of background information that would normally be asked for on such forms [on the other hand, I've filled out plenty of these things in my 'working days', and I remember completing most of the forms with no on-hand addresses or dates, etc.].

cognitive complexity: low	Simple processing of the information requested and the ability to express it in acceptable written format (hence some genre-specific ability is necessary); individualization should facilitate much of the task.
high	Potentially, as the form progresses and the questions become more challenging, the memory and creativity demands will increase [this might be an interesting avenue to explore with different types of forms; the farther the examinee gets, the higher the score...]
communicative demand: low	Complete individual control, one-way; basic reading comprehension of form and ability to respond to prompted information.
high	Relatively high stakes in actual task (job or no job is on the line); more authentic if there is a degree of time pressure (often fill in a job application form at the place of employment, prior to interviews, etc.)

Task: Writing a cover letter in response to a job advertisement

prompt

Read through the following job advertisements from the *New York Times*. Based on your personal background and experience, decide which job you would be most qualified for. Then write a brief (one-page) cover letter to the employer, describing your interest in the job and briefly outlining your relevant job experience or education. Try to address in what way you are a good candidate for the position.

code: low	Job notice vocabulary; professional letter format; register for professional letters; varies to some extent with the life/professional experience that individual examinees have (thus, a college freshman with little job experience would tend to focus on jobs that have less demanding code in terms of the want ads).
high	Code varies with individual and the job for which they are applying; could depend on the particular source of the job ads.
cognitive complexity: low	Comprehending language of job notices; appropriate professional writing style; demand will come from the nature of the want ads (professional, general, big city, small town, overseas, etc.); amount of information that must be processed; amount of background knowledge, especially in terms of genre.
high	Higher demand from more complex, longer ads; also dependent on individual examinee experience and interests; task has inherent processing demands that require memory and background knowledge (format, individual attributes, etc.).

| communicative demand: low | No interaction and authentically little time pressure; unidirectional (absolute control); two modes only (reading and writing). |
| high | Perceived stakes could be pretty high, although will vary with job type and individual; must have decent knowledge of want ad vocabulary and letter writing format; communicative success will depend on ability to incorporate the information required by the selected advertisement into a cover letter format. |

Task: Answer questions in a phone interview

prompt

As a follow-up to your job application (cover letter?, position sought ad?), the employers would like for you to answer a few questions. Listen carefully to each question. After each question, answer to the best of your ability.

code: low	Listening comprehension of posed questions; shorter, more basic questions that are directly related to information provided by the examinee in previous tasks; spoken responses in appropriate code (vocabulary, syntax, pragmatics, strategies, etc. — on ACTFL scale this would be the equivalent of Advanced-level competency, which is supposed to represent minimal work-related ability with the language).
high	Complexity of the code could easily be increased within the type of question and the manner in which it is posed; also depends to a large degree on the information previously provided by the examinee [here we run into the rating issue, again, of whether we want to rate within-task success or across-task ability level or both...].
cognitive complexity: low	Easily understood questions with obvious or direct relation to the forms (hence the examinee is prepared for giving an answer); planning time for a response would also facilitate the response, but might be less authentic; basic ability to process the intent of the question and provide an immediate and appropriate response.
high	Much more difficult if there is no planning time allowed (more authentic as well); less direct relationship between the question and previous information; need to process new information in the question and come up with immediate, on-line response that nonetheless meets the basic conditions determined by code, and so forth.
communicative demand: low	Essentially a two-way task involving potentially multiple listeners and questioners and one interviewee; however, control over the answers is in the hands of the examinee (although the questions are unknown until they are asked, so control is severely impaired).

---

high	Time pressure is immediate; stakes are very high and immediately apparent; oral production task generally involves the least opportunity for reflection and necessitates the most on-line processing in order to communicate effectively.

Theme: Those mundane office chores

This theme could potentially involve numerous lower to more intermediate-level tasks within all of the modalities. Possibly the most authentic means of manipulating the task difficulty involves imposition of communicative demands that would be likely in a work environment (e.g., time, stakes, pressure). Access to a computer and to various types of software for implementation would increase the authenticity and types of tasks.

Task: Creating a Rolodex

prompt

The secretaries at your place of employment have decided to go on strike for better working conditions. You must therefore assume some of the duties that are normally handled by them. Alphabetize the set of business cards from various professional contacts. After alphabetizing, fill out a rolodex entry for each so that your secretary will be able to access the necessary corresponding information when he returns to the job.

code: low	This is a very basic task that involves an understanding of the alphabet and the ability to comprehend and transfer pertinent information from business cards (meishi) to a rolodex format card; basic terminology for common entries on the two types of cards (name, phone, fax, telephone, e-mail, position, institution, etc.).
high	The task code can be made a little more difficult by involving a wider range of business card types with varying formats for representing the required information; likewise with the rolodex; differences between the rolodex and the business card format and vocabulary would increase code difficulty.
cognitive complexity: low	This is not a very cognitively challenging task, requiring simple recognition and transferal of information within a very basic understanding of the genre and of alphabetization.
high	Could make the task a little more difficult if the meishi and rolodex entries had to be broken down into various other categories or marked as belonging to categories (e.g., 'after alphabetizing, mark each entry as either a personal or professional contact', etc.); introduction of new cards halfway through completion would present a slight challenge.

communicative demand: low	One-way, complete control; no inherent time pressure; simple recognition and copying of written information; stakes are relatively low.
high	Could step up the communicative demand by adding time pressure.

Task: Taking messages

prompt

Listen to the voice mail messages left for yourself and for your secretary. Fill out a pink 'While you were out' form for each message, noting the essential information from each call. Be sure to keep your forms separate from those that are directed at your secretary.

code: low	Listening comprehension of the essential information from each message; understanding of numbers, figures, names, crucial vocabulary items to be noted; some knowledge required for determining what is essential versus non-essential information; ability to note information in a legible and comprehensible way on a standard message form.
high	Step up the code complexity by having more difficult, complex, unclear information transmitted in the voice mail messages; greater range of vocabulary, reasons for calling, instructions for returning calls, and so forth.
cognitive complexity: low	Easy, straightforward messages with not too much information to note; simple phone numbers, names, and brief instructions; some memory demands, but if allowed to replay the messages, this is eliminated; ability to identify pertinent information and summarize in a clear note-taking fashion.
high	More difficult if messages are lengthier, if there are more messages, and if they are delivered in an ambiguous manner; memory demand is greater if only one listening is allowed; unclear to whom the message is directed; difficult to decipher what the essential elements of the message are.
communicative demand: low	Not very high stakes; low time pressure if the examinee is allowed to play back the messages multiple times (which seems authentic).
high	Less control in the hands of the examinees, as they have no control over the content or delivery of the messages; listening and writing notes; necessity to listen for detail and note in a manner that is effective and efficient; time limit could be artificially established ('you've got a meeting in ten minutes').

Task: Transcribing a business letter

prompt

Listen to the following letter that has been dictated by your boss. Using the Dictaphone, transcribe with as much accuracy as possible the exact words of the letter. The header and footer have already been created for you, thus you should only concern yourself with an exact transcription of the letter.

code:
low
This task is most easily manipulated in terms of code complexity; that is, success with the task is almost entirely dependent on the vocabulary, syntax, pronunciation, clarity, intonation, and so forth of the recorded letter; lower code complexity would involve easy dictation with simple forms and syntax produced clearly and with punctuation included.

high
More complex code would involve lengthier sentences with more complex syntax, less frequent vocabulary, no punctuation provided; the message could involve changes (e.g., 'no, no switch that to ten million, not ten thousand') and language extraneous to the letter content (i.e., directed at the transcriber and not to be included in the letter itself).

cognitive
complexity:
low
Entirely dependent on ability to comprehend and transfer information from spoken to written format; as such, not so difficult because the language is entirely pre-determined (not much thinking going on).

high
On the other hand, the processing demands will increase proportionally with the lack of knowledge of the code (i.e., the less code an examinee understands, the more the examinee will have to 'fill in the gaps').

communicative
demand:
low
Little time pressure inherent, unless a deadline is artificially established; two modalities of listening and writing, although stress here is obviously on the listening comprehension aspects of the task; no face-to-face interaction.

high
Very little control in the hands of the examinee over the kind of language involved in the task; medium stakes (the boss probably expects good work), although the actual exam stakes could be high if the examinee has a tough time with listening comprehension (for example).

Random tasks

Task: Matching a job candidate with a job

prompt

Listen to John's taped monologue on his job priorities and job skills. Take notes as you listen. Now read through the list of want ads below and find the three jobs that best match both John's desires and qualifications.

code:	Easy, efficient delivery by John in an organized and coherent way
low	covering all of the basic job qualifications that are needed for comparison with the job advertisements; delimited range of job types with obvious types that correspond directly with John's qualifications; basic of job qualifications and the language and format of job advertisements; essential to success in the task is an understanding of what things that John says are critical for comparison with the job advertisements.
high	Less obvious delivery by John; lots of extraneous detail; difficult speech characteristics (vocabulary, syntax, organization); extensive range of job advertisements not necessarily grouped according to John's preferences (such as a typical want ad section of a newspaper) and including/requesting various types of information.
cognitive complexity: low	Closer matches between John's desires and qualifications and actual jobs advertised; John is interested in only one particular type of job; simple matter of note-taking of essential details and then matching the details with job type and then specific job advertisement.
high	John's desires and qualifications do not necessarily match up with any job types or specific jobs; some qualifications apply for some jobs while others apply for others; John is interested in jobs in several different areas (that appear in different sections of the want ads); processing involves extensive organization of information provided in different advertisements, good deal of memory.
communicative demand: low	Two modalities (listening and reading); little time pressure in authentic circumstances (but could impose job-related time pressure without threatening authenticity of task); no interaction.
high	Not much control over any of the information, only over the comparison process; stakes seem moderate, although John's future is on the line; not a task with immediate face-threatening consequences.

Area: At the university
sample themes and tasks

Theme: Application to a university

This theme involves the examinees in tasks that should be well-known to them already, or at least not entirely foreign (as the target population consists of university-level students). The tasks cover a range of processes that are more or less typical for students applying for admission to a given department in a university. Most of the tasks focus on reading and writing modalities, and they range from repetition of basic personal information to more creative responses to directed queries from the university. The tasks can be manipulated to a varying degree within each of the difficulty domains. Background knowledge should be somewhat obviated in this theme, due to the similarity of experiences shared by the university-level examinees. However, familiarity with the genre of each task might play a significant (and difficult to discern) role in task success/failure.

Task: Applying to the university

prompt

You have received the following application form in the mail from the university. Fill in the form to the best of your ability. Keep in mind that these forms are used by the university to screen potential candidates for admission, so try to be as complete as possible with your answers.

code: low	Basic comprehension of vocabulary, forms, and format of application form; hence quite low level task, inherently; written form of answers to various items [Here's a thought — what about the differential difficulty of written representation of the language for examinees with L1s that don't use the Roman alphabet?]
high	Individual questions could pose greater difficulty, again (such as in the job application) ranging from the quite basic (name, gender, residency, etc.) to listing (please list any honors and awards) to the much more difficult and open-ended (please write a short explanation of why you would like to attend university); thus, the code would increase with difficulty for each section or type of item [easy to rate?]
cognitive complexity: low	Dependent again on the item types; should increase proportionally with code difficulty; the initial recall of personal information items should present little processing demand (mainly memory and the ability to transfer to writing).
high	Later items introduce greater cognitive complexity, including creativity, understanding of underlying assumptions regarding what tone, and so forth in writing.
communicative demand: low	Control is in the hands of the examinee, although the prompts are entirely up to the application form; no time pressure inherent; simple reading and writing; generally little need to go beyond simple recounting of personal information.
high	Stakes are pretty high, as admission to the university is partially contingent on successful completion of this task (although the task itself is not so challenging to complete); some of the final prompts in the application could present greater communicative demand in terms of presentation of self (voice, pragmatics, etc.) and general writing issues.

Task: Corresponding with the department chair

prompt

The chair of the department to which you have applied has received your application and has a few questions that require further explanation. Respond to the best of your ability to the follow-up questions based on your application form. Each question is followed by ample space to write an appropriate response.

code:
low

This task essentially offers the opportunity to expand on the previous task with more open-ended questions with written responses; code depends on types of questions asked and how formulated; lower code complexity would use brief questions with obvious answers (specific personal information, academic information, etc.); written responses with appropriate syntax, vocabulary, pragmatics, and so forth.

high

Higher complexity code would involve more complex questions asking for lengthier responses in possibly ambiguous ways (motivation for wanting to study here, why should we accept you, etc.).

cognitive
complexity:
low

Depends a lot on the types of questions asked; minimally, recall of information, elaboration of previously given information; less creativity or processing of the intent of the queries.

high

More complex issues addressed involving processing of intent of the queries, assumption of other knowledge, background information available or not, and so forth.

communicative
demand:
low

Control over the responses, but not at all over the questions; two modalities (reading, writing) could be pretty easy; no interaction involved; probably no time pressure.

high

High stakes due to importance of the responses; control of content of communication is, to a great degree, in the hands of the department chair (the prompts).

Task: Phone interview with the department chair (making a case for yourself)

prompt

After receiving more information regarding your application to the department, the department chair would like to follow up on a few other issues by telephone. She has sent you the following instructions by e-mail, and has asked that you call when ready to discuss them. In her e-mail she has asked that you choose a single concept or issue that you consider central to your proposed field of study. You will be given three to five minutes during the telephone interview to explain the concept or issue and to explain why you think it is of central importance to your field. When the question is posed, deliver your planned response, remembering to keep it within the five minutes allotted to you.

code: low	Code complexity is fully in the hands of the examinee here (and therefore, the more complex the code produced, the higher the rating, at least within this category); code depends on background knowledge of topic chosen for explanation, complexity of the topic itself (in terms of vocabulary required, etc.); production of ideas in spoken format (with the inherent code issues — intonation, pragmatics, syntax, etc.).
high	Again, code is subject to examinee choices and execution; not inherently high or low, although the type of activity might be considered best executed with more complex code components (academic voice, formal speech, etc.).
cognitive complexity: low	Minimally, requires an understanding of the request and the genre of speech that is expected; background knowledge, memory, and creativity or ability to extemporize are all called upon; more planning time would facilitate cognitive processing.
high	Less planning time allowed would increase the cognitive processing load; less familiarity with such speech events would increase the processing load (might, therefore, be easier for grad. students).
communicative demand: low	Control is in the hands of the examinee in terms of content, presentation style, and so forth; lengthier planning time; no interaction (one-way); single mode.
high	High stakes (a lot on the line); high stress during delivery (solo speech-giving to an audience has got to be one of the most stressful, on-line things to do for international students); planning time could be reduced, and examinee must bear in mind time limitations during delivery.

Task: Inquiring about financial support

prompt

Congratulations! Your application was successful and you are now accepted to the university. In the acceptance letter, you read that financial assistance is available from a number of different sources within the department and at the university. However, the acceptance letter provides no specific information regarding types of assistance, amount of assistance, or the application process. Write a brief letter [e-mail?] to the department chair, requesting more information regarding different types of assistance, amount of assistance from different sources, and what you need to do to apply for financial assistance.

code: low	Requires understanding of formal letter-writing pragmatics, format; necessitates corresponding vocabulary (if minimal and somewhat given in the prompt — perhaps this could be a rating criteria: 'goes beyond prompt in requesting x'); general writing

conventions, syntax, and so forth; questioning techniques, politeness forms, terms of address.

high	Inherently a rather high code task; higher code complexity can be introduced by examinee; expansion of code to incorporate specifics within each of the categories mentioned in the prompt (e.g., for types of assistance, 'loans, scholarships, GA-ships', etc.); more appropriate overall tone (politeness, format, etc.), the higher the code; if no examples are given, memorized greetings and closings will be necessary ('sincerely yours, xxx').
cognitive complexity: low	Less processing demand given familiarity with task, understanding of intent and outcomes of task; ability to seek information in a polite and efficient manner.
high	Higher processing demand if genre is unfamiliar, if range of possibilities is not understood; formal writing imposes some demands for attention to details of form and format.
communicative demand: low	Inherently little time pressure; stakes are not too high (no serious results if the task is not perfectly executed); no on-line communication involved, so low stress; single written modality.
high	Writing in a formal vein could cause some difficulty for examinees who are not used to communicating in this manner; this would probably drive up the stress factor

Theme: Registration at the university

This is a typical theme that just about all university students in the US have to face on a semesterly basis. Background familiarity with similar tasks could again play a large role in ease with which the tasks are successfully accomplished. Generally, the tasks stress careful attention to detail, the ability to compare several different sources of information regarding a general body of information, and the ability to take actions that summarize or further process the results of the comparative processes. Difficulty of the tasks seems to be most dependent on the cognitive processes required to deal with computing of details and requirements. The code seems pretty standard, although familiarity with similar code genres would seem to most affect task success.

Task: Selecting the courses you want and are eligible to take, using advice from your adviser

prompt

Familiarize yourself with the following list of courses. Pay close attention to which courses you are eligible to take as a new student and which courses require pre-requisites. Now listen to the comments left on your voice mail by your adviser. Note which courses your adviser suggests as well as any other pertinent information in the message. Finally, fill in the weekly calendar with the course name, instructor, and room number for all of the courses for which you will register.

---

code:	Course list is limited, well-organized, and represents obviously the
low	pertinent course information; message from adviser provides explicit information regarding which courses should be taken in what order, how many courses should be taken by a first semester student, and so forth; language used by adviser is concise, clear, easily understood; basic reading and listening comprehension.
high	Course list is more extensive (could be the entire list of university courses offered) and must be narrowed down by examinee; adviser's message is more ambiguous, with extraneous information, giving multiple options (depending on examinee's preferences); difficult language use.
cognitive complexity: low	No extraneous information from adviser to get in the way of decision-making; easy correspondence between courses offered and courses recommended by adviser; obvious choices ('it is highly recommended that a first semester take the following courses...'); less total information to process; basic comparison of two sources of information.
high	Greater amount of information to process; involve preferences, multiple possible schedule combinations available and recommended by adviser; conflict between what is being offered and the order of classes recommended by adviser; desired classes overlap in time slots, so choice must be executed.
communicative demand: low	Only receptive modalities (listening and reading), but must engage in active manipulation of the information; no on-line changes or active production is required (minimal transfer of corresponding schedule decisions to a pre-determined weekly calendar); one-way task; low stress and stakes are not much higher; no inherent time pressure.
high	Very little control in the hands of the examinee over information being communicated; time pressure could be introduced (you need to finish this task before the registration phone lines close on the last day of registration, five minutes from now).

Task: Registering by phone

prompt

Look back over the courses that you have selected from the list of courses. Now follow the instructions provided regarding telephone registration. You will need to refer to certain information provided on the two forms as you register. [This task requires a telephone registration system, and it might be difficult to simulate without the real thing in place at the assessment venue.]

code:	Basic familiarity with telephone and automated phone services
low	(e.g., what's a 'pound key'); reading comprehension of telephone registration information (numbers to dial, information to have

available when registering, course codes, etc.); listening comprehension of options within the automated service, prompts and corresponding actions with phone keys (adding a course, dropping a course, etc.)

high   Code complexity is pretty standard for this task (and similar across university settings); could be stepped up by adding options, using more extensive or technical explanations, and so forth; generally is not variable from the basic technocratic code.

cognitive complexity:
low   Understanding of registration process, interaction with telephone and a computer on the other end of the line; basic instruction following in a flow-chart format; no memory demand; easy inputting of codes; comprehension of prompts and corresponding actions to take; no new information to process on-line; here again, background familiarity with similar processes could greatly facilitate success with such a task.

high   Difficult or ambiguous prompts could be added; lengthier code numbers, more code numbers; higher degrees of inferencing of action required based on information provided; new information supplied during registration on-line (need to process 'this class is full', etc.); more options and unclear which options to consider in which order.

communicative demand:
low   No pressure in terms of producing live (to be received by other humans) communication per se, but lots of other communicative demands; planning time will reduce some of the demand.

high   Immediate time pressure, once the telephone system has been engaged; higher stakes due to consequences (whether you get your classes or not); two-way task, sort of, with information being traded back and forth between examinee and computer; on-line processing of what the computer voice prompts as well as any new information it provides; continuous switching between reading, listening, and number-punching modalities; less planning time increases pressure.

Task: Calculating and paying your fees

prompt

After registering, you have received a payment by mail form. Fill in the requested information regarding your courses, your residency status, and any other necessary fees (you will need to refer to the fee schedule on the reverse side of the payment form). Total the fees in the blanks provided. Then pay your tuition and fees using the VISA card provided. Be sure to record all pertinent information in order for your fees to be processed.

code: Essential understanding of the structure of the payment form, the
low   corresponding fees and tuition rates for courses; status as a student

| high | The payment form structure can be made more or less obvious, with extra spaces and extra information that may not apply to the examinee; heavy emphasis on reading comprehension of legalese and financial details. |

| cognitive complexity: low | All students have the same fees; tuition costs are obvious per/class figures and easily calculated; tuition status and other details are given on the form; VISA card is pretty straightforward and hard to screw up (as long as examinee includes signature); simple math. |

| high | Multiple fees that needed to be added on depending on student status and different course types (lab fees, health fees, whatever); multiple type of tuition status that must be determined by examinee; difficult calculations that require careful attention to detail. |

| communicative demand: low | No inherent time pressure (paying through the mail); no on-line stress from immediate, productive communication; primary modality is reading comprehension (with incidental filling in of corresponding blanks). |

| high | Pretty high stakes, as admission to classes normally rides on the payment of fees. |

and the corresponding fees and tuition costs; ability to transfer required information from the VISA card to the payment form.

Theme: In-class presentation

The in-class presentation theme is a common one for most students at universities in the US. The development and execution of a successful presentation involves a number of stages, many of which are not readily apparent to students from university environments where such presentations are not common. Depending on the topic or subject area of the presentation, demand can be quite high across the three task difficulty areas, with especially high communicative pressure. Cognitive complexity can also be quite extensive if examinees are not used to similar tasks. The theme itself can be rather easily varied with similar task types based on different presentation types (e.g., deliver a presentation comparing two readings). The theme is also unique in that it incorporates exposure of some of the rating criteria to examinees prior to the presentation task itself. It should therefore retain a much higher degree of authenticity with respect to real-world tasks of similar type.

Task: Plan your presentation

prompt

You have been asked to give a presentation in one of your classes. The presentation should describe your reasons for pursuing your current degree, and it should be between three and five minutes in duration. The audience for your presentation will be your classmates (and the teacher of the class); hence, you should develop your presentation accordingly. The first step you need to accomplish is the planning of your presentation. The final product of this stage should be a set of notes, in outline format, upon which you will base the presentation.

code:
low
Fundamentally, this task turns on an understanding of the genre of in-class presentations and the accompanying language codes; the content area (defined as the reasons for pursuing a degree) should not prove beyond the ability of any examinee enrolled in college (I mean, if they have come this far, they must have some reasons for being at the university); knowledge of enough of the code to express rationale for pursuing a degree [this is another circumstance where the examinee can self-select a higher code]; basic ability to note key issues for presentation in an organized manner.

high
To some extent, then, it depends on the examinee's choice of vocabulary, forms, organization, and so forth; code could thus be made more complex by detailed or specific information regarding the field of study, inspiration for following this course of studies, what the individual hopes to get out of it, and so forth; successful performance will include an organized outline that assists in the delivery of the presentation.

cognitive
complexity:
low
Cognitive processing simply involves the gathering of rationale for pursuing some degree at this university; simple noting in an organized format of the basic elements and key details of the presentation; greater familiarity with this type of task (academic presentations) will reduce the processing difficulty; lots of planning time facilitates the task; basic ability to decide what will work in this kind of presentation and what does not fit.

high
Much higher demand if the examinee is not familiar with this type of task; can be made more complex by the examinees themselves if they attempt more in the presentation; addition of more detail, lines of motivated argument, connections to the future (job plans, goals, etc.) should step up the demand; organization of greater detail increases the processing demands; less planning time increases demand.

communicative
demand:
low
No interaction at this phase in the planning of the presentation; single modality (noting of pertinent information and organization of this information); stakes are not so high at this stage (simply reflecting on reasons for attending university); more time for execution reduces pressure; basically examinee is in absolute control of what will be presented (except for the initial decision of content area, although this is quite broad).

high Time pressure could be reduced (without losing much authenticity); communication per se is very limited at this stage, although in planning, the final execution must certainly be kept in mind and will play a significant role.

Task: Develop a handout

prompt

The next stage in the development of your presentation is to create a handout with pertinent information for your audience. Your handout should be based on the major points that will be raised in your presentation and it should note any extra information that needs to be given in a visual format.

code: This task presupposes minimal knowledge of the code associated
low with the creation of a handout for presentations; includes format, structures, amount of information to include, how best to organize, what information should not be included; also basic code knowledge of vocabulary, syntax, and so forth appropriate to the genre of presentation handouts; appropriacy with respect to the presentation content and delivery style may be the major factor in rating the code employed on the handout.

high If the basic handout code is unfamiliar, then this will obviously be a very difficult task; higher code complexity will accompany examinee choices of types of information to be addressed in the presentation, how much information to be covered in the presentation, use of handout as something more than just a summary of the main points of the presentation (presence of extra information, directions to new information, creativity, aesthetic appeal, etc.); examinees will essentially determine the code complexity as they develop the presentation and the handout.

cognitive The primary cognitive difficulty for this task is to tie the handout
complexity: into the presentation notes in an effective manner; the examinee
low has to be able to foresee the presentation and the manner in which the handout will be manipulated; cognitive processing should be less extensive for an examinee who is familiar with the handout genre.

high Obviously, cognitive processing will be more intense for an examinee unfamiliar with the handout genre; also, the more complex the examinee plans the presentation and the interplay with the handout, the more difficult the processing of the role of the handout (and therefore the creation of the handout).

communicative Examinee is in complete control; task is one-way and has a single
demand: modality (writing up the handout); stakes are still not very high
low (although they could feasibly be growing at each stage as the

reality of the presentation draws nearer); no interaction is necessary; time pressure could be minimized authentically.

high   Less preparation time; communication itself is a little more real in this task, as the product would feasible be presented to an audience (who would then judge the merits of the information communicated); meta-level thought regarding communication must be increasing in this task, as all elements of the presentation have to be considered simultaneously in the construction of the handout.

Task: Practice your presentation

prompt

With a partner, practice your presentation. Each partner should provide written feedback to the other regarding the strengths and weaknesses of the presentation. Consider issues such as time used, points raised, language use (pronunciation, vocabulary, etc.), voice quality, clarity, organization, potential interest for an audience, and so forth (please refer to the rating form for areas of feedback). This task is completed after each partner has had a chance to deliver a practice presentation and has received and read through the feedback from the other partner.

code: Code complexity here is based on three areas: the categories and
low   language used in the rating form, the language of the partner's presentation, and the corresponding language use in written feedback; as such, the task encompasses a wide range of knowledge (understanding of the different genres and different modalities), and covers a potentially wide range of vocabulary, syntax, pragmatics, etc.; further code consideration must be given to the manner in which feedback is to be supplied and recommendations are to be made.

high   The code can be easily made more complex by manipulating the rating form to include a broader range of more detailed categories that require greater knowledge and greater attention to the partner's language production; there is probably a good degree of inherent code difficulty in the forms that are to be used for providing feedback to the partner.

cognitive   Most basically, this task requires that the examinee process the
complexity: information in two sources (the rating form and the partner's
low   practice presentation) and then transfer that information into a coherent written format; as such, the cognitive processing involved in the task is inherently pretty difficult; demand for giving own presentation should not be too high, given notes and handout.

high   Cognitive processing is increased along with the complexity of the rating form and the complexity of the presentation [the more problems in the partner's presentation, the more difficult it becomes to provide constructive feedback — but what if there are no problems, yet the examinee feels compelled to provide some kind of feedback to get through the task? — I guess it could be argued that the examinees have to exhibit confidence in their own cognitive capacities to judge the other presentations, and that this is an inherent value of the task itself]; greater cognitive complexity if the examinee is not used to this kind of feedback provision; high concentration required during listening phase.

communicative demand: low — Communication comes in a written form, so it's not as face-threatening as spoken, but still pretty touchy; examinee does have some control in terms of what will be given as feedback, but this is also influenced by the expectations of the situation (pragmatic, politeness, efficiency, etc.); communication of own presentation should not be too difficult, as it is already planned and accompanied by a handout.

high — Interactive task between two individuals; communication of impressions or judgments regarding the relative strengths and weaknesses of the presentation makes this a high stakes task (face is threatened for both individuals); pressure to process information on-line when listening, relate the information immediately to the areas that will be rated (knowing that feedback will be used by the partner to improve the presentation); little control by the examinee over what the nature of the information is; higher stakes again for own presentation, the first presentation of the self in an on-line, high pressure situation (but ameliorated by the fact that it is actually a practice run, so it's okay to mess up); heavy listening component prior to writing of feedback, so pressure is on to maintain concentration.

Task: Deliver your presentation

prompt
Now deliver your formal in-class presentation, incorporating any feedback that seems pertinent. This is the real thing, so try to do your best and to stay within the time limit. Your presentation will be rated according to the form that you saw in the practice phase. Break a leg!

code: low — Minimally, the code will entail the language use of the examinee in delivering the presentation; success will incorporate pragmatics, vocabulary, syntax, pronunciation, and so forth into the presentation; recommendations of the partner should also be incorporated at this stage; minimally, the presentation should demonstrate an awareness of the rating guidelines (which were seen in the previous task), should incorporate the handout, and should be delivered in an organized fashion.

high	More complex code will demonstrate understanding of the genre, will follow an organized route in involving the potential audience in the presentation content, will show sensitivity to the categories in the rating form.
cognitive complexity: low	This task involves little cognitive complexity in terms of meta-level reflection or thinking; the basic cognitive task involves processing the information gathered in the previous stages of the theme (and which should be well-planned into the presentation by now) in terms of spoken output; requires some memory demand as well as the ability to speak thoughts in a comprehensible fashion; awareness of time limits.
high	Cognitive processing should not be too difficult for examinees who have done public speaking; demand goes up for those unfamiliar with such tasks; if more complex issues are tackled, then demand will increase; ability to control nervousness.
communicative demand: low	Examinee is in complete control of this task, with all communication being unidirectional; heavy emphasis on the speaking modality, although the handout should not be forgotten (nonetheless, essentially a single modality task); no interaction is necessary, given a monologue format for the presentations.
high	This is a high-pressure, high-stakes task with lots of face on the line (formal speaking in front of an audience can prove quite unnerving); time pressure is inherent, with the time limit being strictly adhered to.

Theme: Responding to a lecture and readings

This theme involves the integration of two sources of information (academic lectures and published writing) to eventually create a written product. The theme could easily be expanded to entail a fourth task, an oral presentation of the findings from the previous three tasks [the previous presentation theme could be easily adapted to follow this theme, substituting the presentation topic with the content area from the current theme, for example]. Difficulty level of the tasks is most obviously manipulated by changing the code involved in the original lecture. For an authentic execution of the task, some sort of database, library, and so forth is necessary in order for the examinee to conduct a legitimate search for relevant literature. Barring such capacity in the assessment situation, the literature search task could be reduced to a specific set of predetermined articles, from which the examinee should pick two for the tasks at hand.

Task: Summarize the lecture

prompt

Listen to the following lecture and take notes as necessary [should we give an option of three or four different lectures here — I know it's trouble in terms of reliability, but on the other hand it eliminates background fairness issues, or does it?]. After the lecture is completed, write a brief summary of the main points of the lecture.

code: low	Basic topic-specific vocabulary; lecture style, syntax, strategies in delivery of the lecture that must be comprehended; the topic itself will determine the difficulty of the code here; additionally, the delivery of the lecture will exert an effect (pronunciation, rate of speech, volume, etc.); easy to maintain at a lower level, although there must be a bottoming out point, if it is an academic lecture, somewhere above the lower intermediate ability levels; minimal ability to manipulate written language in summarizing the lecture; much of the code is provided for the summary by the lecture (in terms of vocabulary, relevant structures); main points must be identified and regurgitated comprehensively.
high	Easy to step this up by simply choosing a much more complex topic/content area for the lecture [here's a thought: what about having two of these themes, identical except for the distance from background of the individual examinee; that is, the examinees would listen to one lecture in their areas of expertise and one lecture completely outside their expertise — we often are faced with these kinds of issues, especially as undergraduates at US universities, where we have to take core courses across different disciplines; the point would be to compare performance on both the familiar and the unfamiliar; difficulty would come in determining the background knowledge and interest areas of the examinees, but it seems like it would be easy enough to estimate, no?]; increase code demand in the delivery of the lecture by having quicker speech, more detail, less organization, less direct pointing to main ideas, and so forth; code in the summary can be stepped up by the examinee and should be easily identifiable.
cognitive complexity: low	Demand comes in the form of identifying the salient information from the lecture that needs to be noted in order to write a coherent summary; less processing involved if the lecturer directly indicates the main points; simple, flow-chart type organization facilitates task success.
high	Increase processing demand by introducing extraneous information in lecture; meandering or otherwise unclear organization; unclear what the main ideas of the lecture might be; greater amount of information increases the demand in terms of processing received information into a coherent written summary.
communicative demand: low	Two modalities (listening and writing); no interaction required; little distraction from the focused listening activity (as it is delivered by a single speaker and is uninterrupted).

high   Little control over information that is input (and therefore only marginal control over what needs to be communicated in written format); high time pressure involving on-line processing of aural input and concurrent note-taking; stakes are pretty ambiguous, although could be construed as marginally high if the examinees accept the authenticity of the classroom type task.

Task: Find relevant literature

prompt

Using your notes and summary, find at least five bibliographic references (in the library) that deal with some aspect of the lecture content. All of the references should deal with generally the same aspect of the lecture, although they may take a variety of points of view. Record these references in APA style, as you would in the reference or bibliography section of a term paper.

code: Minimally, the code here involves knowledge of a source of
low   references and how to employ the source for identifying relevant materials (e.g., ERIC system and the accompanying computer commands/applications necessary for operating it); also requires knowledge of the APA system for referencing; ability to comprehend titles and abstracts of potentially relevant sources; if computer search capacity is not available, then the task could involve a set of printed titles and abstracts that the examinee would have to read through in order to identify five relevant sources (and then list, APA reference style); obviously, reading comprehension of related academic vocabulary and forms goes without saying, making this a relatively high-end task from the get go.

high   Actually, the printed title and abstract option might pose an inherently lower level task than the computer search task; in terms of code, there is more range of knowledge to deal with in the computer-based search; anyway, for the printed option, the code complexity could be stepped up by inclusion of marginally relevant articles with similar code (and subtle differences), rendering the differentiation, in terms of code, more complex.

cognitive   Necessitates ability to extrapolate from the general information
complexity: (and/or details) presented in the lecture to themes that might be
low   relevant and identifiable in other sources of information (the literature); necessity of processing the relevance of a bigger field of articles, and then to extract five articles related to the topic in the same general way (e.g., five articles on oral proficiency assessment, if the lecture is about approaches to oral assessment); minimal ability to transfer relevant information into the reference list (author, journal, page numbers, etc.); APA manual could be made available (authentically, we usually have it on hand, even if we don't always look at it...).

high Higher processing load will be required if more sources must be sifted through, if the topic is ambiguous or hard to nail down, if nothing (or everything) can be related to the lecture topic; some kind of informed basis for decision making plays a greater role if things are not relevant; obviously cognitively more demanding if the topic is unfamiliar; efficiency in execution of this task might form a basis for rating it (i.e., the more cognitively prepared the examinee is to do the task, the easier it will be and the more efficiently it will be dealt with).

communicative demand: low
Individually driven task with no interaction required; more control is in the hands of the examinees (they get to pick the sources they want), but the overall content is still determined from the outside; low stress with no inherent time pressure (unless we make efficiency an explicit rating criteria); heavy reading comprehension component with some very structured written communication (but minimal).

high Higher stakes? Maybe, due to the academic feel of the task (thus, the examinees knows that in the real-world analog to this situation, they will be judged on their success in executing this task); control is actually ultimately imposed from outside, and there is, in some sense, a correct solution to the task (i.e., referencing five completely irrelevant sources would not constitute success with this task).

Task: Compare/contrast two sources with the lecture

prompt
Now select two of the reference sources and read the articles. After reading and noting relevant information, write a short paper comparing or contrasting the two sources and the lecture. This paper may take the perspective of a critique of the topic from multiple points of view, or it may critique one of the points of view using the other two as evidence. Include the lecture and the two sources in a reference section at the end of the paper, and be sure to cite where appropriate in the body of the paper.

code: low
Minimally, this task necessitates understanding of the vocabulary, forms, and organization of academic writing (hence, it seems pretty advanced); also requires ability to comprehend the points of view or arguments expressed in the different sources of information (lecture and the two articles); obviously, if the content area is familiar to the examinee, the code will pose fewer problems.

high Greater code complexity will issue from less familiarity with the content area; writing style (and vocabulary, organization, etc.) of the articles may be more or less complex (depending to some extent on the genre, the journal type, etc.); written code can be stepped up by the individual examinee and will therefore form, to some extent, part of the rating criteria for the written response.

cognitive complexity:
low — Again, familiarity with content and genre will play a role in determining how difficult it is for the examinee to process the information in an efficient and effective way; essentially involves the understanding and transfer of vital information from the three selected sources into coherent, cogent writing; processing load may be alternately higher or lower on the examinee, depending on preparedness for academic reading and comprehension, on the one hand, and academic writing, on the other hand.

high — Higher processing load for longer, more complex articles; also higher demand accompanying requirements for longer, more complex writing on the part of the examinee; this is inherently a quite advanced task.

communicative demand:
low — Much more individual control over the communication content here (even though the content area is still top-down determined); no inherent time pressure (although probably will have to be imposed in testing situation); no interaction on-line with people (rather with information); integrated reading and writing.

high — Probably pretty high stress and high stakes, given that this task represents a real-world task in academic settings and would likely result in at least a grade (thus, face-threatening).

Area: Domesticity
sample themes and tasks

Theme: Housing

This theme revolves around a set of tasks that are typically faced by most university students at some point in their university careers. The tasks are all almost exclusively based on the ability to read, comprehend, and process written information and to listen to and understand related information. They require varying degrees of cognitive processing complexity, primarily in the form of comparison of information from one source with information from another source and the seeking of like information. The code seems generically intermediate (within the reading and listening modalities), and task difficulty appears to be most easily manipulated according to cognitive processing requirements, primarily in terms of the amount and variety of information to be processed in the task. The tasks should all be readily understood with minimal prompt explanation (we hope...).

Task: Look for a place in the housing advertisements
prompt

Look through the following notes about the housing needs that you and your future housemates share. Using the information from these notes, go through the housing advertisements of the newspaper and try to find any suitable options that

---

fit within the parameters created by you and your housemates. Circle all of the possibilities as you identify them. Be sure to pay close attention to the details in each advertisement.

code: low	The code for this task is not inherently very difficult; requires minimally an understanding of the format, forms, and vocabulary of housing advertisements (including the meaning of figures and abbreviations); also necessitates reading comprehension of notes.
high	Code could be made more complex to an extent by expanding the range of criteria that are listed in the notes about the housemates, including more complex and varied needs or demands (pets, smoking, color of the house, lots of light, etc.); code from the advertisements is pretty stable.
cognitive complexity: low	Basic reading comprehension; requires processing of the minimum required conditions for an acceptable housing situation (number of rooms, style, cost, gender of roommates, etc.); ability to skim/scan for the established requirements and to eliminate all advertisements that do not correspond; fewer ads renders less processing.
high	Step up the cognitive load very easily by increasing the amount of information to be processed (more roommates, greater number and variety of demands); less correspondence between the requirements and the majority of the ads; greater number of ads to sift through (and less organization of the ads, e.g., into price ranges).
communicative demand: low	One-way task with no interaction or production required; single modality (reading comprehension); no inherent time pressure; stakes are pretty low at this stage (unless this is a pretty urgent situation…).
high	Time pressure can always be manipulated artificially, and stakes could be manipulated somewhat in this one (e.g., 'your roommates have entrusted this task to you and will knock off your first months rent for the work you are putting into it…').

Task: Using information from a rental agency

prompt

Another possible method for finding appropriate accommodations is by using a rental agency. Listen to [could easily be changed to "read"] the descriptions from the rental agency about the different houses and apartments (on their rental hotline). Select the category of housing that most closely fits what you and your roommates will need. As you listen to the descriptions within this category, take down all pertinent information. Now match this information with the list of further specifications that you have. Circle all of the possible rentals that meet your requirements.

code: low	Minimal familiarity with telephones and recorded information; comprehension of categories available and the category of housing that is being sought (based on the notes from the roommates); ability to select category by punching in the corresponding touch-tone code; comprehension of the salient vocabulary and structures used within the rental advertisements that are accessed; note taking of salient points for all possibilities.
high	Code difficulty increased by explanation of categories, ambiguity of which categories correspond best to the predicted needs of examinee and roommates; range of information provided regarding the individual rental units could be increased, including extraneous as well as salient information that would have to be disentangled for appropriate note taking and later decision making.
cognitive complexity: low	Complexity takes the form of processing in two stages (selecting the appropriate category to listen to, then noting salient information for the further selection of possible rental units); minimize the cognitive load by using fewer and more obvious categories of rental units to choose from (organized by price, by number of rooms, by location); minimize processing by using short, clear descriptions of individual units that either obviously correspond or obviously do not correspond to the requirements of the roommates; fewer options renders the processing load lighter.
high	Increase the load by having more categories of rentals to choose from and less obvious choice of correspondence with needs; increase amount of information and number of possibilities in the individual descriptions; descriptions can be more or less obvious or ambiguous; choices can contain varying degrees of correlation with the needs (so the examinee has to listen carefully to the entire ad to identify whether or not each rental unit is a possible or not; e.g., one unit might fit all of the requirements except for the fact that no pets are allowed, etc.).
communicative demand: low	No productive interaction is required of examinee; stakes do not seem inherently very high (although they could be imposed artificially in the prompt).
high	Time pressure is pretty intense due to the need to process immediately the recorded messages (although there is authentically the opportunity to re-listen in such situations); three modalities are involved as well as various sources of information that must be cross-referenced; individual has almost no control over the communication that occurs in the task.

Task: Filling in the rental application

prompt

Listen to the messages from your future roommates on your answering machine. Pay careful attention to the information given, and take notes as needed. Then fill out the rental application, including information for yourself and for all of your roommates.

code: Minimal recognition of relevant vocabulary and forms
low corresponding to biographical information required in rental application (numbers, dates, addresses, occupations, etc.) presented in aural and written modalities; ability to note in a way that will be comprehensible for filling out the forms; standard information organized in like and logical way in the messages as well as on the application form.

high Greater variety of information (including extraneous) provided in messages (requires parsing of salient information) in differentially organized manner; greater range of information requested on application form.

cognitive The basic cognitive load here comes in the form of identification
complexity: of salient information that corresponds to the application form;
low noting of same information; less information presented in an organized format renders the processing difficulty lighter; one-to-one correlation between the information requested on the form and the order and type of information provided in the messages.

high Greater amount of information requested and provided; no one-to-one correlation between order and type of information requested and provided; more extraneous information to be sorted through.

communicative No authentic time demand on this task, as the messages can be
demand: replayed multiple times; stakes are not inherently high (but can
low be imposed); number of roommates involved is variable, but does not add to communicative demand.

high Individual has no control over the amount or type of information being communicated or requested; three modalities and multiple sources of information contribute to the final communication (the filling out of the application form).

Task: Advertising for a roommate

prompt

It seems that one of your potential roommates decided to move to another city at the last minute, just before signing the lease to your new place. Look through the sample 'Roommate wanted' advertisements. Then create an ad of your own. Use the information from one of the apartments that you found most appropriate for your requirements.

code: low	The basic code for productive completion of this task is essentially provided in the sample advertisements; necessitates an understanding of the elements of the advertisements and the corresponding elements that must be included in the examinee's advertisements (header, abbreviations for apartment structure, jargon for other requirements); knowledge of what needs to be included and what information is superfluous (as such ads often charge by the word).
high	Range of sample advertisements to gather information from; greater range of information that must be included in the advertisement being written; inclusion of special issues that may not be found in the examples but which must be included in the new ad.
cognitive complexity: low	Simple ability to transfer new information into the format provided by a similar advertisement; less information and obvious example advertisements decreases the processing load.
high	Greater processing load comes from less correlation between the information that must be inserted into the new ad and the example ads provided; more information and information whose saliency for the advertisement is ambiguous steps up the cognitive difficulty (how does the examinee deal with the inclusion of unknown or indiscernible information?).
communicative demand: low	No interactive communication; little inherent time pressure for completing the task, although in a sense there is some time pressure due to the imminent lease which must be paid for.
high	Examinees have no control over the information to be communicated (although they must decide the appropriate information to be included in the ad — there is going to be a 'most correct' answer to this item); stakes are potentially higher here, as the communication will eventually occur with a broad audience, and success with the communicative act will depend on how the advertisement is written; two modalities (reading and writing) but more sources of information must be accessed over the course of the task.

Task: Filling out a change of address form

prompt

Your roommate has broken the third metacarpal bone in his writing hand. You have volunteered to help him when he needs to have written work completed. He has just called and left a message on your answering machine. Listen to the message. Then fill out the change of address form that he left with you.

---

code: low	Minimally requires comprehension of the information left on the answering machine (vocabulary, forms, pragmatic/strategic aspects); ability to parse salient information for the change of address form and note same information; transfer of same information to change of address form (thus understanding of the categories on the change of address form from the post office).
high	Hard if not impossible to manipulate the complexity of the change of address form; increase the code difficulty by increasing the range of information left on the machine (rendering understanding of code saliency more difficult); authentically, this is a pretty immutably low-level task.
cognitive complexity: low	Simple comprehension and transfer of salient information; ability to process the appropriate biographical data for the corresponding categories on the change of address form.
high	More difficult if more information is provided and if the required information is 'buried' in superfluous detail (e.g., 'okay, my old address is 2386 Miso Street — by the way, were you at that party the night we blew up the living room...', etc.).
communicative demand: low	No interaction; no inherent time pressure.
high	Examinee has zero control over the information required or the information provided; three modalities (listening, reading, writing); stakes are somewhat high (you don't want to screw up this task or your roommates mail will disappear into oblivion).

Task: **Using a catalogue to order things for your new apartment**

prompt

You and your roommates have compiled two lists each, one containing household items that each of you already has and one containing household items that each of you thinks are needed for the new place. First compare the different lists and create one master list of things that are needed but that none of you have. Then look through the catalogue provided. Identify any of the things that you have on your needs list. Fill out the order form for any corresponding items.

| code: low | Two sources of code here are the lists and the catalogue; lists could be kept to a minimal range of easily identifiable household items (sofa, lamp, silverware); use of similar or identical terminology on the different lists will facilitate the compilation of a master list; catalogue is immutable in terms of complexity (except for choice of catalogue itself); requires understanding of the identification numbers used for different items, the vocabulary used for different items (although pictorial |

	representation makes it easier), and the information required within the order form.
high	Greater range of more esoteric household items that are less easy to recognize (cutting board, drapes, shower mat, etc.); differential naming of similar items within the different lists and from the catalogue (renders master list more difficult to compile); see above for catalogue difficulty (which does not change).
cognitive complexity: low	Necessitates comparison of multiple lists and compilation of a single list that is the union of the disparate sets of items; easier with fewer items that are similarly listed; similar naming of items in catalogue; simple organization to the order form within the catalogue; listing function requires very little processing.
high	Greater amount of information and disparity of information provided in the different lists; variable naming of similar items and from catalogue; lengthier catalogue will require more processing.
communicative demand: low	No interaction is required; single modality (reading with incidental filling in of form and lists); production only involves listing of items (thus easy to communicate); no time pressure; stakes do not seem very high.
high	Examinee exercises no control over the type or amount of information provided and to be communicated.

Theme: Paying those pesky monthly bills

The bill-paying theme represents another set of generic and common tasks that practically everyone (adults, that is) is accustomed to. The primary prerequisite for successfully completing these tasks resides in an understanding of the code that accompanies financial matters, bill statements, check-writing, and so forth. Beyond an understanding of the implications of the code, the only real difficulty inherent in these tasks is constituted by the mathematical computation required (cognitive processing). Language is employed in these tasks in an almost exclusively receptive manner, with only incidental writing following the comprehension that is the crux of the task.

Task: Calculating and paying your monthly bills

prompt

It is nearing the end of the month, and the responsibility for paying the household bills happens to be yours. Read through the following stack of bills. Using the checks and envelopes provided, pay any bills that are due within the next thirty days. Pay careful attention to the information provided. If a bill is past due, be sure to include the overdue fee.

code: low	Minimally requires familiarity with vocabulary, forms, and structure of monthly bill statements from a variety of sources (phone, rent, cable, gas, water, electricity, etc.); understanding of due dates, make checks payable to, address for the envelope; basic familiarity with check-writing practice (numbers versus words, where to sign, date, memo, etc.); keep easier by using a straightforward structure for the bills, checks, and envelopes.
high	More difficult if the organization of the bill is not as obvious; mitigating details might step up the code complexity (automated bill deduction from account that is not always very obvious, credit to your account from a mistake in their billing, etc.); broader range of bill types; checks do not have any information provided (e.g., temporary checks that require sender's address, etc.).
cognitive complexity: low	Pretty simple task, actually (with any familiarity of the task); just requires identification of appropriate information and the transfer of same information to a check; addressing of envelope; fewer bills and less variation in bill/check format will reduce the processing involved.
high	Greater processing required for more bills with greater formatting variety; not much can be done in terms of increasing the complexity of this task.
communicative demand: low	No interaction required; no inherent time pressure (on a daily scale rather than an instantaneous scale); communication only involves reading the bills and filling in checks and envelopes (two modalities, nominally).
high	No control over the information being communicated; high stakes due to the consequences of not successfully completing the task.

Task: Depositing money into the bank

prompt

You have just been paid for your two jobs, and you have received some other checks in the mail. Based on the recent bank statement providing your current balance, and making sure to cover the total amount of money that will be paid out in bills over the next month (see previous task), fill out a deposit form for your checking account. Make sure that you have covered any checks that might be drawn on your account over the next month. Fill out a second deposit form to deposit the remainder of your money into your savings account, except for fifty dollars cash received.

code: low	Requires familiarity with paycheck format, bank statements, deposit slips (and deposit process); basic mathematical ability;

fewer check types and organized bank statement will facilitate
code difficulty.

high   More complex if the checks come in varying forms and if the
bank statement is less clearly organized; not much variation of
code on this task, however.

cognitive
complexity:
low

Minimally requires mathematical processing of amount due in
bills as compared to amount already in the bank and added to
the amount of money available as income; remaining
calculation involves the subtraction of fifty dollars from the
money left over after checking deposit; otherwise the task has
minimal processing demands in terms of filling in the correct
numbers on different forms and comprehending the
representations of money in different forms (bank statement,
checks, etc.); fewer checks.

high   More checks and more operations required to get to the final
calculations will step up the cognitive complexity in this task.

communicative
demand:
low

No interaction or on-line production; no inherent time
pressure; simple reading and writing in a very structured format.

high   No control over the information provided; high stakes (need for
attention to detail and accuracy in order to avoid financial
problems).

Theme: Credit

These tasks involve an understanding of some aspects of the credit system that
operates in the US. As such, they are much facilitated (and to some extent
dependent on) cultural understanding of the process. Nonetheless, they should be
common enough in the target (US) culture that many students will be
authentically faced with their real-world execution. Emphasis is again on reading
comprehension of figures and facts as encountered in the different materials.
Written production is added as a means of examinee ability to function
successfully with information that must first be gathered from various sources and
then comprehended. Even though the tasks might pose quite new and culturally
specific situations to the examinees, this is perhaps one of the benefits of the
theme. The potential learning benefits seem obvious.

Task: Comparing credit card offers and arguing for the best
choice

prompt

Compare the information from three different student credit card offers. Decide
which credit card is best for you (there is not necessarily one right answer —
which card you choose will depend in large part on what seems most important to
you). Now summarize (in writing) what you consider to be the differences

between the three, and then defend your choice of which card is the best offer for a student like yourself.

code: low	Hard to manipulate this one in terms of the code; generally, most credit card offers have the same kind of information, deals, fine print, and so forth (they are generally required by law to display certain salient facts, although the format that they display in can certainly change); basically, this task requires an understanding of the salient elements of the different credit card offers and recognition of the aspects that are not necessarily important in making an informed decision; ability to use vocabulary and structures for defending a particular choice; understanding of student needs and wants; ability to compare/contrast the offers; pragmatics and strategies for defending a choice.
high	Task seems inherently difficult due to detail of code and familiarity required to relate to code; vocabulary, understanding of credit system, abbreviations, numbers, percentages (e.g., 5.9% APR), credit limitations, and so forth make the code relatively difficult; forms and vocabulary required for expression of choice are pretty academic; code will be to a certain extent increased or decreased by the examinee (source for rating criteria).
cognitive complexity low	Somewhat dependent on the amount of information and the format of the offers; could be minimized by the use of similar summaries of credit card offers covering the same categories (fees, deals, APR, credit limits, etc.); monologic representation of the opinion with evidence and rationale for choice; requires incorporation of personal background into the equation for calculating the most appropriate credit card (higher limit, no yearly fee, low APR, etc.); willingness to make a choice and back it up.
high	Made more complex by the inclusion of multiple types of input that come with credit card offers in the mail (introduction letters, flyers, different representation of the information necessary for making an educated choice); requires reading between the lines to really understand the terms; must be individualized and include personal rationale that is explained in such a way that the choice is well-defended; again, the examinee will step up the cognitive complexity individually, according to familiarity/willingness/ability.
communicative demand: low	Individual comparison of salient information and expression of a choice; no inherent time pressure; low stakes (nothing on the line); individual is in control of the productive aspects of the task; two modalities (reading and writing).

high   Varies from examinee to examinee; must be able to individualize the choice and talk about why a given card seems to be the best choice for them; writing itself presents higher communicative demand, given academic association with this modality (greater demand than speaking in terms of attention to form).

Task: Calculate your semester expenses

prompt
You have a vague feeling that you are not going to have enough money to support yourself while going to school over the next semester. Calculate the amount of money you will need for the next semester (using the bill estimates provided). Be sure to include living expenses as well as university-related expenses. Next, calculate your income for the next semester. Be sure to include money you already have in the bank, income from work, and the money that your grandmother has promised to send you. How much money does it seem you will be short?

code: Code involves understanding of various sources of financial
low   information (bills, bank statements, budget estimates, etc.); ability to interact with numbers and simple mathematical operations; easier if there is less range in terms of sources of costs and income; easier if the information is organized in a format that is logical to follow.

high   Code is made more complex if the range of information and sources of information are diversified and come in less organized fashion; still, the math is not inherently difficult, and the task would authentically maintain more or less the same sources of income and expenditure for most college students (tuition, housing, food, etc.).

cognitive   The processing of information that occurs in this task involves
complexity: the compilation of various sources of information regarding two
low   issues (income and expenditures) and a mathematical comparison of the outcome; processing will thus be simplified by fewer elements that contribute to the compilation (e.g., fewer expenditures).

high   Greater number of sources of information to be considered will increase the cognitive complexity.

communicative   No interaction or productive communication in this task; no
demand: inherent time pressure; simple reception and comprehension of
low   numbers and sources (reading and mathematical calculations only).

high   Examinee has no control over the information to be handled in the task; stakes are pretty high, as an accurate assessment of the situation will determine further course of action.

Task: Applying for an emergency student loan

prompt

Based on the calculations for your semester expenses, fill in the following emergency student loan application. Be sure to provide accurate information and to fill in the open-ended questions (regarding the nature of your immediate financial needs) in a convincing manner.

code:
low   Basic understanding of the information requested on the application form (biographical data); comprehension of instructions; ability to write concise answers to questions posed on the forms ('what is the cause of your financial need?', and 'explain how you will pay back this emergency student loan').

high   Task is pretty generic; code could be made more complex by requesting greater range of information or further types of open-ended, personal explanations; basically the same code from university to university, however.

cognitive
complexity:
low   Processing is minimal for the biographical information (simply fill in the requested data); necessitates use of figures and sources from previous task; writing explanations in response to open-ended questions requires processing of the information provided in the previous task and the presentation of this information in a sincere and coherent way that will be agreeable to the loan officers (necessitates pragmatic abilities and understanding of the situation).

high   The open-ended questions pose the only cognitive processing challenges within this task (hence more would prove more complex); without pragmatic understanding of the situation surrounding this task and individuals who engage in the task, the processing will be intensified (through uncertainty, etc.).

communicative
demand:
low   Two modalities (reading and writing) and pretty straightforward communicative intent that must be transmitted in the task.

high   High stakes (with lots of face and outcomes on the line here — possibly more so for international students than for US students); inherent time pressure, as these things usually have to be completed at the student financial aid office; little control over the information that must be understood and communicated; semi-two-way task, as the writing should be directed with a specific reader in mind.

Area: Travel
sample themes and tasks

Theme: Planning a vacation

These tasks involve the examinee alternately in extensive processing of various sources of information (in terms of comparison of requirements with possibilities) and in production that uses conclusions based on the information. The tasks are alternately based on higher cognitive demand versus higher communicative demand. They presuppose a basic understanding of the rather jargon laden travel industry code (and therefore might be biased to those who have done more traveling). Although the tasks are posed in terms of lots of listening and speaking, they could easily be transferred into internet-based tasks (without losing any authenticity).

Task: Decide where you can go based on your 'Advantage Miles'

prompt

You are planning a vacation with one traveling companion, and you have volunteered to arrange and pay for the tickets. You would like to use the Advantage Miles that you have accrued over the past several years. Read through the list of travel destinations that you and your companion agreed would be nice places to spend an entire two week vacation. Now read through your Advantage Miles statement and the conditions that apply. Identify all of the vacation spots on your list that you would be able to pay for with Advantage Miles. Now call up your friend and leave a message listing all of the possible vacation destinations.

code:
low
Success with this task will depend on understanding of the vocabulary and forms use in the Advantage Miles statement; necessitates simple reading comprehension of rules and regulations; ability to locate the individual account information and identify what kinds of tickets can be purchased (understanding of field-specific vocabulary — domestic, international, economy class, etc.); background knowledge of where the vacation cities are is essential; pronunciation of city names.

high
Code is pretty immutable on this particular task; the difficulty comes in parsing out the applicable information on the Advantage Miles statement (but these are quite standard).

cognitive
complexity:
low
Simple comparison of the information provided on one part of the form with the information provided on another part of the form and with the list of vacation cities; second part of the task depends on the first; pretty basic task, given understanding of the code involved.

high
Slightly more difficult if more destination cities have to be decided on (bigger initial list), but this gets to be something of a

geography test; the point is to see whether examinees understand the Advantage Miles process.

communicative demand: low	No inherent time pressure; stakes should be pretty low; the primary modality is reading (with incidental speaking at the end).
high	No individual control over any of the information being processed or produced.

Task: Booking a flight

prompt

Now that you have decided on a travel destination, you need to make airline reservations. Listen to the following questions from the airline reservations agent. After each question, provide the requested information. Refer to the Advantage Miles information from the previous task and to the travel calendar provided for necessary details.

code: low	Requires understanding of notes on a calendar (regarding dates of travel, name of companion, time of travel, what class, etc.); understanding questions from agent (which tend to be standard); ability to speak about the travel details (answering questions with specific information).
high	Basic code for making airline reservations; responses that are elicited from the customer do not need to be delivered in any kind of complex formulations (often a simple single-word response is sufficient to transmit the necessary information); could be made more difficult by having a chatty reservations agent who imbeds questions in other information (but these phone agents are paid to keep people moving through the system, so not too authentic).
cognitive complexity: low	Inherent demand here is to produce a response in an on-line and timely fashion; in an authentic situation, success might be dependent on the opportunity to request repetition (thus, allow for repetition of taped question if requested); processing is pretty minimal in terms of the amount and complexity of information that must be transferred (it should all have been determined in the previous task).
high	Processing will be more difficult if the questions are not immediately understood; not allowing request for repetition might make it more difficult; this would actually be a good task to implement in a live role-play format (as negotiation of meaning often occurs in such situations) [but then it would be really unwieldy, like oral interviews].

<table>
<tr><td align="right">communicative
demand:
low</td><td>This is an inherently tough communicative task; there is little that can be done to simplify the communicative demand involved in an authentic manner.</td></tr>
<tr><td align="right">high</td><td>On-line, interactive (if simulated) two-way task; very little control over the information being requested and produced; immediate time pressure to produce detailed information; pretty high stakes due to the need to produce (although failure does not have dire consequences); three modalities required (reading, listening, speaking).</td></tr>
</table>

Task: Choosing a hotel

prompt

Listen to the message that your travel companion has left for you on your answering machine. [Could easily substitute here: refer to the e-mail message that your companion sent you and that you printed out.] Note any information regarding the selection of hotel accommodations in your vacation city. Now locate your city in the travel guide book that is provided. Select the hotel that best suits the information provided by your travel companion.

<table>
<tr><td align="right">code:
low</td><td>Listening comprehension of hotel accommodation preferences of companion (basic vocabulary: double room, view of the ocean, less than $150 a night, etc.); ability to locate information in travel guide book; understanding of similar hotel recommendations (meaning of stars, seasonal price changes, etc.); note taking ability.</td></tr>
<tr><td align="right">high</td><td>Could complexify the code by varying the language used on the message; greater range of parameters set by traveling companion; guide book has immutable code that is pretty standard and understandable.</td></tr>
<tr><td align="right">cognitive
complexity:
low</td><td>Processing of the information provided by travel companion in order to select the appropriate hotel; relatively easy comprehension task with little processing demand, given initial understanding of the code.</td></tr>
<tr><td align="right">high</td><td>Could be stepped up by creating difficult requirements from the travel companion; this might make it more difficult to process a base-line okay hotel; on the other hand, it might make it easier to decide which hotel would be the 'best'.</td></tr>
<tr><td align="right">communicative
demand:
low</td><td>No interaction required; listening and reading modalities (with incidental note taking); stakes are not so high (as consequences are not bad for the specific task, although the examinee wants to please the travel companion).</td></tr>
<tr><td align="right">high</td><td>Examinee has little control over the information (provided on both ends); time pressure is somewhat high during listening</td></tr>
</table>

(although this can be ameliorated authentically by allowing repetition of the taped message).

Task: Booking a room
prompt

Now you need to book a room in the hotel for yourself and your companion. Refer again to the information from the message in order to book your room. Now listen to the following questions from the hotel desk clerk. After each question, provide the requested information. [this could very easily be converted to an e-mail task: after each prompt, type in the requested information; press control x when ready to send, etc.]

code:
low
Basic understanding of hotel accommodation forms and vocabulary; listening comprehension and ability to produce the corresponding requested information (based on notes taken in the previous task); easier if hotel clerk is concise, clear, and organized.

high
Code could be made more complex in two ways; either increasing the types of information requested by the clerk or the types of needs presented earlier by the travel companion will complexify the code; either could contain superfluous information that would have to be parsed out; obviously, production characteristics of the clerk could be altered as well (rate of speech, volume, accent, etc.).

cognitive complexity:
low
Rides on an understanding of the questions asked, familiarity with the task, and the information provided earlier; like the airlines reservation task, the answers to prompts from the clerk do not have to be complex (often single word answers — 'single, double', etc.); easier if there is less information to be processed and if the answers are already available from the previous task (thus no need for creativity in response); allowed to request repetition.

high
Processing is more difficult if more information is requested, if the information is not readily available from the travel companion notes, and if the examinee has to create new information on-line (also, repetition or not of the desk clerk's requests?).

communicative demand:
low
Again, this is a highly communicative task requiring immediate production/interaction, thus demanding.

high
High time pressure in an essentially interactive task; stakes are a little high (due to face-threatening nature of immediate interaction); three modalities (reading, listening, speaking) with stress on spoken production; very little control over the information being requested or provided.

Theme: At the airport

These tasks stress receptive comprehension skills that are applied to specific bits of information which must be processed in order to successfully move through the stages of the airport. Production always follows comprehension in these tasks, and ranges from simple identification of appropriate information to on-line vocal responses to specific questions. Understanding of an imposed (if standard and very formulaic) code forms a basis for all of the tasks, and communicative difficulty is high on a number of the tasks.

Task: Find your flight

prompt

At the airport, you want to find out where and when your flight is boarding. Look at the flight departure screens and try to identify your flight. Note the salient information regarding your flight from the departure screen.

code: low	Simple understanding of what constitutes salient information in the situation (gate, time, flight number, on time or not, etc.); ability to locate the appropriate information in the ticket and on the screens for corresponding airline/flight.
high	This is a basic recognition task that is pretty immutable in terms of code complexity; either the examinee understands the airport code or does not.
cognitive complexity: low	Processing involves simple comparison of the information in the ticket with a larger set of information on the screens; isolation of appropriate flight information on screens; ability to process what the information means (use fill in the blanks on the ticket cover for different categories such as boarding time, boarding gate, etc.).
high	No way to really make this task more complex in terms of processing; it seems to be a mini-task, but one that is necessary in an authentic airport situation; could incorporate efficiency into rating criteria (how long does it take the examinee to locate the appropriate information?).
communicative demand: low	One-way task in a single modality (reading from two sources); no interaction required; pretty basic recognition type of communication.
high	Generally high time pressure and high stakes (as this is usually one of the first things we do when we get to the airport, in order to get the travel process rolling); no control over the information.

Task: Solving airline ticket problems

prompt

At the airport, thirty minutes before your flight, you have discovered a conflict between the ticket you were issued by mail and the flight schedule that is currently being posted on the departure screen. Read through the departure screen and ticket information to find the discrepancy. Then explain the problem to the clerk at the ticket counter, using specific details from the written information. Try to come up with a solution to your problem, using the assistance of the clerk. [Or not? — do we want to just test their ability to explain the situation?]

code:	low	Basic understanding of time, numbers, airline flight scheduling; reading comprehension of ticket and departure information; general travel vocabulary; appropriate register and pragmatics for interacting successfully with airline clerk.
	high	Understanding of different options posed orally by the clerk may be more difficult, depending on the vocabulary and forms used; the problem itself could involve a more specific type of code (e.g., the flight does not seem to exist versus the departure time is different).
cognitive complexity:	low	Ability to compare times/locations/dates/other information; necessitates grasping of the essential problem with the ticket (which can require more or less processing, depending on the given problem); ability to express difficulties in a straightforward, coherent way; lower if solution to problem is obvious and available before going to change the ticket (can be suggested by the examinee).
	high	Higher if decision making occurs on-line, in interaction with clerk; if new information must be acquired from clerk and incorporated into given knowledge; more processing for different nature of problem.
communicative demand:	low	Can be a relatively individual task, depending on the amount of information provided (but information given is not controlled by the individual, rather that which is produced); requires some interaction with clerk, but could be nearly 100% handled in the examinee's explanation.
	high	High time pressure and high stakes situation make this task more demanding; waiting in line, having to solve the problem within a few minutes, having to process information provided by the clerk all increase the communicative demand; involves three modalities in interactive way (reading, speaking, listening).

prompt

Now that you have resolved your flight information, you need to check in at the gate. Listen to the questions asked by the stewardess at the gate. After each question, provide the requested information.

code: low	Standard airport check-in procedure with accompanying code (did you pack your own bags, how many bags will you be checking, traveling alone, would you prefer smoking or non-smoking, window or aisle, etc.); success depends on understanding the questions that are posed and producing (vocally) appropriate responses.
high	Could be more difficult if the airport is on security alert; involves greater range of questions to be answered with sometimes not obvious responses (understanding of why they are asking these questions can play a role).
cognitive complexity: low	Simply necessitates comprehension of questions being asked and the ability to process answers based on general knowledge that is either formulaic (yes, I packed my own bags), random (window or aisle), or based on information from previous tasks; authentically, there would be the opportunity to request repetition.
high	Somewhat more processing may be required in a security alert situation, although should not be too much more complex; more information requested will naturally require more processing.
communicative demand: low	Two modalities (listening and speaking) and the communication itself involves basic productive capacity.
high	Immediate time pressure of boarding; high stakes in on-line interaction that requires immediate, appropriate responses; little control over the information requested (although more over the information produced); two-way task.

Task: Boarding

prompt

Listen to the following boarding calls and other information provided over the loudspeakers at the departure gate for you flight. Indicate which of the announcements is your boarding call. Refer to your ticket for relevant information.

code: low	Necessitates listening comprehension of variety of information provided in often hard to discern, formulaic speech over the airport loudspeakers; understanding of which call corresponds with the information provided on the ticket or boarding pass; easier if there are fewer messages to parse out and if the messages

are produced audibly (although more authentic if examinee cannot understand a single word...).

high   More difficult code with more distractions (background noise), greater variety of messages being transmitted.

cognitive   Pretty basic recognition task; processing involves discernment of
complexity: intent of each message and the given audience that is named;
low   fewer messages, all directed to boarding, should make lower processing load.

high   More messages to parse out; greater variety of messages directed towards boarding as well as other audiences [does examinee have to listen to all messages, or simply indicate which one applies when it occurs?].

communicative   Single modality (listening comprehension); no interaction or
demand: production required, rather simple recognition.
low

high   Immediate time pressure to recognize appropriate call; high stakes (don't want to miss your chance to board your flight); no control over the types and amount of information being presented.

Task: Trying to find your lost bag

prompt

After arriving at your vacation destination, you find that the bag that you checked has not turned up in the baggage claim area. Fill out the lost baggage form in order to claim your bag. Refer to the notes that you keep in your briefcase for just such emergencies.

code: Necessitates basic understanding of the information requested on
low   the form; ability to comprehend information recorded in notes regarding the lost luggage; pretty standard code for this one (form requesting physical description of bag and contents as well as value); knowledge of other information (where to be contacted, etc.).

high   Could be somewhat more difficult if different kinds of information are requested or if more information is recorded on the notes about the luggage (types of luggage could be strange: golf bag; multiple pieces of luggage?); generally this is a pretty standard task with not so much variability.

cognitive   Comprehension of basic form and the ability to process the
complexity: appropriate corresponding information from the notes; less
low   demand if there is less information requested and less information to be explained (from the notes).

high	Higher processing difficulty if there is more information requested and if the notes contain more information regarding the bag(s) or if there is information that is ambiguous and tough to explain.
communicative demand: low	Single modality (reading with incidental writing); no interaction required.
high	Examinee has little in the way of control over the information being communicated; relatively high time pressure and stakes (given severity of the situation); requires some production in terms of the description of the bags, contents, and so forth.

Theme: Other travel tasks

Task: Picking up the correct family from the airport

prompt

As part of your job at the university, you have to pick up international visitors from the airport from time to time. Today, your boss has asked you to pick up a family arriving from overseas. Unfortunately, the family is coming on a family charter with multiple other families. Listen carefully to the description of the family that your boss has left on your voice mail (of course, he forgot to mention their names). Take notes as necessary. Then pick out the correct family from the different sets of photos that you have on file at the office. This photo will help you to identify the correct people at the airport.

code: low	Code complexity is determined by the descriptions on the voice mail; requires basic vocabulary for describing physical attributes of people of a variety of possible combinations; fewer members of the family with a more restricted range of attributes will make the code less complex; obviously, delivery of the salient information could be more or less complex (speech rate, extraneous detail, etc.).
high	Code is actually quite standard and basic; could be modified to include a very wide range of physical attributes for a variety of family members; complexify speech characteristics of the boss on voice mail.
cognitive complexity: low	Processing basically involves understanding the message and noting appropriate information for identification of family; requires attention to detail; less difficult with less total information and fewer photos to be sorted out; more obvious connections (or lack thereof) between descriptions and photos; not much in the way of heavy processing load.
high	Task processing can be made more complex by increasing the amount of description, the number of family members, and the number of photos to be sorted through; less obvious correlation

between the photos and the descriptions will increase processing load.

communicative demand: low	One-way task, with no interaction involved; single modality (listening comprehension with incidental note-taking); time pressure may not be inherently high (or low).
high	Stakes are pretty high (examinee wants to get the correct family); time pressure could be authentically applied (have to get to the airport in the next thirty minutes, so efficiency is essential).

Area: Health and recreation/entertainment
sample tasks

Task: Deciding on a movie

prompt

Read your friend's note describing when he can go to the movies and what kind of film he would prefer to see. Then listen to the list of movies from the three different movie theaters. Pay careful attention to the show-times and the brief movie descriptions. Note titles and times that seem appropriate. Now match up your friend's times and preferences with as many films as you think fit. Call your friend and leave a message on his answering machine giving pertinent information about any of the films that fit his requirements. Finally, suggest one film that seems preferable to you (be sure to state a reason for your preference).

code: low	Reading comprehension of written notes; movie lingo vocabulary, genres, forms (e.g., horror, thriller, action-packed, glued to your seat, show-times); listening comprehension of movie description and noting of pertinent information; knowledge of what constitutes pertinent information; oral production of movie possibilities and forms (pragmatic, syntactic, words) for defending choices; easier if friend's preferences are couched in organized, clear notes using less complex forms and vocabulary; movie messages follow similar easy format (basic forms and vocabulary); examinee determines the code complexity of the phone message (and can be rated accordingly); basic understanding of time forms.
high	More complex code involves greater range of requirements as issued by the friend in a less-organized fashion; movie descriptions also have expanded range of forms and vocabulary (more like a movie review); again, examinee determines own code complexity in leaving a phone message.
cognitive complexity: low	Essentially requires examinee to compare two sources of information across several categories (primarily time and movie type); note-taking is crucial in order to eliminate high memory demand; task will require less processing if the sources of information are organized/aligned in the same format and involve

restricted amounts of information; ability to make a decision based on summary of information and transfer decisions in oral presentation; times and possible movies match up.

high   More processing involved if there is more information to be processed in the notes, in the movie reviews/descriptions, if there are more movie possibilities; movies that fit the friend's requirements do not all match up in terms of times when friend can go to the movie; organization of presentation of information in the film descriptions is different from organization of friend's requirements.

communicative   Emphasis on listening comprehension (key to task); stakes are not
demand: very high (this is a luxury task).
low

high   Involves four modalities (with emphasis on reading, listening, and speaking, with incidental note-taking); time pressure is inherent in having to immediately process the movie information as presented in the descriptions and immediately produce information on the message; although interaction is not really on-line, immediate productive capability is required (in listening as well as in leaving a message on the friend's machine); examinee has little control over the information that is communicated (in any direction).

Task: Choose the most appropriate film

prompt

Your friend did not like any of the movies you suggested, and he has changed his mind about the type of film he wants to see. Listen to his message on the answering machine (noting any important information). Then look through the movie reviews section of the Sunday paper to identify any films that he might enjoy. Call him back and leave a message describing the film that you think best fits his requirements. Be sure to mention the show times and location of the film you choose.

code: This task starts with listening comprehension of the friend's
low   message (simple vocabulary, forms, pragmatics of refusals/requests/expression of preferences); note-taking of salient information upon which further decisions will be based (understanding of which items are relevant to decision making); reading comprehension of movie reviews (pretty standard format, abbreviations, rating system, etc.); spoken production of salient information; easier if initial message is clear (standard pronunciation, slow rate of speech) and involves a restricted range of information (forms, vocab., etc.); examinee determines the complexity of the final message (to some extent).

---

high	Code is made more complex by use of hedging strategies, diversions, and so forth on the part of the friend; greater range of vocabulary, forms, and strategies in the message; movie reviews could be made more complex, although authentically they tend to follow a standard, somewhat complex format; examinee complexifies code in message by including greater range of vocabulary, forms, and so forth (but is a complex code necessarily going to receive a higher rating? — how about code appropriacy as a rating criterion?).
cognitive complexity: low	Less information given by friend in a more organized format that closely parallels what will be found in the movie reviews; reviews are brief, organized, and to the point with easily understood coding/rating system; basic task involves scanning multiple sources of written data in search for the best match for a finite set of data that must be transferred from the message; transfer of information back into spoken format.
high	More information presented in phone message in a more complex and less parallel manner; reviews include larger amounts of task-extraneous information organized in a less obvious manner; greater number of movies and possibilities for matches to the original phone message; time conflicts.
communicative demand: low	Lower time pressure in the main portion of the task (as it is reading); still low stakes, and scale is essentially solo.
high	Time pressure does play a role in original listening and in final speaking with the machine; information is still beyond the control of the examinee, although manipulation of the information is the examinee's responsibility; all four modalities

(emphasis on listening, note-taking, reading for details, persuasive speaking).

Task: Planning the weekend

prompt

Several friends are coming to visit you (e.g., in Honolulu) this weekend. Look through the three following lists: arrival and departure schedule and pre-determined schedule of activities, the things your friends would like to do while in town, and the weekend entertainment section of the newspaper. After comparing these three sets of information, write out a weekend activity schedule that includes all activities that can be matched up from the three sources of information. Start by including all activities that have already been scheduled.

code: low	Code complexity here basically depends on an understanding of written information regarding scheduling (times, dates, preferences, etc.); easier code will have limited range of activities

that need to be fit into a schedule; arrival/departure times are obvious and correspond with other activities; requires basic understanding of tourist/entertainment possibilities.

high   More complex code will involve a greater range of activities to be reviewed in the 'weekender' section of the newspaper as well as a greater range of activity types that are suggested by the visitors; scheduling is not as obvious (various times, dates, locations for arrival/departure, activities, etc.).

cognitive   Processing here is in terms of two sources of written data,
complexity: comparing the two for similarities/differences; transfer to written
low   agenda is pretty simple follow-up to the major comparative task; will be easier if there is less information to be compared, if the descriptions in the 'weekender' section are organized, clear, and brief.

high   More difficult processing if the scheduling conflicts are more extensive (people arriving at different times that conflict with activities, etc.); greater amount of information to be processed in terms of what the guests want to do, what activities are being offered on the various dates; less organization and clarity, and greater amount of information in the 'weekender' section of the paper will create greater cognitive load.

communicative   Task focuses on the single communicative event of reading
demand: comprehension and comparison of written information in various
low   sources (with incidental summary-style writing); language production is limited and is very informal and free form; no inherent time pressure; stakes are ambiguous [could be manipulated depending on the roles of the visitors — just friends? parents? consular officials who need to be impressed with examinee's organizational capacities?, etc.].

high   Examinee has no control over the information that is provided as input, rather only over the manipulation of the information.

Task: Getting directions to the party

prompt
You have to drive several friends to a party tonight. Although you have a map of the area where the party is going to be held, you are unsure of exactly where the party is going to be. Listen to the directions that the party's host has left on your answering machine. On the map, trace the route to the party as it is described by the host.

code: Code complexity is based on the delivery of directions by the host
low   and the corresponding points on a visual representation of the area (a map); less complex code would involve limited range of vocabulary and forms to describe route, limited extraneous

information, straightforward route itself; delivery would be easier if kept slow, clear, organized.

high   Higher code complexity would involve greater range of vocabulary, forms, extraneous information; map could be made more complex in terms of size exhibited, convolutedness of route; delivery could be stepped up in terms of rate of speech, lack of clarity in pronunciation or organization, and so forth.

cognitive
complexity:
low   Processing involves simple comprehension of directions and the ability to transfer information to a visual schema; less processing if map area is delimited and obvious; re-listening opportunity (authentic if a message on an answering machine); less total information to be processed in finding route to party.

high   Greater processing load with greater amount of information in terms of directions as well as extra information; map could be more complex, representing a greater area; route could be convoluted; limit opportunities to re-listen.

communicative
demand:
low   Simple listening comprehension of directions (with incidental tracing of route on map); no production required; re-listening opportunity reduces immediate time-pressure.

high   some time pressure inherent, due to the necessity of understanding what is said on the message and the lack of opportunity to negotiate meaning; stakes seem relatively high (i.e., if the message content is missed, then the examinee won't be able to haul friends to the party).

Task: Making the most of a dating service

prompt

A friend of yours is too embarrassed to follow up on her first trip to the dating service. Watch the video that she left at the dating service. Then go through the set of possible dates that the service came up with, taking notes from the video information as you see fit. Now create three lists: one for those possible dates that match her requirements, one for those possible dates whose requirements your friend matches, and a final list for your recommendations of the best possible dates.

code:
low   Essentially, understanding this code requires comprehension of audio-visual information presented in a video-tape format; forms and vocabulary are likely to be relatively immutable with this genre of speaking (basic information about personal attributes, interests, hobbies, requirements for romantic interests, etc.); easier if range of topics is delimited to a few, basic and organized themes; code for note-taking and listing will issue from code delivered in video format; delivery in this format tends to be

general conversational speech (could be manipulated to use slow, direct speech with standard pronunciation, etc.).

high   Authentically, this code should be maintained at a pretty generic level; however, could be stepped up by providing a greater range of information in video format (interestingly, subtle code variations could be inserted in this task in terms of physical attributes of the potential dates on the video — and the requirements provided by both ends of the match-ups); themes addressed in the videos could vary from individual to individual in a less-organized manner; delivery could vary and take a more complex format (fast speech, other audial complexities).

cognitive complexity: low   Amount and types of information form the keys to successfully processing this task; information must be noticed, noted, and developed into a set of criteria whereby further sources of information can be evaluated; comprehension of information provided in visual and audio formats is essential; less overall information and greater similarity of organization between the different videos will reduce cognitive load (also fewer total videos).

high   Greater processing load if the amount of information provided (within videos and in terms of total number of videos) is expanded; disparity between the organization of information presentation will complexify as well.

communicative demand: low   Production only involves the creation of a set of lists; basically task is entirely dependent on understanding and noticing of visual and spoken information.

high   Multiple sources of information from different individuals (such as a multi-scale task, although interaction is not required); pretty high stakes, given overall task purpose; some time pressure, as the individual videos must be understood as they present information in a conversational manner; examinee controls only the processing of the information, but not the amount or quality of informational input (or output, for that matter).

Task: Giving medical advice

prompt

Familiarize yourself with the chart covering symptoms of various common illnesses. Then listen to your neighbor describing the symptoms that her child is exhibiting. Use the chart to check off the corresponding symptoms for your neighbor (who can speak but not read English). What is the probable sickness? What should your neighbor do (refer to the advice section on the chart)? Explain the probable illness and what steps the neighbor should take.

code:	Code complexity here depends on two factors: type of illness and
low	corresponding symptoms, and description of symptoms by neighbor; less complex code would entail a brief description of very common symptoms (stuffy head, runny nose, fever, aches and pain, etc.), simple anatomical terms, perhaps the use of visual representation of anatomy as well; complexity of the code used in the medical guide is immutable (chart with corresponding symptoms flowchart); structure of the book, use of index and/or table of contents is also essential; ability to express the basic information from the book in a spoken format (examinee determines the code complexity used to produce speech).
high	Code could be made more complex by including rarer symptoms and a broader range of symptoms as delivered by the neighbor and to be identified in the medical guide; delivery of symptoms could be varied (neighbor is non-native speaker, so we have standard vs. non-standard L2 production; neighbor could also be under a lot of stress, very worried about the child, quick delivery, etc.); differences between lay and medical expressions for the symptoms and ailment could be quite divergent.
cognitive complexity: low	The task rides on an ability to identify the salient features of the illness as described by the neighbor and to match these features in a checklist of common ailments; the book itself presents some processing difficulty, using the index, and so forth in order to identify the appropriate section; less processing demand if the symptoms are few, localized and/or characteristic of a common ailment; delivery of information by neighbor is organized and without extraneous information; transition of the information from the book to speech presents little cognitive challenge, if understanding has already taken place.
high	Higher processing complexity if the symptoms are manifold and not localized or characteristic of a common ailment; delivery of the neighbor could render greater cognitive complexity if upset, irrational, disorganized, and so forth; less understanding translates into greater cognitive load in terms of production.
communicative demand: low	Basically a communicatively demanding task; no formal language requirements involved here (more along the lines of doing whatever it takes to accomplish the task).
high	Task is essentially two-way (even if audio taped), containing the exchange of information between two parties; control of the information is not really in the hands of the examinee (except for the processing of the information and the reporting, but no creation of information is involved); requires three modalities, all actively engaged and equally important (listening, reading, speaking); quite high stakes, as a child's health is on the line;

time pressure is also high, for similar reasons, and because of the immediate nature of the task.

Task: Be careful with medicine

prompt

Your friend's daughter is allergic to a number of ingredients found in many common medicines. She is also currently taking several types of medication. Read through the list of allergies and medication that your friend's doctor has given her (she does not understand the language in the list very well). Now compare the lists with the various medicine labels. Which of the medicines are safe for the child to take? Circle the labels for all safe medicines.

code: low	Code complexity is dependent on the types of allergies and ingredients listed by the doctor (generally pretty sophisticated vocabulary); medicine labels usually have warning paragraphs giving any counter-indications; if not, the ingredients are always listed; task rides on the ability to recognize information from one list and to identify whether or not it interacts negatively with information on another label (authentically pretty immutable); could be easier depending on the types of allergies and ingredients listed.
high	More complex if their is a greater variety of allergies and ingredients on both the list and the labels.
cognitive complexity: low	Fairly low level of processing here; no need to understand what the allergies or ingredients actually are, rather simply to compare for presence or absence; less information requires less processing.
high	Label organization may play a role in processing difficulty; greater number of items to look for and compare between the sources of information increases the demand.
communicative demand: low	No production or interaction required; simple recognition of written information (reading modality); no inherent time pressure.
high	Stakes would seem quite high, given the potentially fatal outcomes if information is misunderstood/miscommunicated; no control over the information being processed.

Task: Convince your friend to quit smoking those nasty cigars

prompt

Read the following article about the health risks involved in smoking cigars. Then read the brief e-mail message from your friend extolling the virtues of cigar smoking. Now write an e-mail response, arguing for your friend to quit smoking cigars. Try to counter the points raised in the message from your friend by using evidence from the article.

code:	Cigar article complexity is similar to that of an article from a
low	daily newspaper, slightly easier than *Time* or *Newsweek* reading level (this will form the basis for the code involved); friend's e-mail can be variable (easier would involve very general vocabulary in basic structures, e.g., 'Cigars are not as dangerous as cigarettes,' etc.); code complexity of the e-mail response will be determined by the examinee (but based on the evidence presented in the article, which might be taken as a minimal range for success).
high	More complex code will involve greater variety of arguments from the friend (using more vocabulary in a variety of structures); code of response will be more or less complex depending on the extent to which variety of evidence is incorporated into the writing.
cognitive complexity: low	Processing involves the understanding of the two lines of argument and a recognition of where they address comparable issues (identifying point/counterpoint information in the full body of information); the arguments must then be transferred in an organized, argumentative fashion into a piece of persuasive writing; lower demand if the arguments from the friend are fewer and directly addressed by the article on cigar smoking.
high	Higher processing demand will be required if there are a greater number of arguments in the friend's message and if the arguments are not directly addressed in the article on cigars (therefore requiring inference or adjustment of some kind in order to respond).
communicative demand: low	No time pressure; two modalities (reading and writing — thus no immediate comprehension/production pressure) rather equally balanced; examinee exercises some control over the communication of findings (voice, pragmatics, etc.).
high	Stakes are pretty high, as this is likely to be a touchy subject for the cigar-smoking friend (and there is an obvious health risk on the line); written communication will require more attention to formal aspects of the language, attention to detail to convey the exact meaning desired.

Task: Getting advice from TEL-MED

prompt

You are worried about the health condition of several colleagues in your office. Using the TEL-MED health information service, find out as much as you can about the relationship between diet/exercise and heart disease. After you have gathered enough information, write up a brief office memo (no more than one page) describing the most important points to keep in mind with respect to this issue.

---

code: low	In order to access the information, the examinee must be able to operationalize the information provided in the TEL-MED system (using the phone key pad, understanding the prompts and when to punch what buttons); code for the different taped messages in TEL-MED is pretty generic (lay medical terms, slow rate of speech, pleasant conversational tone, basic syntax); success will depend on the ability to cover a range of messages, to note appropriate information, and to transfer important points into an e-mail message; written code complexity will constitute a combination of code from gathered information and examinee's input (in terms of structure, organization, etc.).
high	Code complexity is quite immutable for this task, as the TEL-MED information does not change; the only alteration in code will be dependent on the appropriacy of the examinee's own written production.
cognitive complexity: low	Depends on the examinee's ability to locate, comprehend, and reproduce information that is relevant and that is drawn from multiple sources; task is quite challenging, due to the amount of information involved and the fact that it must be first accessed and then assimilated into a coherent message that will be read by numerous colleagues.
high	Cognitive load will also depend on the extent to which the examinee actually accesses and incorporates the full range of possible information (in this way, cognitive complexity could form a basis for rating — i.e., the more complex the processing engaged in by the examinee, the higher the rating of success for this task).
communicative demand: low	Examinee has extensive control over the amount of information accessed and the way the information is communicated (creative task grounded in an understanding of various sources of information); no time pressure, as the examinee can listen to the recordings as often as necessary (although at some point, the examinee will either have to understand the message content or move on).
high	Involves three modalities in a step-wise fashion (first reading comprehension which will determine access to listening which will determine what is finally written); high stakes due to the health risks involved and the audience that will be reading the message (and they are all guilty of engaging in risky behavior)

ABOUT THE AUTHORS AND HOW TO CONTACT THEM

John M. Norris conducts research for the National Foreign Language Resource Center at the University of Hawai'i, where he is also pursuing a PhD in Second Language Acquisition and teaching in the Department of ESL. Previously, he worked as an ESL instructor in Brazil. His main research interests include second language research methodology, validity in language testing, and task-based language teaching and assessment. His publications include recent articles in *Die Unterrichtspraxis* and in *New Ways in Classroom Assessment*.
e-mail: jnorris@hawaii.edu

James Dean Brown is a Professor the Department of English as a Second Language at the University of Hawai'i at Mānoa where he teaches in the MA program in English as a Second Language and the Ph.D. program in Second Language Acquisition. He has also taught in Florida, China, and Japan. His book publications include *Understanding Research in Second Language Learning* (Cambridge University Press, 1988), *The Elements of Language Curriculum* (Heinle and Heinle, 1995), *Testing in Language Programs* (Prentice Hall, 1996), *New Ways in Classroom Assessment* (TESOL, in press), and three other co-authored books.
e-mail: brownj@hawaii.edu

Thom Hudson (PhD University of California at Los Angeles) is Associate Professor in the Department of English as a Second Language at the University of Hawai'i at Mānoa. He has worked in the US, Egypt, Mexico and Japan in program administration and university level teaching.
e-mail: tdh@hawaii.edu

Jim K. Yoshioka is a Master's student in the Department of English as a Second Language at the University of Hawai'i at Mānoa. His current interests include ESL writing, sociolinguistics (cross-cultural communication and pragmatics, in particular), curriculum and materials development, alternative forms of assessment, and pedagogy. He is also currently an instructor for the English Language Institute at UH Mānoa, where he teaches courses in academic writing and listening/speaking for international students.
e-mail: jkyosh@hawaii.edu

SLTCC

TECHNICAL REPORTS

The Technical Reports of the Second Language Teaching and Curriculum Center
at the University of Hawai'i (SLTCC) report on ongoing curriculum projects,
provide the results of research related to second language learning and teaching,
and also include extensive related bibliographies. SLTCC Technical Reports are available
through University of Hawai'i Press.

RESEARCH METHODS IN INTERLANGUAGE PRAGMATICS

GABRIELE KASPER
MERETE DAHL

This technical report reviews the methods of data collection employed in 39 studies of interlanguage pragmatics, defined narrowly as the investigation of nonnative speakers' comprehension and production of speech acts, and the acquisition of L2-related speech act knowledge. Data collection instruments are distinguished according to the degree to which they constrain informants' responses, and whether they tap speech act perception/comprehension or production. A main focus of discussion is the validity of different types of data, in particular their adequacy to approximate authentic performance of linguistic action. 51 pp.

(SLTCC Technical Report #1) ISBN 0–8248–1419–3 $10.

A FRAMEWORK FOR TESTING CROSS-CULTURAL PRAGMATICS

THOM HUDSON
EMILY DETMER
J. D. BROWN

This technical report presents a framework for developing methods that assess cross-cultural pragmatic ability. Although the framework has been designed for Japanese and American cross-cultural contrasts, it can serve as a generic approach that can be applied to other language contrasts. The focus is on the variables of social distance, relative power, and the degree of imposition within the speech acts of requests, refusals, and apologies. Evaluation of performance is based on recognition of the speech act, amount of speech, forms or formulæ used, directness, formality, and politeness. 51 pp.

(SLTCC Technical Report #2) ISBN 0–8248–1463–0 $10.

PRAGMATICS OF JAPANESE AS NATIVE AND TARGET LANGUAGE

GABRIELE KASPER
(*Editor*)

This technical report includes three contributions to the study of the pragmatics of Japanese:

- A bibliography on speech act performance, discourse management, and other pragmatic and sociolinguistic features of Japanese;
- A study on introspective methods in examining Japanese learners' performance of refusals;
- A longitudinal investigation of the acquisition of the particle *ne* by nonnative speakers of Japanese.

125 pp.

(SLTCC Technical Report #3) ISBN 0–8248–1462–2 $10.

A BIBLIOGRAPHY OF PEDAGOGY & RESEARCH IN INTERPRETATION & TRANSLATION

ETILVIA ARJONA

This technical report includes four types of bibliographic information on translation and interpretation studies:

- Research efforts across disciplinary boundaries: cognitive psychology, neurolinguistics, psycholinguistics, sociolinguistics, computational linguistics, measurement, aptitude testing, language policy, decision-making, theses, dissertations;
- Training information covering: program design, curriculum studies, instruction, school administration;
- Instruction information detailing: course syllabi, methodology, models, available textbooks;
- Testing information about aptitude, selection, diagnostic tests.

115 pp.

(SLTCC Technical Report #4) ISBN 0–8248–1572–6 $10.

PRAGMATICS OF CHINESE AS NATIVE AND TARGET LANGUAGE

GABRIELE KASPER
(*Editor*)

This technical report includes six contributions to the study of the pragmatics of Mandarin Chinese:

- A report of an interview study conducted with nonnative speakers of Chinese;
- Five data-based studies on the performance of different speech acts by native speakers of Mandarin: requesting, refusing, complaining, giving bad news, disagreeing, and complimenting.

312 pp.

(SLTCC Technical Report #5) ISBN 0–8248–1733–8 $15.

THE ROLE OF PHONOLOGICAL CODING IN READING *KANJI*

SACHIKO MATSUNAGA

In this technical report the author reports the results of a study that she conducted on phonological coding in reading *kanji* using an eye-movement monitor and draws some pedagogical implications. In addition, she reviews current literature on the different schools of thought regarding instruction in reading *kanji* and its role in the teaching of non-alphabetic written languages like Japanese. 64 pp.

(SLTCC Technical Report #6) ISBN 0–8248–1734–6 $10.

DEVELOPING PROTOTYPIC MEASURES OF CROSS-CULTURAL PRAGMATICS

THOM HUDSON
EMILY DETMER
J. D. BROWN

Although the study of cross-cultural pragmatics has gained importance in applied linguistics, there are no standard forms of assessment that might make research comparable across studies and languages. The present volume describes the process through which six forms of cross-cultural assessment were developed for second language learners of English. The models may be used for second language learners of other languages. The six forms of assessment involve two forms each of indirect discourse completion tests, oral language production, and self assessment. The procedures involve the assessment of requests, apologies, and refusals. 198 pp.

(SLTCC Technical Report #7) ISBN 0–8248–1763–X $15.

VIRTUAL CONNECTIONS: ONLINE ACTIVITIES & PROJECTS FOR NETWORKING LANGUAGE LEARNERS

MARK WARSCHAUER
(Editor)

Computer networking has created dramatic new possibilities for connecting language learners in a single classroom or across the globe. This collection of activities and projects makes use of e-mail, the World Wide Web, computer conferencing, and other forms of computer-mediated communication for the foreign and second language classroom at any level of instruction. Teachers from around the world submitted the activities compiled in this volume — activities that they have used successfully in their own classrooms. 417 pp.

(SLTCC Technical Report #8) ISBN 0–8248–1793–1 $30.

ATTENTION & AWARENESS IN FOREIGN LANGUAGE LEARNING

RICHARD SCHMIDT
(Editor)

Issues related to the role of attention and awareness in learning lie at the heart of many theoretical and practical controversies in the foreign language field. This collection of papers presents research into the learning of Spanish, Japanese, Finnish, Hawaiian, and English as a second language (with additional comments and examples from French, German, and miniature artificial languages) that bear on these crucial questions for foreign language pedagogy. 394 pp.

(SLTCC Technical Report #9) ISBN 0–8248–1794–X $20.

LINGUISTICS AND LANGUAGE TEACHING: PROCEEDINGS OF THE SIXTH JOINT LSH-HATESL CONFERENCE

C. REVES,
C. STEELE,
C. S. P. WONG
(Editors)

Technical Report #10 contains 18 articles revolving around the following three topics:

- Linguistic issues: These six papers discuss various linguistics issues: ideophones, syllabic nasals, linguistic areas, computation, tonal melody classification, and *wh*-words.
- Sociolinguistics: Sociolinguistic phenomena in Swahili, signing, Hawaiian, and Japanese are discussed in four of the papers.
- Language teaching and learning: These eight papers cover prosodic modification, note taking, planning in oral production, oral testing, language policy, L2 essay organization, access to dative alternation rules, and child noun phrase structure development. 364 pp.

(SLTCC Technical Report #10) ISBN 0–8248–1851–2 $20.

LANGUAGE LEARNING MOTIVATION: PATHWAYS TO THE NEW CENTURY

REBECCA L. OXFORD
(Editor)

This volume chronicles a revolution in our thinking about what makes students want to learn languages and what causes them to persist in that difficult and rewarding adventure. Topics in this book include the internal structures of and external connections with foreign language motivation; exploring adult language learning motivation, self-efficacy, and anxiety; comparing the motivations and learning strategies of students of Japanese and Spanish; and enhancing the theory of language learning motivation from many psychological and social perspectives. 218 pp.

(SLTCC Technical Report #11) ISBN 0–8248–1849–0 $20.

TELECOLLABORATION IN FOREIGN LANGUAGE LEARNING: PROCEEDINGS OF THE HAWAI'I SYMPOSIUM

MARK WARSCHAUER
(Editor)

The Symposium on Local & Global Electronic Networking in Foreign Language Learning & Research, part of the National Foreign Language Resource Center's *1995 Summer Institute on Technology & the Human Factor in Foreign Language Education* included presentations of papers and hands-on workshops conducted by Symposium participants to facilitate the sharing of resources, ideas, and information about all aspects of electronic networking for foreign language teaching and research, including electronic discussion and conferencing, international cultural exchanges, real-time communication and simulations, research and resource retrieval via the Internet, and research using networks. This collection presents a sampling of those presentations. 252 pp.

(SLTCC Technical Report #12) ISBN 0–8248–1867–9 $20.

LANGUAGE LEARNING STRATEGIES AROUND THE WORLD: CROSS-CULTURAL PERSPECTIVES

REBECCA L. OXFORD
(Editor)

Language learning strategies are the specific steps students take to improve their progress in learning a second or foreign language. Optimizing learning strategies improves language performance. This ground-breaking book presents new information about cultural influences on the use of language learning strategies. It also shows innovative ways to assess students' strategy use and remarkable techniques for helping students improve their choice of strategies, with the goal of peak language learning. 166 pp.

(SLTCC Technical Report #13) ISBN 0–8248–1910–1 $20.

SIX MEASURES OF JSL PRAGMATICS

SAYOKO OKADA YAMASHITA

This book investigates differences among tests that can be used to measure the cross-cultural pragmatic ability of English speaking learners of Japanese. Building on the work of Hudson, Detmer, and Brown (Technical Reports #2 and #7 in this series), the author modified six test types which she used to gather data from North American learners of Japanese. She found numerous problems with the multiple-choice discourse completion test but reported that the other five tests all proved highly reliable and reasonably valid. Practical issues involved in creating and using such language tests are discussed from a variety of perspectives. 213 pp.

(SLTCC Technical Report #14) ISBN 0–8248–1914–4 $15.

NEW TRENDS & ISSUES IN TEACHING JAPANESE LANGUAGE & CULTURE

HARUKO M. COOK,
KYOKO HIJIRIDA,
& MILDRED TAHARA
(Editors)

In recent years, Japanese has become the fourth most commonly taught foreign language at the college level in the United States. As the number of students who study Japanese has increased, the teaching of Japanese as a foreign language has been established as an important academic field of study. This technical report includes nine contributions to the advancement of this field, encompassing the following five important issues:

- Literature and literature teaching
- Technology in language classroom
- Orthography
- Testing
- Grammatical versus pragmatic approaches to language teaching
  164 pp.

(SLTCC Technical Report #15) ISBN 0–8248–2067–3 $20.

THE DEVELOPMENT OF A LEXICAL TONE PHONOLOGY IN AMERICAN ADULT LEARNERS OF STANDARD MANDARIN CHINESE

SYLVIA HENEL SUN

The study reported is based on an assessment of three decades of research on the SLA of Mandarin tone. It investigates whether differences in learners' tone perception and production are related to differences in the effects of certain linguistic, task, and learner factors. The learners of focus are American students of Mandarin in Beijing, China. Their performances on two perception and three production tasks are analyzed through a host of variables and methods of quantification.

(SLTCC Technical Report #16) ISBN 0–8248–2068–1 $20.

SECOND LANGUAGE DEVELOPMENT IN WRITING: MEASURES OF FUENCY, ACCURACY, AND COMPLEXITY

KATE WOLFE-QUINTERO, SHUNJI INAGAKI, & HAE-YOUNG KIM

In this book, the authors analyze and compare the ways that fluency, accuracy, grammatical complexity, and lexical complexity have been measured in studies of language development in second language writing. More than 100 developmental measures are examined, with detailed comparisons of the results across the studies that have used each measure. The authors discuss the theoretical foundations for each type of developmental measure, and they consider the relationship between developmental measures and various types of proficiency measures. They also examine criteria for determining which developmental measures are the most successful, and they suggest which measures are the most promising for continuing work on language development.

(SLTCC Technical Report #17) ISBN 0–8248–2069–X $20.

DESIGNING SECOND LANGUAGE PERFORMANCE ASSESSMENTS

JOHN M. NORRIS, JAMES DEAN BROWN, THOM HUDSON, & JIM YOSHIOKA

This technical report focuses on the decision-making potential provided by second language performance assessments. The authors first situate performance assessment within a broader discussion of alternatives in language assessment and in educational assessment in general. They then discuss issues in performance assessment design, implementation, reliability, and validity. Finally, they present a prototype framework for second language performance assessment based on the integration of theoretical underpinnings and research findings from the task-based language teaching literature, the language testing literature, and the educational measurement literature. The authors outline test and item specifications, and they present numerous examples of prototypical language tasks. They also propose a research agenda focusing on the operationalization of second language performance assessments.

(SLTCC Technical Report #18) ISBN 0–8248–2109–2 $20.